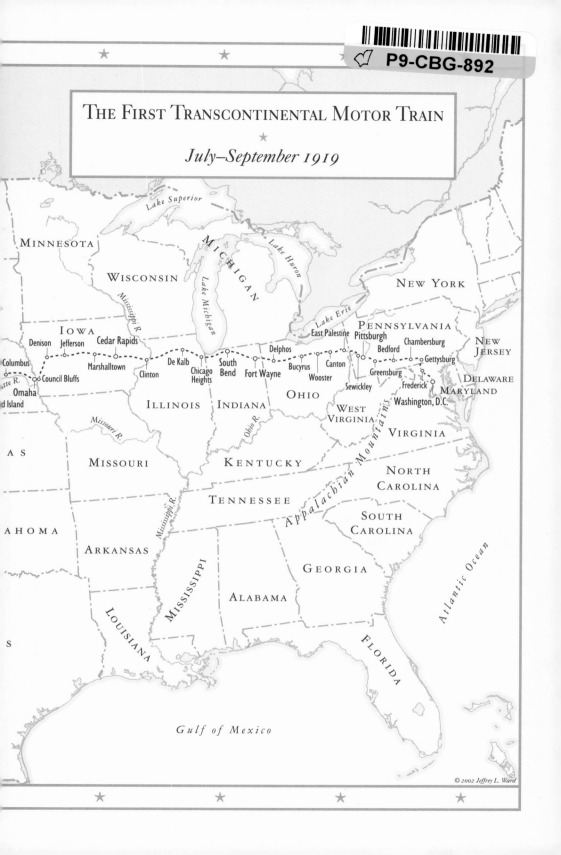

The First Transcontinental Motor Train

★

July–September 1919

Lake Superior

MINNESOTA

WISCONSIN

MICHIGAN

Lake Michigan

Lake Huron

NEW YORK

Mississippi R.

Lake Erie

PENNSYLVANIA

IOWA   Cedar Rapids

East Palestine   Pittsburgh   Chambersburg

NEW
JERSEY

Denison   Jefferson

Delphos   Bedford

Columbus

Marshalltown

De Kalb   South   Fort Wayne   Bucyrus   Canton   Greensburg   Gettysburg

Council Bluffs   Clinton   Chicago   Bend   Wooster   Frederick   DELAWARE

tte R.   Heights   Sewickley   MARYLAND

Omaha   Washington, D.C.

d Island   ILLINOIS   INDIANA   OHIO   WEST
                                                        VIRGINIA

Missouri R.   Ohio R.   VIRGINIA

A S   MISSOURI   KENTUCKY   Appalachian Mountains   NORTH
                                                                CAROLINA

                    Mississippi R.   TENNESSEE

AHOMA   ARKANSAS   SOUTH
                                                        CAROLINA

                            MISSISSIPPI   GEORGIA   Atlantic Ocean

S   LOUISIANA   ALABAMA

                                        FLORIDA

Gulf of Mexico

© 2002 Jeffrey L. Ward

Also by PETE DAVIES

Fiction

THE LAST ELECTION

DOLLARVILLE

Nonfiction

ALL PLAYED OUT

STORM COUNTRY

TWENTY-TWO FOREIGNERS IN FUNNY SHORTS

I LOST MY HEART TO THE BELLES

THIS ENGLAND

MAD DOGS AND ENGLISHWOMEN

THE DEVIL'S FLU

INSIDE THE HURRICANE

American Road

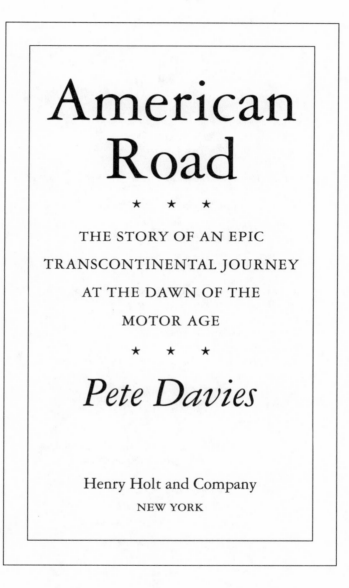

American Road

★ ★ ★

THE STORY OF AN EPIC
TRANSCONTINENTAL JOURNEY
AT THE DAWN OF THE
MOTOR AGE

★ ★ ★

Pete Davies

Henry Holt and Company
NEW YORK

Henry Holt and Company, LLC
Publishers since 1866
115 West 18th Street
New York, New York 10011

Henry Holt® is a registered trademark of Henry Holt and Company, LLC.

Copyright © 2002 by Pete Davies
All rights reserved.
Distributed in Canada by H. B. Fenn and Company Ltd.

Library of Congress Cataloging-in-Publication Data
Davies, Pete, 1959–
    American road : the story of an epic transcontinental journey at the
    dawn of the motor age / Pete Davies. — 1st ed.
        p. cm.
    Includes bibliographical references and index.
    ISBN 0-8050-6883-X (hb)
        1. United States—Description and travel. 2. Overland journeys to the
Pacific. 3. Automobile travel—United States—History—20th century.
4. Travelers—United States—Biography. I. Title.
E169 .D254 2002
917.304'913—dc21   2002017224

Henry Holt books are available for special promotions and premiums.
For details contact: Director, Special Markets.

First Edition 2002
Designed by Fritz Metsch
Printed in the United States of America

3   5   7   9   10   8   6   4   2

For Scott and Jane

Contents

American Road

CHAPTER ONE

★ ★ ★

Zero Milestone

I N 1919, THE United States was in a condition that might best be described as traumatized optimism. Fifty thousand Americans had died in World War I. Over ten times as many more had lost their lives to the calamitous pandemic of Spanish flu that had erupted the previous fall. As if that wasn't bad enough, the country was racked with racial tension, industrial disorder, spiraling inflation, and a widespread paranoia about Bolsheviks on the one hand and profiteers on the other. On a bad day, it could seem as if the entire social and economic fabric was on the brink of unraveling.

Yet amid this postwar turmoil, a tangible excitement was in the air. The United States had been the decisive player in the ending of the war and was now unquestionably the most powerful country on earth. Liberty was this new titan's theme, and the word was used to name anything at hand—from the bonds that had helped fund America's participation in the war to the aviation engines designed by the Packard Motor Car Company in Detroit that had helped fight it. While Europe lay in ruins, the prolific, protean energies of America were building entire new industries in a frenzy of invention and innovation.

No business better captured the booming spirit of the day than the automobile industry. In just two decades, America had moved from an eccentric handful of rickety horseless carriages to the private ownership of nearly 6.5 million vehicles. Detroit was pulling in thousands of people to build them, while Akron drew thousands more to make the tires on which they ran. With Goodyear, Goodrich, Firestone, and others working at full capacity, Akron was growing so fast that the city was said to have standing room only.

New firms sprang up all across the nation. Cars and trucks were made in thirty-two different states by 550 different companies; the industry employed more than a million people. This didn't include accessory manufacturers, garages, repair shops, or car dealers; nor did it include all the men now employed building the roads on which these cars might drive.

Congress had over forty bills before it related to road improvements. The best-known proposal came from Senator Charles E. Townsend of Michigan; the Townsend Bill called for a national system of highways and a federal highway commission to run it. Others wanted defense highways built along the bandit-ridden Mexican border, as well as along the Pacific coast, to confront "the Japanese menace." States in the Rocky Mountains, meanwhile, wanted roads to carry visitors to their new national parks.

The car had brought into being another thriving new industry: motor tourism. Every major newspaper now had an auto section, and it was standard practice in these pages to map out tours for readers. On Sunday, July 6, 1919, for example, the *Washington Evening Star* offered a route map to Atlantic City via Wilmington—but such an outing was not to be undertaken lightly. To be properly equipped, the paper advised, you would need:

- a set of ignition brushes, boxed and labeled
- a tow rope
- a jack and handle, with two blocks of wood to rest the jack on
- a box of plungers for the tube valves
- a three-in-one valve tool
- a tire-pressure gauge
- a wrench for the interruptor points
- a file for cleaning the points
- a voltmeter for testing the battery
- an oil squirt can, filled
- a box of assorted nuts, cap screws, lock washers, and cotter pins
- a spool of copper wire, and another of soft iron wire
- an extra set of electric light bulbs
- clean rags
- a set of fuses
- a folding canvas pail

- a full set of tire chains and a chain tool, with extra cross-links
- a fire extinguisher

Last but not least, you'd need sweaters and rain gear. After all, the paper said, "It might be necessary to change a tire in rain and mud, if nothing else."

If a simple day trip from the capital to Atlantic City involved all that, imagine what it might be like to drive from Washington, D.C., to San Francisco.

THE SPRING OF 1919 was not a good time to be a professional officer in the United States Army, and Dwight D. Eisenhower knew it. Ike was bored, he was homesick, and he was bitterly disappointed that he'd not made it to France before the Great War had ended. Now, as the army demobilized three million men, he envisioned a career spent shuffling paperwork around, growing a belly on a lowly wage behind a desk. He was twenty-eight years old, and he could see few prospects for himself.

Despite his dark mood he had, in fact, been a considerable success. His promotions had been rapid, and less than four years out of West Point he was already a lieutenant colonel. He'd spent most of 1918 in command of ten thousand men at Camp Colt near Gettysburg, Pennsylvania. It was a general's responsibility, and the good-looking blond six-footer from Kansas had worn it well.

Colt was a tank training center; when Ike got there in March 1918, it was chaos. For a start, it didn't have any tanks. After a couple of months a seven-ton French Renault turned up, but though a plant in Dayton, Ohio, was supposed to be building American tanks, no such product had appeared by the time the war ended. Eventually, he got three Renaults, along with two British officers who knew how they worked. He set up a telegraph school and a motor school, and in short order he turned an empty wheat field on the old battleground into a first-class training center. The army never did send him to Europe, because he was too good at preparing other men to go there—but that was little consolation when the war was over and he'd missed it. As one of his biographers noted, when Ike was given the Distinguished Service Medal for "unusual zeal, foresight, and administrative ability," it must have seemed "more a bitter reminder than a welcome award."

The months after November 1918 were a messy, wearisome shuttle from Gettysburg to Fort Dix in New Jersey, to Fort Benning in Georgia, and then in March 1919 to Camp Meade outside Washington, D.C., in Maryland. All this he did alone. Mamie, his wife of three years, and their baby son, Doud Dwight, were half a continent away at Mamie's family home in Denver. There were no married quarters available at Camp Meade; Ike thought of bringing them to live in Baltimore or Washington, but he didn't think he'd see much more of them if he did. Transportation, he noted wearily, "was meager and slow."

With or without them, he would soon lose his rank. His elevation to lieutenant colonel had been a temporary honor brought on by the war, and before long he'd be demoted to captain again. His pay would drop by nearly a third, to $200 a month. He would earn it signing papers to send his men back to civilian life, playing bridge and poker in a fast-shrinking service, and wondering if his own unit had any future at all. The Tank Corps was new, and as a potentially subversive affront to traditional infantry doctrine, it was not held in high regard.

An Indiana businessman who'd been a junior officer at Camp Colt offered Ike a job, and he thought seriously about taking it. Of his mood at this time, one West Point classmate later said, "He was greatly upset. . . . I had the definite impression that he intended resigning his commission." In short, the man who would lead the Allies to victory in Europe in World War II, and go on from there to eight years in the White House, might instead have opted for life as an unknown civilian—but then Eisenhower heard of an extraordinary thing.

That spring, the War Department was proposing to send a convoy of trucks and other military vehicles from Washington, D.C., to San Francisco—a journey whose projected itinerary lay 3,239 miles across the heart of the continent—and it wanted observers from different branches of the army to go along. Specifically, besides men from ordnance, artillery, and the Quartermaster Corps, from the Air Service and from the Corps of Engineers, it wanted two tank officers to make the trip. With his friend Major Sereno

Brett, Eisenhower volunteered right away. The convoy sounded at last like a chance for some genuine adventure.

BY 1919, THE people of Washington, D.C., were well used to cars. In eighteen months of wartime, the capital's population had increased from less than 400,000 to over 500,000. In the same period, the number of government and military vehicles in the city had multiplied tenfold. The congestion had become bad enough that the police felt the need to start a street-safety campaign; already, in the first half of the year, some fifty people in the District of Columbia had died in accidents involving cars.

People were getting used to seeing trucks as well. They were mostly flatbeds weighing a ton or a ton and a half; they had no cab, and there was little more for the driver's comfort than a bench behind the engine. All the same, during the last couple of years these crude, ponderous vehicles had started replacing horse-drawn wagons for local deliveries of ice, groceries, and building materials. Packard claimed that its trucks had been "adopted with unqualified success by thirty different lines of trade in Washington," one of those trades being sculptors—which was understandable in a city rich with monuments.

When Camp Meigs, on Florida Avenue and Fifth Street NE, was hastily knocked together for the army's new Motor Transport Corps, Washingtonians got used to seeing larger vehicles too. Painted uniform khaki, the army's trucks grumbled through the capital on juddering solid tires, slowly toting squads of doughboys and all the myriad supplies that went with them.

Yet for all this growing familiarity with the car and the truck, when the First Transcontinental Motor Train pulled out of the gates of Camp Meigs at eight-thirty on the morning of Monday, July 7, no witness to its departure had ever seen anything like it. No one anywhere in the world had ever seen anything like it, not even in the supply trains behind the Western Front—because this was the largest convoy of military motor vehicles ever assembled.

When they crossed town and arranged themselves in a massive semicircle around the Ellipse in Potomac Park, near the south lawn of the White House, the line stretched beyond the capacity of any camera lens to capture it. In driving formation on the road, even when they could hold the faster vehicles close in line with the slower ones, the convoy was over two miles long. That morning, the first of them were parking by the White House when the last of them were still leaving camp.

No one would have heard anything like it either. The cylinders in these engines had a huge displacement; they gave off a deep, pounding rumble. Among them were Mack trucks, still running on a chain drive, which would have added a ratcheting, clattering roar.

The convoy's principal elements were Companies E and F of the 433rd Motor Supply Train, Company E of the 5th Engineers, and Service Park Unit 595. A medical detachment traveled with them, as did a field artillery detachment, and there were seventeen commissioned officers (including Eisenhower and Sereno Brett) attached to the motor train as observers.

In all, there were eighty-one vehicles, carrying thirty-seven officers and 258 enlisted men. There were forty-six trucks, ranging in size from three-quarter-ton Dodge light-delivery vans to monster Macks with over five tons in capacity. There were Whites, Garfords, Packards, Rikers, and Four Wheel Drives. Most were cargo trucks: two of them carried spare parts, one contained a blacksmith's shop, and two others were complete mobile machine shops. For fuel, two tankers carried 750 gallons of gas apiece, while a third carried the same amount of water.

There were eleven passenger cars for the officers—Whites, Cadillacs, and Dodges—and there were nine Indian and Harley-Davidson motorbikes for the scouts. There were five General Motors ambulances, two ambulance trailers, and four kitchen trailers—two four-wheelers called Trailmobiles and two two-wheelers called Liberties.

There was a pontoon trailer called a Loder, which was, at least in theory, going to get them across the Missouri River at Omaha. There was a three-million-candlepower searchlight mounted on a Cadillac chassis, there was a Maxwell caterpillar tractor—and then there was the Militor.

This last was an extraordinary vehicle, a custom-built "wrecker winch," or "artillery wheeled tractor," that had set the army back the best part of $40,000. With a scooped, hooded cowling on the engine, the Militor looked like an iron box bolted on the back of a huge scarab beetle. It had a powerful winch on the rear end and a hefty sprag, a big iron bar that could be anchored into the ground when the Militor was hauling a lamed or stranded vehicle out of trouble. As things turned out, a great number of vehicles would indeed find themselves ditched or mired—and the Militor would prove to be the convoy's most priceless asset.

Before this spectacular assembly could get on the long road to the Pacific, however, they had to be formally sent off. They first had to dedicate the Zero Milestone.

Slowly the convoy thundered through the heart of Washington. Though it was only a couple of miles from Union Station to the Ellipse, the schedule gave them ninety minutes to cross town; the ceremonies would not begin until ten o'clock. Waiting for them before a speaker's podium beneath an arc of trees, an assembly of notables and high-ranking officers gathered around a stumpy object sheathed in a white sheet.

Chief among them was Secretary of War Newton Baker, a small, bespectacled man in a white linen suit. Assorted senators and congressmen were present, as was General Peyton March, the chief of staff, heading a medaled array of military men, and Brigadier General Charles B. Drake, the chief of the Motor Transport Corps. Just three days earlier, Drake had appointed Lieutenant Colonel Charles W. McClure to be the expedition's commander.

Fresh from twelve months' service in France as an infantry officer with the All-American Division—literally just a few days off the boat—McClure was a weathered six-footer with tombstone teeth and a lean, ascetic air about him. Born in Carlinville, Illinois, in 1883, he'd joined up in 1905, following the example of his father, who had served in the army, and in fourteen years he'd seen service in the Philippines, Mexico, and Europe. Now he had to get this convoy to the Pacific; he was a man with a schedule, and he meant to keep it.

McClure accepted ceremonial wreaths to be delivered across the continent to the mayor of San Francisco and the governor of California. The chaplain of the House of Representatives pronounced a benediction on his enterprise. Others present, meanwhile, hoped to find themselves blessed in more material fashion. Among the crowd were Akron tire magnates Harvey Firestone and Frank Seiberling, of Goodyear; the motor age would run on the rubber these men sold, and now the army was running on it too.

Standing by the podium in the dappled shade of the trees, his left hand lightly resting on it, Secretary Baker spoke of the part that trucks like these now arrayed around the park had played in the war. "The great feat of the motor transport in rushing troops into Chateau Thierry to relieve the French," he said, "will live long in history. This world war was a war of motor transports . . . there seemed to be a never-ending stream of moving transports on the white roads of France." Baker also used a phrase often heard from the mouths of politicians, but in this case it was entirely apposite. He said, "This is the beginning of a new era."

Unveiled from its white wrapping, the Zero Milestone was presented to the secretary of war. It's still there today; it's the zero point, from which all highway distances in the United States from the nation's capital are measured. A plain stone pillar, chest high, with a bronze compass rose on the top of it, on its west side is inscribed, STARTING POINT OF FIRST TRANSCONTINENTAL MOTOR CONVOY OVER THE LINCOLN HIGHWAY VII.JUL.MCMXIX.

The Zero Milestone was dedicated with appropriate oration; at least two officers, however, managed to avoid the flights of rhetoric. Though Eisenhower's orders assigning him to the convoy were dated May 11, he would later cheerfully claim that he and Brett had too little notice to make it into the city from Camp Meade. Instead, they joined the convoy at its first night stop in Frederick, Maryland. One can easily imagine that famous, ironical grin as Ike genially observes in his memoirs, "My luck was running; we missed the ceremony."

THE SPEECHES LASTED about an hour. As they finished, the men of the convoy bent their backs to the weighty business of cranking forty-six truck engines. This was a job that called for care; if one of these brutes backfired, it could easily break an arm. But there were no mishaps that sunny first day, and at eleven-fifteen the pilot car of the First Transcontinental Motor Train departed the Ellipse, guiding the huge convoy north from the capital into Maryland.

The pilot car was not one of the eighty-one vehicles assembled by the army. It was instead a gleaming white Packard Twin Six—America's answer to Rolls-Royce—and it was driven by a man named Henry C. Ostermann. Ostermann was the convoy's pilot because, in the past few years, he had driven from coast to coast across America no less than nineteen times. Or, to put it another way, Ostermann was driving the pilot car *because he was the only man who knew the way.*

Back in the train behind Ostermann was First Lieutenant Elwell R. Jackson. The convoy's most junior officer was thirty-two years old. Born in Trenton, New Jersey, he gave his address as 4613 Wayne Avenue, Philadelphia, but he'd seen little of home in the past two years. Jackson was an associate member of the American Society of Mechanical Engineers who'd joined the Ordnance Department as a reserve officer in August 1917. Posted first to the Midvale Steel Company in Philadelphia, before joining the convoy he'd gone on to lend his expertise to the business of armament supply at different firms in Aurora, Indiana, then in Cincinnati, Springfield, and Dayton, Ohio.

If he were thirty-two today, he'd be a computer geek; but just as software and the Internet are the boom trades of our day, so in 1919 automobiles and engineering were the place for a technically minded young man to be, and Elwell Jackson loved every detail of it. As the Ordnance Department's observer with the motor train, he was wonderfully diligent. No leaky radiator or clogged carburetor would escape his notice.

That first day, Jackson noted that one of the kitchen trailers had broken its coupling, that one of the White observation cars had snapped a fan belt, and that the Militor had to tow a Class B with a busted magneto the last mile into camp in Frederick. Still, the weather was fair and warm, the roads were excellent, and the convoy made forty-six miles in seven and a quarter hours.

On the good paved roads of the East, they had traveled at an average speed just a whisker over six miles an hour. What would it be like when they got to the mud of Nebraska? To the dirt trails of Wyoming, and the deserts of Utah and Nevada? Largely unpaved, the vast continent of North America lay stretched out before them. Could they get to San Francisco at all? And why were they trying to go there?

CHAPTER TWO

★ ★ ★

A Road Across America

AMERICAN ROADS WERE terrible. At the start of the twentieth century there was no organized network of connected highways in any state of the union. In the rural United States as late as 1907, there was not one single mile of paved road. In short, when the car appeared, there was nothing for it to drive on.

In 1901, Ransom Olds designed a lightweight runabout with a curved dash, aiming to sell it at the low end of the emerging market for $650. As a public relations stunt, test driver Roy Chapin drove it from Detroit to the second National Automobile Show in New York. He arrived at the Waldorf-Astoria so splattered in mud that the doorman shooed him away. To get in to meet Olds, he had to use the tradesman's entrance.

In 1902, Olds sold two thousand Curved Dashes—it was America's first mass-produced car—and over the next few years, the industry underwent explosive growth and technological advance. The Ford Motor Company was organized in 1903, and by 1907 Ford's profits topped $1 million. The Model T appeared the following year. In 1909, the United States produced over 100,000 cars—and in Indiana, Carl Graham Fisher built the Indianapolis Motor Speedway.

Unlike the great majority of American roads, the speedway was paved—in brick, to begin with—but Fisher was a man with grander visions by far than just a racetrack. At this point, American drivers still had no certainty when they left a town that they'd find anything even approaching a passable road. In consequence, with more and more people trying to travel in more and more cars, the Good Roads Movement was growing fast—but it remained an incoherent, often sectional hubbub, with little focus or direction.

Carl Fisher changed that. Born in Greensburg, Indiana, on January 12, 1874, he was inventive and gregarious. As a boy, he loved ice skating and canoeing; when he was sixteen and living in Indianapolis, with a group of friends he founded the Zig-Zag Cycle Club and became an ardent racer.

He loved speed, and the thrill of the new; he was also a born salesman. Hawking newspapers, books, and magazines to railroad passengers, he'd saved $600 by the time he was seventeen—which in 1891 was about the same as the average factory worker's annual wage. He used the money to open a bicycle-repair shop and soon became the city's distributor for a string of leading manufacturers. He had a genius for publicity and, in his own words, "more nerve than a government mule." One stunt involved his riding "the largest bicycle in the world" around the city—a contraption over twenty feet tall that he had to mount from a second-floor window.

When the automobile appeared, it was inevitable that Fisher would get involved, and he took to racing cars all over the Midwest. He made up for his poor eyesight with a large measure of reckless courage, and, albeit briefly, in 1904 he was the world record holder over two miles. Unfortunately, the year before in Zanesville, Ohio, his engine had exploded and he'd crashed into the crowd, killing two and injuring a dozen others—only one among many illustrations of how dangerous this new game could be.

Now in his thirties and wearing glasses, "Crazy Carl" quit racing and applied his energies to becoming a successful car dealer. In 1908, foreshadowing the industry's taste for the spectacular, he flew across Indianapolis in a car suspended from a huge balloon. Nor was he content just to sell cars; in 1904, he founded the Prest-O-Lite car headlight company.

Until then, on the rare occasions when people dared to drive at night (or found themselves obliged to do so, because they'd got stuck or broken down), they tried to light their way with lamps hung off the front of the car, burning a mix of lard oil and kerosene. Now Fisher backed a local tinkerer who had the rights to a French patent whereby compressed carbide gas produced a much brighter light.

It was touch-and-go to begin with; explosions in the company's plants were a constant menace, and produced a flood of lawsuits.

Nonetheless, Fisher prospered, and he soon had factories from New Jersey to Los Angeles. At the same time, with three partners, he built the Indianapolis Speedway. The motor business was thriving—but there still remained that one big problem. More and more people were taking to the road, and the road was dreadful.

One day late in the summer of 1912, Fisher drove out into the country with two friends to look for a farmer who they'd heard made good cider. On the way back it started raining, and as darkness fell they got lost. Guessing their way as best they could, they came to a spot where the road forked three ways. Fisher reckoned they were about nine miles from the city—far enough that they couldn't see any light from it—and, obviously, there weren't any streetlamps. It was, he said, "as black as the inside of your pocket."

The car had no top, and the three men were soaked to the skin. They tried to figure out what they should do; then one of them thought he saw a sign on top of a pole, dimly reflecting their carbide-gas headlights. It was too high to read, so they drew matches to see which of them should climb up and take a look. Fisher got the short one, so up he went and struck a match; knowing this kind of thing could happen to you at any time when you set off driving, he'd had the top of a saltcellar sewn into his shirt cuff for just this purpose. Then he held up the match to read the sign. It said, CHEW BATTLE-AX PLUG.

This was ridiculous. Clinging, drenched, to the top of a pole in the unlit countryside not ten miles from the city, yet so entirely lost that he might as well have been halfway up the Amazon, Carl Fisher decided something needed to be done. On September 6, he called a dinner at the Old Deutsches Haus for his friends and colleagues in America's booming new motor trade. After they'd eaten, he got up and told them his idea. He said, "A road across America. Let's build it before we're too old to enjoy it."

At the time it was a notion so bold, so entirely unheard of, that more than a few thought Fisher really was "Crazy Carl." There was, surely, no possibility whatsoever of building such a road. Yet in the next few years, this road he imagined stretching out across America would become the most famous road in the world. It would be called the Lincoln Highway. It would run from Times Square in New York to Lincoln Park overlooking the Pacific in San Francisco—

and, on July 8, 1919, the First Transcontinental Motor Train would join it at Gettysburg on its way to California.

THE FIRST PEOPLE to drive across America were a physician from Burlington, Vermont, named Horatio Nelson Jackson and Sewell K. Crocker, a mechanic he hired to go with him. Jackson had been bet fifty dollars that it couldn't be done; he bought a two-seater, twenty-horsepower Winton in San Francisco, and the pair set off on May 23, 1903.

To avoid the Sierra Nevada, they went north through Oregon. Near Caldwell, Idaho, they took on board a stray bulldog, christened him Bud, and bought him a pair of driving goggles. After sixty-five days—forty-five of them driving, with the remainder spent either fixing the car or waiting for spare parts—they arrived in New York on July 26. They'd covered the best part of six thousand miles on a roundabout route—roundabout being the only kind of route there was.

Over the next few years, virtually all transcontinental crossings were organized and undertaken by the car producers. Sometimes they were test drives, sometimes they were attempts on a new record time for the journey, and sometimes they were races—including an extraordinary race in 1908 from New York to Paris via Seattle, Japan, and Siberia—but they were always publicity stunts. The new industry was fast proving to have a real genius for the art of promotion.

Packard was first off the blocks. In 1903, its sales manager, Sidney D. Waldon, sent driver Tom Fetch and photographer Marcus C. Krarup to San Francisco with a car that came to be known as "Old Pacific"; it was a two-seater with twelve horsepower. Waldon also sent a mechanic for backup, as well as a journalist to cover the story. He directed Fetch and Krarup to drive over Emigrant Gap to Reno, up the Humboldt Valley in northern Nevada, around the north side of the Great Salt Lake, and then clear through the middle of Colorado. They set off on June 20, just short of a month after Jackson and Crocker—and they soon found that the route Waldon had selected was a serious challenge. "I didn't understand the difficulties," Waldon later admitted. "Like a dumb fool, I was thinking from the standpoint of publicity, with pictures of the mountains and the canyons, but what I sent them into was something terrific."

Fetch made it to New York on August 21. It had taken sixty-two days, but Krarup's pictures were good, and the story made a big public impression. As one report rather strikingly put it, "That trip meant considerable to the autoists. It meant that the bean-brained sensationalists that would combat the rising of the sun if an injunction could be served on the Almighty, would have something to 'think on' regarding the progress of the Auto-Car." The report concluded, "The land of the Packard is everywhere." Packard would send a car across the country annually for years to come.

You could tackle the journey only in the summer, and to begin with, barely a handful of people tackled it at all, for the simple reasons that for much of the way there wasn't a road, there wasn't a road map, and there weren't any road signs. Looking back ten years from 1918 to 1908, Elwell Jackson's Lincoln Highway guidebook described the adventure like this:

> You proceeded first to lay in a stock of supplies and accessories only slightly less comprehensive, expensive and cumbersome than Captain Amundsen would require for a dash for the Pole or Stanley for a trip into darkest Africa.
>
> Then you started out pretty much by the compass . . . finding, or endeavoring to find the best road, if roads existed, from town to town along as direct a course as you could lay. You could not tell beforehand how long your trip would take, how much it would cost, which way you were going . . . or whether, in reality, you would ever reach your destination or not.

Convoy pilot Henry Ostermann made his first crossing in these conditions in 1908. At that time, he said, an amateur driver needed to allow at least sixty days for the journey—and would need to be prepared for it to take as long as ninety.

This, when he stood up in the Old Deutsches Haus in 1912, was the state of affairs that Carl Fisher meant to change. "What we wanted," he said later, "was to get roads that would go some place, so we could get in our automobiles and ride over them."

FISHER'S ORIGINAL NAME for America's first transcontinental road
was the "Coast-to-Coast Rock Highway." He imagined it graded
and graveled all the way; he plucked a number out of the air and
said it would cost $10 million to build; and he invited the auto-
mobile industry to build it.

This may seem an astonishing idea now, but in 1912 it didn't
seem likely that the government would be building roads anytime
soon, while the carmakers and their associated industries clearly
stood to benefit. Fisher was clever, too, about not asking for the
cash there and then. He suggested instead that all concerned
should pledge one-third of 1 percent of their gross revenue to a
highway fund, with the provision that this money would be called
in only when the total pledged hit his target of $10 million. He
aimed to have the money in place in less than four months, by the
start of 1913, and to get the road built by May 1, 1915. He had a
monumental vision of a cavalcade of twenty-five thousand cars
crossing the continent to open the highway, with the Panama-
Pacific International Exposition in San Francisco that summer as
their destination.

The first response looked good. Frank Seiberling, president of
the Goodyear Tire & Rubber Company in Akron, Ohio, pledged
$300,000 immediately, without even consulting his board. Roy
Chapin (the same man who'd driven the Olds Curved Dash from
Detroit to New York in 1901) was now president of the Hudson
Motor Car Company; he subscribed to the project, as did the man-
agement at Willys-Overland, which ranked second in sales at this
time, behind Ford.

A. G. Batchelder, secretary of the American Automobile Association, wrote to invite Fisher to New York to promote his highway. The idea was so inspired, he said, that "someday there will be
erected to you one of the finest pieces of statuary obtainable." As
smart as he was impulsive, Fisher demurred. "Dear Batch," he
replied, "I am not much on statuary—and right now I think it is a
good idea to pull out personally and take away from our subscribers
the idea that this road plan is mine. If any particular noise is made

for any particular person or small clique of persons, this plan is going to suffer."

All the same, driven by the grand beauty and ambition of his scheme, he toiled with all his energy to see it realized. Dictating floods of letters, keeping his stenographers working nights, touring the headquarters of one firm in Detroit after another, urging, arguing, persuading, within thirty days he had $1 million dollars in promises, and $10,000 more coming in every day.

Fisher worked especially hard on the press. He wrote to Elbert Hubbard, "the sage of East Aurora" in Erie County, New York; Hubbard edited magazines called the *Fra* and the *Philistine.* "Of agitating good roads there is no end," Fisher told him, "but I think you'll agree that it is high time to agitate less and build more." He went on:

> As you know, Mr. Hubbard, the highways of America are built chiefly of politics, whereas the proper material is crushed rock, or concrete. We believe one magnificent highway of this kind, in actual existence will stimulate as nothing else could the building of enduring highways everywhere that will not only be a credit to the American people, but that will also mean much to American agriculture and commerce. Will you pitch in and help?

Hubbard agreed enthusiastically; he called the highway plan "this big and splendid work." He said of the material Fisher submitted for his magazines that it was "certainly way up. It carries the red corpuscle, and anyone can see that it is written hot out of your heart."

The key was Henry Ford. With 118,000 Model T's on the city streets and dirt tracks of America, Ford was now making about three-quarters of the country's cars. Knowing that if this titan of the trade came in with them they were home and dry, Fisher went to see him personally. Arriving at the factory, he was told that the great man was at the Michigan State Fair; Fisher didn't know Ford or where to find him there, but he saw a smart-looking newsboy and offered him ten dollars if he could find Ford in fifteen minutes.

The boy was back soon enough; he told Fisher, "Mr. Ford is down there looking at the pigs."

In the livestock exhibit, the two men leaned with their arms on the top rail of the pigpens. As the highway's official history describes the moment, "Dark, magnetic Fisher convinced lank, conservative Ford that the plan was righteous and worthy of support." Ford told Fisher to come to his plant in the morning, and he'd sign up to back the transcontinental road. Fisher was jubilant; he went out for a champagne dinner. The next morning, he arrived at the factory—and Ford's secretary brushed him off. Stubborn, eccentric, unpredictable Henry Ford had changed his mind.

Fisher appealed to him through his business manager, James Couzens, through Thomas Edison, through Indiana Senator Albert J. Beveridge, even through the White House. Vice President Charles Warren Fairbanks wrote Ford urging him to join in—and told Fisher that if his letter to that effect wasn't strong enough, he'd write another one more forcefully yet.

Ford didn't budge. In later years, his son, Edsel, would personally contribute a good deal to the project, but Henry Ford himself never backed the highway. The reason given (in a letter sent to Fisher by James Couzens) was, typically, both brusque and prophetic. "Frankly," said Couzens, "the writer is not very favorably disposed to the plan, because as long as private interests are willing to build good roads for the general public, the general public will not be very much interested in building good roads for itself. I believe in spending money to educate the public to the necessity of building good roads, and let everybody contribute their share in proper taxes."

Which is pretty much the way things turned out. By 1913, however, Carl Fisher's idea was becoming a crusade that would march on with or without Ford—and the man who would lead that crusade was Henry Joy.

HENRY BOURNE JOY need never have worked a day in his life. Entering this world on November 23, 1864, two blocks from the post office building in Detroit, he was, by his own happy admission, "born with a silver spoon." His father, James Frederick Joy, was a railroad magnate. He'd given Abraham Lincoln his first big case for the Illinois Central, and in the 1870s he was president of the Michigan Central.

Henry used to play in his father's offices at the railroad's brick-and-frame depot downtown ("when I did not make too much of a nuisance of myself") and he was fascinated with technology from early in his life. When his parents took him to the Centennial Exposition in Philadelphia, he fell in love with the enormous Corliss engine that powered the machinery hall, "with its vast moving parts, and huge walking beam high in the air." He sat day after day on the platform with the engineer, who let him fill the oil cans and go around the machine with him as he oiled it. He said simply, "I was enraptured."

Like Carl Fisher (albeit substantially better off) he grew up with a strong sense of adventure and was vividly thrilled at the copious inventiveness of the industrial age. After a couple of years in his early twenties prospecting and mining in Utah, he started taking up the reins of his father's many interests in Detroit; expanding his range, he acquired shares and directorships in a string of banking, transport, energy, and agricultural businesses.

He was a member of Detroit's aristocracy before the advent of "Gasoline Society"; in 1892, with his wedding to Helen Hall Newberry, he married into the city's first family. Oliver and Walter Loomis Newberry had opened a dry goods business in the lakeshore settlement in 1826. As the city grew they moved into real estate and shipping, and were soon among the richest men in America. In the mid–nineteenth century, with his partner James McMillan, Oliver's nephew John Stoughton Newberry started a firm known simply as Newberry & McMillan, Capitalists. By the time of his death in 1887, John Newberry was a director of just about every major business in Detroit; Joy's bride, Helen Newberry, was his daughter.

At the turn of the century, the city had a population of around 250,000. It was a thriving industrial center making ships, steel, steam engines, stoves, and paint, and Joy was at the heart of it. With his brother-in-law, Truman Handy Newberry—who would later be secretary of state for the navy under Theodore Roosevelt, and then beat Henry Ford in the race for a Michigan seat in the

United States Senate—he invested in steamship lines and sugar refineries, railroad firms and land deals. They dined in comfort at the Detroit Athletic Club, they ran pleasure boats on Lake St. Clair, they passed their summers sailing at Watch Hill in Rhode Island, they built mansions at Grosse Pointe, and they appeared in the society columns with their wives' dresses and jewelry noted to the last expensive detail. In the Gilded Age, few were more golden.

In the circumstances, Joy need never have lifted a finger to do more than buy another tranche of shares—but he was far too alive a man to fritter away his days counting dividends, and he was far too excited at what technology held in store for the future of his country. He had vivid memories of a trip to London with his father in 1884, when he was twenty years old, and of meeting the British chancellor of the exchequer, Sir Hugh Childers. Childers told the Joys that "England had reached the zenith of her power . . . that America was developing with inconceivable rapidity as a world influence, in production, in manufacturing, in mining and in agriculture, which would give it a standing in years to come that would challenge the world." Henry Joy wanted to be involved in that challenge, to create and to build; he was, in short, a man ripe for the automobile age.

He bought his first Packard in 1900. The story is apocryphal, but it involves Joy and Truman Newberry, on business in New York, passing a salesman in the street. The salesman has a pair of cars by the sidewalk; he tries to interest the two Detroit men in looking them over, but they're pressed for time and turn him down. Then a fire engine rattles past. Evidently a fellow with a sharp eye for an opportunity, the salesman says, "Jump in. I'll take you to the fire." So they do, and he does, and Joy and Newberry are sufficiently impressed that they buy both cars there and then.

The cars were Packards, and whether the story's true or not, it's certainly the case that Joy liked his first Packard well enough that when the company announced a new model for 1902, he placed an order straightaway. At the time, when a leading citizen ordered a car, that was news. Throughout his life, Joy kept stacks of clippings on all manner of subjects; dated November 7, 1901, one of them is headlined, NEW AUTOMOBILE WHICH HARRY JOY HAS ORDERED.

The story said, "Henry B. Joy has placed an order for a new automobile, which is expected to be one of the best in this part of the country. . . . The machine will be strictly modern in every-thing. It is of twelve horsepower, weighs 1,900 pounds, and has three speeds ahead and one reverse, the maximum rate of speed being twenty-eight miles an hour."

Six months later the car arrived; once again, this was news. Dated May 14, 1902, the story read, "IT'S A BLUE DEVIL. . . . Henry B. Joy's new $2,500 Packard automobile stood in front of the Detroit National Bank this morning for several hours, sur-rounded by a crowd of curious people. It is a gasoline road machine with blue body, red wheels and plenty of brass work, highly pol-ished and giving the machine an elegant appearance."

A couple of weeks later, Joy had his car in the papers again. Disgruntled autoists were complaining that the "speedonometers" used by policemen on bicycles were measuring their speed incor-rectly—so Joy took Judge Murphy for a spin around the Boulevard Speedway to prove that cars were safe, with policemen in pursuit trying to prove that their measurements were accurate. A reporter from the *Detroit Journal* said that the cars sounded like lawn mow-ers, that the judge passed out cigarettes to all present, and that after his ride he concluded, "Well, I'd like to own an auto myself."

Pretty soon, Henry Joy would be the man who could sell him one. Now a confirmed "auto fiend," an ardent fan of these "petro-leum projectiles," he wasn't content with buying his new Packard; he liked it so much that he drove it back to the factory in Ohio and bought the company as well.

JAMES WARD PACKARD had a small business making electrical appa-ratus in Warren, Ohio. In 1899 he started making cars in the cor-ner of his plant, and he struck it rich in 1902, when he won Henry Joy as a customer. Selling out to Joy, he invested the proceeds in his original company, which went on to become one of the largest of its kind in Ohio; Joy, meanwhile, moved the car firm to his home city. This removal of Packard to Detroit, wrote a journalist nine years later, was "the connecting link between the romance of the geniuses and the romance of the industry."

Joy put in $25,000, realized fast that it wasn't remotely enough, and raised his stake to $100,000. He rounded up other shareholders from the glittering circle of his friends and family in Detroit, and the new Packard plant opened in the fall of 1903. It had two acres, 247 workers, and a total investment of $500,000—all from Joy and his associates, because the banks wouldn't touch it. The new business, it was later said, "was unable to obtain a dollar's worth of credit. . . . Detroit financiers considered the making of motor cars a folly." Defying the bankers, Joy looked at the future of the automobile and posed a simple, fine, indeed a classic American question. He asked, "What is the limit?"

Joy was a man of medium height and jovial mien, though with a temper one wouldn't want to cross; he was lively company, and he buzzed with energy and ambition. Now forty-one years old, he was depicted by a journalist as "well put up, not tall, nor stocky. . . . He is strong and wiry, and not the man one would take hold of without counting the cost. He shakes hands like an American, and he talks like one too."

He had served on the U.S.S. *Yosemite* in the blockade of Cuba during the Spanish-American War; he wasn't afraid of a challenge. "I drove myself like a steam engine," he wrote twenty years later. "I drove myself like a slave!" He promoted a new model Packard in 1906 by driving it from Detroit to the New York showroom in three days flat; and he would soon be tackling more ambitious expeditions altogether.

Joy was well enough known that in 1908, with Benjamin Briscoe from the Maxwell Briscoe Motor Company of Tarrytown, New York, he represented the American automobile industry before Congress. He appeared before the Committee on Ways and Means, lobbying for tariffs on foreign cars to protect domestic firms. American labor costs, he claimed, were two and a half times those of their European competitors. But if other companies were hurting (and very few of the early car companies lasted long) plainly these labor costs weren't affecting Henry Joy very much.

Three weeks after he'd spoken to Congress, at the ninth annual Automobile Show at Madison Square Garden, the latest Packard was displayed on a giant mirror set in a bed of concrete, so you could see under the chassis without having to lie on your back. At the same time, on fifty-one acres with six hundred feet of lakeshore frontage in Grosse Pointe Farms, Joy was starting work on Fair Acres, a three-story mansion with sixty-five rooms. He had a forty-two-foot cruiser on Lake St. Clair and a sixty-five-foot motor launch called *Spray II* at Watch Hill. He had dealerships in thirty-seven cities across the continental United States, with others in Paris and Honolulu. By 1909, his original two-acre plant had grown to eighteen acres and employed four thousand people.

The plant was on East Grand Boulevard in central Detroit. It was a mile long, and it was the largest maker of luxury cars in the world. By 1911 it sprawled over seventy-eight acres, with a rail line, a water tower, its own lumberyards, and laboratories. It was the biggest single plant in Detroit. Seven thousand people now went to work there, and there was $14 million in orders on the books for 1912. The following year, Packard sold over eighteen thousand cars—and four thousand trucks as well.

Amid this torrent of production, an original 1899 Packard Model A was kept in pristine condition to remind all involved how the business had been born. "It looks," said one observer, "something like an automobile." Car plants in the late 1890s had been "little 15×20 shops stuck around on alley corners." Now they were "industrial palaces . . . so vast that they astonish even men accustomed to vast things." They had canteens and restaurants; they had acres of glass, giving the workforce an airy light unimaginable in the Victorian mills of older industries.

The money involved was staggering. Consider, for example, the horror in Ford's accounting department early in 1911, when it was found that $68,000 had gone missing. Everybody ran around trying to track it down—until it turned out the missing money was Henry Ford's monthly dividend. He'd stuffed the check in his vest pocket and forgotten to cash it.

At the other end of the payroll, jaws hit the floor all over America when, in 1914, Ford announced that the minimum wage for an eight-hour day in his factories would be five dollars—over twice the average American wage. People said (not for the first time, or the last) that Ford was mad, but it worked. He would continue to outsell all his competitors for another thirteen years.

Meanwhile, on East Grand Boulevard, Henry Joy reported

contentedly in April 1914, "By a flood of orders the Packard Motor Car Company is marooned on a pinnacle of success." This same year he became a director of the Federal Reserve Bank for the Chicago area and joined the board of the United States Chamber of Commerce.

In little more than a decade, the car industry had ascended from nowhere to the very summit of American society. On December 20, 1911, the Automobile Club of America held its twelfth annual banquet at the Waldorf-Astoria. The guest of honor was President Taft; also present at the top table were Count J. H. von Bernstorff, the German ambassador to the United States, John Dix, the governor of the state of New York, and Colonel John Jacob Astor.

Astor was on the banquet committee. Other stellar names helping to organize the affair were Flagler, Frick, Pierpont Morgan, Vanderbilt, and Chauncey M. Depew—once memorably described by Joy's father as "Vanderbilt's Man Friday"—along with Truman Handy Newberry and Henry Bourne Joy. You couldn't buy cachet like this; you couldn't move in higher circles without boarding a rocket.

As for Packard's reputation at this time, it was simply matchless. Elbert Hubbard wrote, "The Packard is a car for a patrician. It belongs to the nobility, and is of the royal line. It is conceded to be without a superior in reliability, workmanship, and luxurious and artistic finish. To own a Packard is the mark of being one of fortune's favorites. It satisfies ambition, soothes aspiration, and gives a peace which religion cannot lend."

The company's slogan preened with smooth confidence; it said simply, "Ask the Man Who Owns One."

SIDNEY WALDON WAS Packard's sales manager; he believed in testing their cars to the extreme. He sought "a destructive ordeal over the worst roads he can find," a goal that led him in 1908 to drive a Packard the length of rural Cuba. He knew all about bad roads, and he also knew Carl Fisher—because in June 1912 Fisher had become Packard's dealer in Indianapolis. Now Waldon introduced Fisher to his boss. Fisher said bluntly, "Joy, the way things are going in this country, we will get an American highway system about the year 2000."

Joy was the perfect man to approach. He had power, prestige, money, and influence, and the need for good roads had been on his mind for years. In the *New York Herald* in 1905 he'd written, "The advent of the gasoline motor has opened a new era and broadened the scope of human ability [but] in America, the abominable road conditions which generally prevail, both in the cities and in the country, have been and continue to be the chief handicap in the development of the home industry."

He knew from his own experience how bad those road conditions were. On May 8, 1911, he'd set off from Detroit with his chief engineer, Russell Huff, to test-drive a new Packard. Their destination was Wyoming; they were "dressed for roughing it, Mr. Joy in a suit of khaki, sombrero and flannel shirt." When they got to Omaha, Nebraska, Joy asked his local dealer where he'd find the road west.

The dealer told him, "There isn't any."

"Then how do I go?"

The dealer told Joy to follow him, and he'd show them the way. They drove west until they came to a wire fence. Here the dealer said, "Just take down the fence and drive on and when you come to the next fence, take that down and go on again."

"A little further," said Joy, "and there were no fences, no fields, nothing but two ruts across the prairie."

The Packard company decided to back Fisher's road in December 1912. At a board meeting at the beginning of the New Year, Joy pledged $150,000 (1 percent of a projected $15 million turnover) to help get it built. The effect was electric. It was, said one observer, "proof that not everyone would wait for Mr. Ford."

Joy said, "If a transcontinental highway can be fathered . . . the good roads improvement which will result within the next ten years can hardly be conceived of in advance. . . . [Such improvement] would benefit almost every person in the United States."

One of the first things they had to do was give their road a better name. The Coast-to-Coast Rock Highway, after all, hardly rang with glamour. Elbert Hubbard wanted it called simply the

American Road. Then, at a meeting on April 14, 1913, in Joy's office in Detroit, Fisher suggested that they call it the Lincoln Memorial Highway. He'd always idolized Lincoln and had pictures of him on the walls of his home; as for Joy, he was an active Republican whose father had known Lincoln personally. They agreed upon it then and there. It was a perfect name, patriotic, resonant, inspiring; it was the ideal name for their ideal road.

The Lincoln Highway Association was formally incorporated the following month, with its headquarters at 2115 Dime Savings Bank Building, Detroit. Henry Joy was appointed the organization's first president; other directors included Carl Fisher, Roy Chapin, and John Willys from the motor business, Frank Seiberling of Goodyear, and Albert Gowen from the cement industry. Joy warned them, "The enterprise has strewn in front of it insurmountable difficulties." That, however, had never stopped these men from trying large things before. But how do you go about promoting and building a road thirty-three hundred miles long?

BY THE SUMMER of 1913, it was clear to the directors of the newly formed Lincoln Highway Association that Fisher's original plan wasn't viable. They had promises of money and free cement worth over $4 million, and that was no mean tally—but it was less than half Fisher's target. Besides, it was equally clear that building a road across America would cost a great deal more than $10 million, even if they could raise that much.

Nonetheless, the project had taken on a life of its own. Standing to gain from it as they did, the western states especially were zealous in their backing for the road. The Denver Chamber of Commerce sent cars to scout a trail to Salt Lake City. Utah and Wyoming sent delegations to affirm that if the highway went through their territory, they'd fund the construction work themselves. Cities as far south as Santa Fe and Phoenix clamored to get on the route—and apart from money, the route was the first and biggest question. Just where exactly was this road going to go?

Joy was determined that the Lincoln Highway should be the best and most practical road they could devise, running from New

York to San Francisco by the shortest, most direct route. To secure
the backing of the states along the way, he planned to launch the
project by announcing the route at the annual Governors' Conference in Colorado Springs in August 1913. As the announcement
drew near, a rising flood of demands to be placed on the road
poured into Detroit from hundreds of western communities. They
could chivy and beg as much as they wanted, but it would do them
little good. As far as Joy was concerned, directness was all.

He followed common sense, and he followed history. West of
Omaha, topography drove the road up the valley of the Platte and
through the South Pass in Wyoming, as it had done the Union
Pacific and the forty-niners before it. At Salt Lake City, it parted
company with the railroad; it went south of the lake and the Great
Salt Lake Desert, following the Pony Express and the Overland
Stage through central Utah and Nevada. Finally, from Reno, it
crossed the Sierra Nevada to the north of Lake Tahoe, passing into
California through Emigrant Gap. This was the toughest piece of
mountain terrain on the whole length of the highway; at this point,
Joy also drew an alternative route running south of Tahoe from
Carson City to Placerville, rejoining the main line at Sacramento.
This "Pioneer Branch" was the only place on the road where, of its
own volition, the association offered tourists two options. The reason for this was never really explained, but the two branches of the
highway around the lake remained on their maps throughout the
road's existence.

Joy knew, when these and all their other decisions became public, that there would be turbulent agitation for realignments from
one ocean to the other. Prepared to face that, on August 26 he presented the route to ten state governors at a private meeting in the
Antlers Hotel in Colorado Springs. His address was vintage Joy,
managing (like himself) to be both short and orotund, punchy and
high-toned.

"The appeals of sections have been heard," he declared. "The
arguments of all interests have been and are being weighed." But
should the road go to every major city, every site of scenic beauty,
every point of interest across the country? Such a road, he said,
"would indeed be a devious and winding journey in this great

America of ours." Therefore, he continued, "the decision must be confined to one permanent road across the country to be constructed *first,* no matter how desirable others may be and actually are."

He concluded by making a comparison that would recur again and again. He said, "It seems to us but yesterday that the Panama Canal was begun, and yet almost tomorrow it will be open to the world." Privately, he and his fellow directors thought building the highway would take twenty years. They knew it was a wonderful idea; in reality, they also knew it was just a line on a map.

Joy CALLED THE association "a committee of idealists." They were, of course, manufacturers of cars, tires, and cement, whose sales would soar as America built roads. It would, however, be unwise to be too cynical about this. When Joy talked about "the great patriotic work," he meant it; the martyred Lincoln had been an idol of his in childhood. Besides, these were the kind of Americans for whom making money and patriotism were indivisible; making money was synonymous with building America.

Moreover, like Fisher, Joy recognized that any crudely obvious use of the road for his own ends would soon backfire. When the route was announced, his name and that of the Packard company were repeatedly identified in the ensuing press coverage. Seeing this, Joy wrote to his staff at the Dime Savings Bank Building and said, "I notice mention is made of Packard. This is directly against my wishes. It hurts the whole proposition by creating prejudice— and rightly so."

Whatever they thought of Joy and his motives, the western governors had political and commercial imperatives of their own. As a result, some of the negotiations that followed their presentation were, said Joy, "rather delicate and strenuous." Governor William Spry of Utah, for example, had a power base in Ogden and had been given to understand that the Lincoln Highway would go there from Wyoming before turning south to Salt Lake City. In the public proclamation of the route after Joy's address in Colorado Springs, that wasn't the case, and Spry's telegram of September 12 to Carl Fisher is unequivocally worded. "Under no circumstances can I endorse that route, and unless change is made . . . shall be compelled to withdraw my support." At this early stage, the association could not be sufficiently sure of itself to risk such displeasure. In short order, they assured Spry that Ogden would be on the route.

As for Governor Ammons of Colorado, he was aghast to learn that the highway didn't enter his state at all. At the cost of disregarding their basic principle—that the Lincoln Highway should be one road, running only by the shortest, most direct route—the association hastily placated Ammons by adding a clumsy dogleg south to Denver from Big Springs, Nebraska, which then jogged back north to rejoin the main line at Cheyenne.

From the beginning—inevitably, and as Fisher had feared—the road was built as much of politics as it was of crushed rock. Soon, however, the association would feel a great deal more confident of its public standing (not that its members were much lacking in self-belief to begin with), and future disputes over routing would be faced down more firmly. In July 1914, when Woodrow Wilson asked that the line be changed between Philadelphia and Gettysburg to include Baltimore and Washington, Joy turned down even the president—though as he was a confirmed Republican, one might imagine he enjoyed that.

As for the Denver dogleg, that was soon dropped from the map. In 1915, when the first guidebook came out, it contained this warning for the traveler at Big Springs: "The tourist wishing to follow the official Lincoln Highway straight west through Cheyenne, Wyoming should not be diverted at this point by markers or signs indicating that the Lincoln Highway turns southwest here to Denver. Numerous markers have been placed here to mislead the tourist." As one historian dryly observes, "Colorado's never had a good word for the Lincoln Highway since."

JOY HAD TRAVELED to Colorado with Carl Fisher and the association's first secretary, A. R. Pardington. On the train back to Detroit from the conference, these three drew up a proclamation of the route for the general public. It was published on September 10, 1913, along with Joy's address to the governors, now titled "An Appeal to Patriots." Some 150,000 copies were mailed to newspapers and magazines, to car dealers and manufacturers, to road boosters and legislators and chambers of commerce. The association didn't have enough people to handle this; instead, Joy had his staff at Packard work through the night to get it done. He asked all his dealers and agents to fly Lincoln Highway pennants and the Stars and Stripes side by side, and to hang portraits of Lincoln in their showrooms. He also sent a personal appeal to every owner of a Packard, along with the proclamation of the route, urging them to display it. Pointing once again to the Panama Canal, he said, "Without dreams the world could accomplish little!"

The goal was to raise both money and enthusiasm. To keep the pot bubbling, the association asked the governor of each state along the route to declare a public holiday on October 31 and to dedicate the highway to Lincoln's memory on that day. They asked the clergy of the nation to preach about Lincoln in their sermons in connection with that dedication; these holy plaudits for the road were then recycled as press releases.

Come the day, there were parties and parades from New York all the way to San Francisco. Towns dressed themselves in the national colors, mayors spoke, and bonfires and fireworks lit up the night. After the celebrations in Omaha, the *Sunday Bee* said that within the next few years, the road would be so well built "that it will last forever."

THE ASSOCIATION'S WORK, said Joy, "is not the work of a moment, it is not the work of a year; it is not the work even of a decade. It is the work of a generation."

"It looked," said Sidney Waldon, "like a wild dream."

In 1913, there was nothing west of Pittsburgh that even remotely resembled a connected road system. Along the entire length of the route—as first drawn out, 3,389 miles—only 650 of those miles were macadam or stone.

In Detroit, meanwhile, they had no money. By the start of 1914, the association was $21,700 in the red. To keep the road alive, it did four things. First, to cover the immediate shortfall, Joy put in $7,000 from the Packard company and wrote to his fellow directors saying, "Won't you please put your shoulder to the wheel and help me clean it up?" He got money from Carl Fisher, from

Roy Chapin at Hudson and John Willys at Willys-Overland, from Frank Seiberling at Goodyear and Albert Gowen at Lehigh Cement. Mostly they put in $2,000 apiece; five other cement companies chipped in, as did Harvey Firestone, T. Coleman Du Pont, and William Randolph Hearst.

Second, they stoked the publicity machine; for the next few years, their public relations would be prolific and immaculate. They published guidebooks, they filled newspapers and magazines with pictures and stories, they helped Wyoming draft its highway laws, they made a documentary movie, they produced lapel buttons, pennants, radiator badges, stickers, and stationery. In the history of boosterism, it was as lively a campaign as there's ever been—and the army convoy in 1919 would be its crowning moment.

The third thing they did was change their objectives. There was no possibility, as Fisher had dreamed, that a finished road would be ready by 1915; they had to set themselves more modest and attainable goals. One was to get the whole route signposted and to persuade local authorities all along it to rename it the Lincoln Highway. The other was to build "seedling miles," which turned out to be a quite brilliant piece of marketing.

The association had decided that poured concrete was the future. Now they set about converting the nation. Up to this point, many people had at best been indifferent to road building; if it meant paying more taxes, they could be actively hostile. To persuade people otherwise, the association offered free cement to any community willing to find the labor to pour it. The first concrete mile was laid near Malta, Illinois, in October 1914; others followed in Iowa, Indiana, and Nebraska. They were object lessons in how good a road could be—but the real genius of the idea was that each one was built way out in the countryside. People had to toil through mud and dust to reach them. They would then have a mile of smooth-riding bliss before bouncing and slithering into the rutted dirt again. Naturally, they went home wanting the rest of the road paved too—and then the cement firms had only to wait for the bond issues to pass and the phone to ring.

These, then, were three of the four things that the association did to keep its plan in motion. It put up money, produced floods of publicity, and kept its aim on what was practically attainable: painted signposts and poured seedling miles. The fourth thing they did was hire Henry Ostermann.

OSTERMANN WAS BORN in Tell City, Indiana, in 1876. His father, an opera singer from Luxembourg, died when he was one year old. His mother, an actress, didn't long survive her husband, so Henry was raised by his older sisters in New York. He became a newsboy in the city when he was six years old, and a hotel bellhop when he was ten. At fourteen he joined the navy; he deserted in Lima, Peru, was arrested, and then discharged in California. He drifted awhile, picking oranges and working West Coast steamers, before traveling for two years with Buffalo Bill's Wild West Show.

In his twenties he worked on ranches in Montana and North Dakota, then became a flagman on the Illinois Central. Promotions to brakeman and conductor followed, until in 1906 he invented a new kind of grain door for freight cars. He built up a business making these; in 1913, he started a car dealership in Deadwood, South Dakota. Then he lost everything in an ill-judged investment—so he went to work selling memberships for the Lincoln Highway Association.

He got the job in October 1913, on a salary of $350 a month. Ostermann proved to be astoundingly good at promoting the road out in the field, among the people who would actually have to vote the bond issues and get the thing built. He was a handsome, swarthy man with a bristling, silver-blond mustache and a wolfish charm. When the association's perpetual financial difficulties led to his salary being axed a year later, he soon got it back. They didn't want to lose him; he was "a direct asset on a self-sustaining basis because of the personal contact which is constantly maintained, and has been extremely helpful in many instances."

The association had appointed unpaid state and county "consuls" all along the route, and some three hundred of them were now pushing the work across the country. They were mayors, car dealers, garage owners, hoteliers, and local businessmen who could see the advantages of being on the transcontinental road. Twice a year, Ostermann went back and forth in his Packard Twin Six visiting these people, addressing meetings, and getting the car, with its Lincoln Highway logo on the side, pictured in the papers.

From the Atlantic to the Pacific, he was well known and much liked. While Joy argued and cajoled in the highest circles of Gasoline Society, Ostermann turned the wheel on the road. He was ideally suited to the job. He'd crossed the continent twice already before the highway was born, in 1908 and 1912; now he did it for a living, often with his wife, Babe Bell, along for the ride.

At the start of June 1919, a month before the army's motor train set off from Washington, D.C., Babe Bell died in Detroit. How Ostermann felt we can't say—but it certainly wouldn't have stopped him from leading out the convoy. In all likelihood, nothing short of physical illness or forcible restraint would have stopped him from doing that. After all, he was the man who'd thought of it in the first place—and his inspiration was brought about by the demands of World War I.

BACK IN OCTOBER 1914, Packard had received an order for 180 trucks from the Allied armies in Western Europe. A thousand men stormed the factory gates on East Grand Boulevard trying to get a piece of the work. The plant ran around the clock. A new truck was produced every forty minutes, and the order was filled in five days.

Although the armies of Europe could see the worth of these new motor vehicles, the American army wasn't much interested. There had been a proposal that the army build a car as early as 1900, but Quartermaster General Ludington rejected it: "He considered that the condition of the average roads traversed in military operations, unpaved and often deep with mud, made them entirely unsuitable for automobile use."

The army continued to be hostile to motor vehicles for another decade; it wasn't until 1911 that it tried to develop a motor truck for military use. The effort didn't get very far, because the army didn't have any money—it took two years just to write the specifications—but this is when the links were first forged between Detroit and the military.

Meanwhile, the Lincoln Highway Association wanted the government to get into the road-building business. One line of approach was to push legislation; another was to promote so-called military highways in the service of the national defense. This was of a piece with the growing pressure for "national preparedness," a cause loudly espoused by Henry Joy; it was also about enlisting the army in the Good Roads Movement.

To this end, in July 1915, twenty-five cadets from the North-western Military Academy of Lake Geneva, Wisconsin, drove to San Francisco over the intended route of the Lincoln Highway. They had an armored machine-gun car, an armored wireless station, two "balloon destroyers," an ambulance, and three cars for provisions, cooks, and officers. Colonel R. P. Davison, the expedition's commander, duly reported, "As a military necessity, the Lincoln Highway should be constructed so that the heaviest artillery could be rushed from one coast to the other with the rapidity and efficiency which German roads have allowed in Teuton maneuvers."

This was fine in principle; in practice, the army still had very few motor vehicles to rush from either coast to anywhere. If it couldn't go by train, in the U.S. Army in 1915 it most likely went by wagon or mule. Then, on March 9, 1916, Pancho Villa raided the border town of Columbus, New Mexico. Stores and houses were looted and burned; seven American soldiers and eight civilians were killed. President Wilson ordered General Pershing to take ten thousand men on the "Punitive Expedition," pursuing Villa into Mexico—and at last Detroit had its chance.

Two days after the raid, the Southern Department of the Army ordered two motor companies of twenty-seven trucks each. They were to haul munitions and supplies, and one of the two companies was to be built by Packard. The order came in to East Grand Boulevard at five o'clock on a Monday afternoon. By three-thirty the following afternoon, the trucks had been built and were loaded on a special train from Detroit to El Paso. Their steel frames were painted a dull battle gray, their wheels and tires were steel and solid rubber, and they had bullet-proof hoods—to protect the engine, but not the driver.

Regardless of the latter drawback, no less than one thousand of Joy's workforce volunteered to go with their trucks to Mexico. Thirty-four drivers were selected from the eager crowd. One of them cried out, "Leave your overcoat behind. We are going to a hot place where the night blooming cactus grows." In the heady rush of departure another said, "Send us some bats and balls. We forgot them."

When they got there Herbert Wilcox, a Packard driver, wrote to his mates in the factory that this first shipment had driven six hundred miles into Mexico, resupplying the cavalry in the nick of time. The soldiers had been eight days on short rations; they'd had to kill sixty horses that they couldn't feed.

Joy followed them south at the end of March. He had a customized Twin Six shipped express to Columbus, then drove across the border toward Chihuahua to see how his vehicles were faring. Ever alert to the public relations opportunity, he sent back pictures to the *Detroit Free Press*. He mounted a captured machine gun on the hood of his car for the cameras and bounced merrily around Mexico, dishing out tobacco to the troops and their Indian scouts.

He was "roughing it de luxe." He reported to the paper that "the roads are not roads at all, and . . . the trucks are obliged to fight their way across unbroken country."

General Pershing dubbed the two truck companies the Flying Squadron, though in truth you could hardly say that they flew; it was slow, hot, filthy, arduous work. Lieutenant Colonel J. M. Walker of the engineers subsequently reported, "The keeping of the road from Columbus to El Valle, 175 miles, open for truck traffic was rendered possible by the fact that every man—soldier or civilian—on the job made up his mind that it should be done. This statement includes the personnel of the Truck Trains, trucks frequently being hauled by hand through seemingly impassable mud or sand." Nonetheless, it worked. In the words of the Quartermaster Corps' historian, "Any lingering doubts as to [motor transport's] superiority over animal-drawn transportation were forever settled."

Packard got an order for a second batch of twenty-seven trucks in April. By the summer the army had bought 588 trucks, 57 tankers for gas and water, 10 mobile machine shops, 6 wreckers, 8 tractors, 75 cars, and 61 motorbikes. Convoys left Columbus daily all through 1916, carrying thousands of tons of food, water, clothing, mail, medicine, and munitions to Pershing's men. They may never have caught Pancho Villa—but for the eight different motor manufacturers involved, he was awfully good business.

IN HIS INIMITABLE way, Henry Joy had urged Americans to wake up and get ready to join the world war for years before they finally did so. On January 9, 1916, he wrote an extraordinary piece for the *New York Herald* whose subheads read as follows: "Reviewing Recent History, Mr. Joy Feels Shame at Being American Citizen . . . Says Heritage of National Honor Is Slipping Through Our Fingers—Nation's Policy in Dealing with Murders by Teutons Blot on Record."

One hundred and twenty-eight Americans had died on the *Lusitania*. The German submarine campaign was widely considered an inhuman outrage, and Joy felt that vehemently. He berated Wilson's administration for "doing practically nothing to place the United States in a state of military and naval preparedness . . . babbling boobs continue to babble of peace and neutrality when there is neither." He also ripped into Henry Ford's "sentimental mushiness," complaining that his rival's pacifism attracted "undesirable notoriety" to Detroit. The country, he said, was "supinely quiescent." He went on fiercely to ask, "Shall we not redesign our beloved Uncle Sam? Ought we not to depict him as a blind, bloodless cigar store Indian, with a wooden head, a wooden heart and wooden insides? We are all in the sewer of disgrace together."

Two months later, Pancho Villa hit Columbus. As Pershing crossed the border, Secretary of War Newton Baker called out the National Guard. Ford said that any of his workers who joined the Guard would lose their jobs. Protesting against the rush to war, he paid the *Chicago Tribune* $887.04 for a full-page ad titled "Humanity—and Sanity, by Henry Ford." The *Tribune* gave the money to the Navy League, calling Ford "a serious opponent of genuine patriotism."

Joy returned from Chihuahua, railing that both the size and the condition of the U.S. Army were so poor as to be "an invitation to Mexico to fight us" and saying that he only wished all the "bloodless, gutless pacifists" had been in Columbus when Pancho Villa came to town. The *Detroit Labor News* called Joy "our esteemed flag-flapping friend of motordom . . . Henry B. Joy-ful [is making] so many mental somersaults that it's really very hard to follow him." Nonetheless, the paper went on, "Now you may be joyful, for the interests want war with Mexico. We hate to suggest what they have reason to gain by it."

Shortly afterward the *New York Times* reported, "Preparedness Means Millions for Motors. Officer of Quartermaster Corps Says Army Increase Plans Will Call for Heavy Purchases of Trucks." What Joy called preparedness, Ford called militarism. He said war was "an enormous crime," and that he'd "rather end his days in poverty than make a profit out of war or preparedness." Joy retorted that Ford might take a different view if his factories were in Belgium instead of Michigan. The *Chicago Tribune* called Ford an anarchist. Ford sued for $1 million in libel damages.

In Europe, the bloodshed continued—and then, on April 2, 1917, Woodrow Wilson spoke to Congress. "The day has come," he said, "when America is privileged to spend her blood and might for the principles that gave her birth and happiness and the peace which she has treasured. God helping her, she can do no other."

The United States entered the world war. Eighteen months later, the army owned over eighty thousand trucks. One in five of them was a Packard.

ENTRY INTO THE war wrought phenomenal dislocation on the American economy. Pershing left Pancho Villa to his own devices and set off for France, facing the infinitely greater challenge of building and leading the American Expeditionary Force. On June 6, 1917, he cabled Washington that he wanted one million American men on the Western Front by May the next year. Hundreds of Liberty ships began sliding down the slipways of scores of shipyards; every kind of industry turned itself over to war production. To get the men and materiel to the ports of the eastern seaboard, the government took over the railroads—but the rail system was soon overwhelmed.

Since the trains couldn't cope, the army had to get on the road. In November 1917, the Council of National Defense set up the Highways Transport Committee. Its chairman was Roy Chapin—

formerly Oldsmobile's test driver, now the president of the Hudson Motor Car Company and a director of the Lincoln Highway Association as well.

The association was on the inside track. When the army started organizing truck convoys from industrial centers to seaports, it was the Lincoln Highway they drove on, and it was Henry Ostermann in his Packard who led the way. After all, who knew the road better than he?

The first convoy left Detroit for Baltimore on December 17, 1917. In ferocious winter conditions, it took them two weeks to go 580 miles—but out of thirty vehicles that set off, all but one of them made it. Soon convoys were rumbling day and night onto the highway through Ohio and Pennsylvania from Chicago, Detroit, Cleveland, and Akron. Through six weeks of blizzards, fifteen hundred men worked ten-hour shifts to keep the road clear through the Alleghenies. The snow drifted sixteen feet deep; huge bonfires blazed by the roadside to keep the men warm.

It was during this heroic struggle against the weather that Ostermann conceived the idea of sending a convoy the entire length of their American road. It couldn't be done during the war—the men in France needed bullets, shells, guns, and gas masks, and the army needed every truck it could lay its hands on to carry them—but as soon as the war was over, Detroit started pushing the idea in earnest. As its own history tells it, in 1919 the First Transcontinental Motor Train was arranged "at the instance and with the assistance of the Lincoln Highway Association."

Sadly, even as the association pulled off its greatest coup, Henry Joy was no longer directly involved. When America entered the war, he resigned his presidencies at both Packard and the association and signed up as a lieutenant colonel in the supply service of the nascent Army Air Service. After all, at his instigation, Packard had designed the Liberty engines that powered the army's planes. Then he suffered an attack of angina—the first stirrings of the heart trouble that would eventually take his life.

Even so, you couldn't keep him quiet. When the convoy set off from Washington, he was on vacation at the Longs Peak Inn in Estes Park, Colorado; to mend his heart, he'd decided to go hiking. Promoting the Townsend Bill and its plan for a federal highway system, he cabled the motor train's commander, Colonel McClure, with a long message of support and encouragement. He said, "The sending of the convoy . . . is the realization of the vision of the founders. . . . The prayer of the Lincoln Highway Association is that the work of establishing a national system of main arterial highways may be taken up with a vengeance and pushed to completion."

The men of Detroit had gotten their way. They had the army and the government behind them. America stood on the brink of a new world, and the defining feature of that world would be "automobility."

CHAPTER THREE

★ ★ ★

"We're Going to Get There; That's All"

WHEN THE FIRST Transcontinental Motor Train left Washington on July 7, 1919, the people who'd organized it had several objectives in mind. One of them went largely unspoken, but it was vitally important all the same.

These were difficult times, with much strife and grieving, and America needed celebration—so, after the enormous national effort of the war, from one ocean to the other the army meant to show off an impressive array of the equipment that had helped win it. It was a way of saying thank you to the people. They'd bought their Liberty bonds, and now the convoy would show them where their money had gone. It would, in a sense, be one giant, rolling, transcontinental party.

This feel-good factor aside, the official aims of the exercise were fourfold. They were set out in detailed press releases—mostly written in Detroit—that spurred front-page coverage nationwide. First, the convoy would put this equipment through as grueling a trial as could be devised. Since the army had acquired all these trucks, what exactly were they capable of? For manufacturers and military men alike, this was the ultimate test drive. Certainly, no one had ever dreamed before of sending such a quantity of vehicles across the unpaved vastness of America. Eisenhower would later say, "We were not sure it could be accomplished at all."

Second, along the way, the convoy's observers would conduct detailed studies of the terrain and the driving conditions, as they affected their different branches of the service. The key questions were, Could the military make practical use of a highway across the continent? And if they wanted to get men and equipment from one ocean to the other by road, what would that involve? Because the truth is, they really didn't know. Incredible though it may seem today, in 1919 so many American roads were still so bad, and motorized transport was still so new to the army, that the convoy didn't have a decent road map. Instead, Colonel McClure was using a Lincoln Highway guidebook.

The motor train's third stated purpose was as part of a recruitment drive. With three million troops either demobilized or very shortly to be so, the army needed new men. In this regard, the convoy was only one of many stunts and attractions (albeit a pretty large one) that the armed forces put on at this time to draw fresh recruits.

Finally—and by far the most important to all concerned—the motor train was "the government's contribution to the Good Roads movement." In a nutshell, Washington had decided it was time to get into the road-building business.

In what must have been sweet music to Detroit, the Motor Transport Corps' chief officer, General Charles B. Drake, described the convoy's purpose as follows: "To demonstrate the practicability of long distance motor commercial transportation and the consequent necessity for the expenditure of governmental appropriations to provide necessary highways."

Now, you may well ask what business it was of the army to promote "motor *commercial* transportation." Nonetheless the Good Roads Movement, said Drake, was one in which the army was "vitally interested"—so traveling from coast to coast on the Lincoln Highway, the convoy was the army's way of promoting good roads. It was also, as things turned out, a way of proving how very badly the country needed them.

BEING IN LARGE part a public relations exercise, the convoy naturally had a publicity officer. He was a bumptious young lieutenant named William Doron, and unfortunately—unlike the Lincoln Highway Association—he was hopeless.

Elwell Jackson, the diarist who sent daily telegrams back to the Ordnance Department noting their progress and the performance of their vehicles, subsequently wrote a detailed report on what happened. His verdict on Doron was scathing. What work he did in preparing people for their passage, said Jackson, "was in a large measure counteracted by the exaggerated or misleading statements he issued."

Mitigation for Doron might be pleaded insofar as the expedition had been cobbled together with disorderly haste; invitations to the dedication of the Zero Milestone went out only five days before the convoy was due to depart. This was little excuse, however, for his lyrical claim that the men of the convoy were "the flower of the Motor Transport Corps."

They were nothing of the sort. Jackson noted tersely, "The majority of the enlisted men of Co.'s E & F of 433rd Motor Supply Train were raw recruits with little or no military training, many of whom had not driven a motor truck before." Many had joined the outfit at the last minute, and discipline in the early weeks "was conspicuous by its absence."

Eisenhower concurred. He reported afterward, "Discipline among the enlisted personnel of the M.T.C. was almost unknown . . . they lacked training and good officers." In consequence, amid much "unseemly conduct," some trucks drove too fast, others stopped wherever they felt like it, and vehicles were unnecessarily damaged by the capricious treatment handed out to them by green rookies at the wheel.

Looking back nearly fifty years later, Ike recalled, "The convoy had been literally thrown together and there was little discernible control. All drivers had claimed lengthy experience in driving trucks; some of them, it turned out, had never handled anything more advanced than a Model T. Most colored the air with expressions in starting and stopping that indicated a longer association with teams of horses than with internal combustion engines. It took a week or ten days to achieve any kind of march discipline."

Part of the problem was Colonel McClure; these were not his men, and this was not his convoy. Since February, the planning for the expedition had instead been in the hands of Captain Bernard H. McMahon, a genial Californian from Salinas. It might be argued, of course, that the indiscipline of the men on departure should therefore be laid at McMahon's door, and that the army was right to appoint McClure as his superior. Nonetheless McMahon was, noted Jackson, "the idol of his men and always had their interests at heart."

McMahon was placed in a delicate position. "The wholesome effect of his personality," said Jackson, served to keep the men going, but McClure "was decidedly unpopular." McClure told Eisenhower that, being handed the convoy on short notice, he'd had no chance to drill the men before they left, and no say in the selection of the officers he had to work with. They were, in short, going to have to learn how to run this thing as they went along.

FREDERICK, MARYLAND, IS an attractive, well-preserved small town of old brick buildings and many churches. On their first day out from Washington the convoy rolled in here at six-thirty in the evening, with the Militor towing a broken-down Class B.

The men camped a short way east of the town center at the county fairgrounds on East Patrick Street. The officers shared two-man tents; the men slept on the trucks, on camp beds, or on the open ground. They had "shelter halves," but they bothered putting them up only if it threatened to rain.

First call was at four forty-five in the morning; reveille was sounded five minutes later. Mess was served off the kitchen trailers at five-thirty, the vehicles were inspected at six, and soon thereafter two scouts left on motorbikes to post direction signs on the road ahead. By seven o'clock, the convoy was under way. They drove into town, turned right at the Square Corner, and rumbled up North Market Street toward the Emmitsburg Pike and Pennsylvania.

Moving along what's since become U.S. Route 15, the convoy headed north through lush farmland bordered to the west by the low rise of the Catoctin Mountains. After ninety minutes, the diligent Elwell Jackson noted the fan adjustment letting go on a Standard Class B. Then, on the Middle Creek between Emmitsburg and Gettysburg, they came upon their first conundrum.

The roof on the covered bridge was too low for the bodies of some of the trucks, and the bridge itself was too weak for the heavier vehicles. While the bigger trucks forded the creek, inching over rocks through the water, the lighter ones edged gingerly through the bridge. Standing beside the driver, one of the men hacked boards out of the roof until his truck could pass. As he did so, the convoy's film crew captured him easing their way through the journey's first obstacle.

The film crew was supplied by the Signal Corps; with a group of journalists, they were following the motor train in a trio of brand-new Willys-Overland Mysteries. Their moving pictures would be shown in cinemas all across the country—because if this was going to be an epic adventure for the army men, for the motor business it was going to be a wonderful advertisement as well.

WEAK BRIDGES AS they neared the Pennsylvania line held them up for two hours. They forded the creeks and took muddy detours around roadwork. Ten tons fully loaded, one of the machine shops stuck in the mud. Two Macks in tandem couldn't pull it out; with 165 horsepower under its quirky bonnet, the Militor managed it.

Lieutenant Howard Shockey, an M.T.C. supply officer, told the *Gettysburg Times,* "That bridge we just passed was entirely incapable of withstanding heavy traffic or allowing our cars to pass. These old wooden bridges are a thing of the past, and it wouldn't be a bad idea to run over them and break them down to show how poorly they are constructed."

Given what was happening elsewhere, this might have been more tactfully expressed. Traveling ahead of the trucks while they dealt with the bridges, at ten o'clock that morning Colonel McClure arrived at the hamlet of Greenmount, just south of the Gettysburg battlefield. Waiting for the convoy, he found a delegation of a dozen state and city officials and local businessmen, before whom he was considerably embarrassed.

Lieutenant Doron, the convoy's hapless publicity officer, had told the local notables that they'd be playing host to the motor train that night. He had, said the *Times,* stated positively that the train would stop there—an assurance that now proved incorrect.

Understandably, Gettysburg was somewhat put out. The town had made the Nixon Field ready for the convoy to camp in; the local Red Cross had arranged for shower baths for the soldiers at the town's college and the Kurtz Playground. For their evening's entertainment the local band had been secured for a dance, and all concerned had been looking forward to a display from the convoy's huge searchlight. Now none of this would happen.

McClure told the waiting delegation that he appreciated their hospitality, and he thanked them for their interest. He said he was sorry they couldn't stop, but his orders were to proceed to Chambersburg, and that was what he had to do.

The main body of the convoy arrived at Greenmount four hours later. The local worthies watched the men eating lunch—one egg sandwich and a cup of coffee each—and then the trucks pressed on through the town's Center Square, and away west on the Lincoln Highway.

DID NOT STOP HERE, said a curt headline in the *Times.* "Efforts of Citizens Wasted." As with the matter of the enlisted men's discipline, this did not augur well. Worse, however, was the worry that if they had had trouble crossing a small creek on their second day out, how on earth would they cross a whole continent?

TRAVELING AHEAD OF the convoy in his shining white Packard, Henry Ostermann made a better show of the public relations job altogether. For good roads, he declared, reaching with practiced ease for the automotive metaphor, "Pennsylvania right now doesn't need to take a back seat for any state in the union."

At this early stage on its journey to the Pacific, the Lincoln Highway followed a shortened version of the old Pittsburgh & Philadelphia Turnpike through the Alleghenies—the road that's since become U.S. 30. The third edition of the highway's guidebook had appeared in 1918; it was in the pages of this most recent edition that Elwell Jackson wrote his daily log.

From Gettysburg, said the guide, "Good bituminous macadam roads prevail. The mountain roads are particularly good . . . the Pennsylvania State Highway Department [has] spent hundreds of thousands of dollars to bring the road up to its present boulevard condition." Pennsylvania was indeed far ahead in the matter of building good roads. The state's highway department had been created in 1903. From 1911, its charge had been to build an entire state highway system, and the need for this was obvious. In 1911, there had been 43,282 motor vehicles registered in the state. Over the next six years, that number soared eightfold to 349,720.

The highway department's report for the years 1917 to 1920 said, "With the old methods of transportation, the public traveling by highway seldom extended over a radius of ten miles, from farmhouse to warehouse, to post office or store. With the advent of the automobile it reached to county seat, and from county seat to county seat, from center of population to center of population, and the demand was for a smooth hard surface all the way."

That demand had not been there to begin with. On the contrary, country people had at first been vehemently opposed to cars. Cars were toys for the rich, and they scared the horses. All over America there were tales of farmers strewing broken glass on the roads, or burying rakes in them with the tines pointed upward. When people broke down (as they often did) it was a point of honor to lean on your fence and call out to the flustered driver that he should get a horse. In Pennsylvania there was even a "Farmers' Anti-Automobile Association," with this engaging set of rules:

1. *Automobiles traveling on country roads at night must send up a rocket every mile, then wait ten minutes for the road to clear. The driver may then proceed, with caution, blowing his horn and shooting off Roman candles, as before.*
2. *If the driver of an automobile sees a team of horses approaching he is to stop, pulling over to one side of the road, and cover his machine with a blanket or dust cover which is painted or colored to blend into the scenery, and thus render the machine less noticeable.*
3. *In case a horse is unwilling to pass an automobile on the road, the driver of the car must take the machine apart as rapidly as possible, and conceal the parts in the bushes.*

As for paying taxes to fund road building so wealthy joyriders could frighten your animals, that was out of the question. In 1913, a proposal for a bond issue for highway improvement in Pennsylvania failed to get past the voters. Then, as Henry Ford's mass production drove prices down, farmers started buying cars, small trucks, and tractors, and sentiment changed fast. By 1918, when the state's electorate approved a staggeringly vast bond issue of $50 million for their roads, only four out of sixty-six counties voted against it. In Pennsylvania, the convoy was preaching to the converted.

THE CONVOY RUMBLED through the villages of Seven Stars, Mc-Knightstown, Cashtown, and Fayetteville to Chambersburg. Jackson noted that the roads were excellent, though some of the trucks had trouble on the grades of Piney Mountain all the same; the Macks and Packards were "lazy on hills."

They made Chambersburg at five-thirty. At the South Second Street show lot two blocks from the middle of town, scores of people came to stroll through their camp. The Queen City Band played a concert in the field, and the searchlight played over town. The weather, said Jackson, was fair and warm.

The next day clouded over a little, but on the road things carried on well. Half a dozen vehicles had niggling little mechanical glitches, but there were no major problems. They met steep grades and crested passes over twenty-two hundred feet without incident. Jackson noted with satisfaction that the day had afforded "excellent driving for untrained personnel."

That night in Bedford, they were met by a crowd of two thousand—pretty much the whole town. General Drake came from Washington to greet them; there were speeches and dancing in the street. The convoy's "official speaker," Dr. S. M. Johnson of the National Highways Association, proclaimed, "We are crossing the continent to impress upon all leaders of public action in the world that the next step in the progress of civilization is to provide road beds upon which rapid transit motor vehicles may be operated with economy and efficiency. This is true, not only of backward peoples, but also of the most advanced nations, including our own."

Indeed it was true. Eisenhower noted that they had now taken twenty-nine hours' driving time to cover 165 miles—an average speed of less than six miles an hour. He added, "Before we were through, however, there were times when the pace of our first three days would seem headlong, and the four speeches at Bedford only a slight taste of the hot air ahead."

THE ROAD WAS improved all the way from Bedford to Greensburg, much of it paved in brick. Nonetheless, said the guidebook, "care should be exercised." The way runs through gorgeous scenery, through rolling green hills with wooded crests—but even today it twists and bucks up fog-laden slopes, through steep bends over Bald Knob Summit, down sharp grades past the village of Buckstown, and on over a long string of climbs and drops past Stoystown.

Then there's Laurel Hill Summit, 2,684 feet at its highest point, followed by a striking descent down the face of a forested and precipitous hillside to Ligonier. Ironically, this road today carries signs reading TRUCK ALERT. One of them advises truck drivers to avoid U.S. 30 altogether.

The convoy left Bedford at six-thirty in the morning, battling in low gear up the first steep climb out of town. Awaiting their arrival sixty-three miles down the road, Greensburg was in festival spirit. It was, indeed, having the biggest party in its history.

Its residents were holding a parade to welcome home the veterans of Westmoreland County from the war. In a town of fifteen thousand, the crowd was estimated to be three times that size. Soldiers, sailors, marines, and Red Cross nurses in their white uniforms marched down Pennsylvania Avenue to Fourth Street, along Fourth to Main, and from there to the high school to have souvenir badges pinned to their chests. Civil War veterans went with them in cars; veterans of the Spanish-American War marched alongside the young men and women back from Europe. Bands paraded between them, and the sidewalks were thronged with cheering, flag-waving crowds every step of the way.

From the high school the parade turned east, heading for Miller's Grove on the edge of town along the Lincoln Highway. There were around a thousand veterans in all; at long tables under the trees, every one of them was fed at a clambake. There was a special bar set up, complete with a brass rail—though with Prohibition in force for ten days now, it served only lemonade.

Following the parade to the grove, a traffic jam of cars and pedestrians clogged the road out of town for the best part of three hours. Before the meal was served the Reverend Dr. Charles Schall, pastor of the First Presbyterian and chaplain of the Fourth Corps, gave the invocation. Afterward there were boxing bouts, a display of fancy rifle shooting, and performances by (among others) Frank Stanton, the "original chanticleer," and a magician named Señor Leigh de Coursey.

Amid these entertainments, the arrival of the convoy would be an extra layer of spectacle. Unfortunately, at four-thirty that afternoon, a storm blew in. At Miller's Grove, the gala atmosphere was marred when John Saville of Poplar Street was killed by lightning. On the highway, the weather didn't help the convoy much either.

East of Greensburg, the road was slick from an earlier rain in the morning. Heavy rain continued on and off through the day. On the slopes and turns of the Alleghenies brakes were dragging, motors overheating, trucks stalling. One of the Garfords burned out its engine bearings when the crankcase opened up and all the oil drained out. Coming down one of the slopes a Dodge delivery lost control, careened into one of the ambulance trailers, and stove a hole in its radiator. The Militor took both Garford and Dodge under tow, and a disabled kitchen trailer too.

It got worse. Late in the afternoon the convoy was cresting Laurel Hill Summit, slipping down the steep grade toward Ligonier, when the storm hit. Lightning burst all about them. Amid the thunderclaps and the pouring rain, one bolt hit a tree fifty yards behind a GM cargo truck. Stunned, the driver skidded clean off the road and away down the hillside. Luckily, no one was hurt—with no cab on these trucks, and traveling anyhow at a snail's pace as they crept down the hill, the men on board were all able to jump clear. Soaked and shaken, they watched their truck tumble down the hill.

The cheerfully shameless Lieutenant Doron would later make the most of this drama. Farther west (where no one could know any different) he thrilled newspaper readers with tales of this vehicle being literally blasted off the face of the hill by the lightning strike. "The truck itself," he declared, "crashed to a thousand splinters in a canyon a hundred feet below."

It wasn't quite that bad. Interviewed in Iowa, Ike put the damage at not more than $200. Either way, however, the truck was unrecoverable; McClure cabled Washington to send a wrecking party. If he stopped to try and salvage the vehicle himself, he said, he'd fall behind schedule.

Missing out on the gala, the convoy struggled into Greensburg at eleven o'clock that night. Traveling these sixty-three miles through the rain and the mountains had taken sixteen and a half hours. Still, they were able to contribute to Greensburg's big day at least somewhat.

The town's fireworks had been soaked in the downpour, making that evening's display literally a damp squib. Pushing on ahead of the trucks, the searchlight crew made up for that by planting their light on Point Lookout, then blazing the three-million-candlepower beam onto Seton Hill, the county courthouse, the high school, and various other local landmarks.

While thousands stared wonderstruck at the fierce light shining down on Greensburg, McClure went off to send Washington another telegram. Amid news of the day's difficulties, it carried another telling jab at the unfortunate Lieutenant Doron. "Previously arranged publicity," snapped McClure, "puts us in all towns one day later than actual arrival causing considerable confusion disappointment and loss of cooperation."

Convoy pilot Ostermann, meanwhile, was smoothly spinning his line again, this time to the *Daily Tribune*. "Pennsylvania right now," he said, "doesn't need to take a back seat in the union in the matter of highways." It's possible, of course, that the men leaping from their truck as it slithered down the mountainside may have taken a different view.

ON FRIDAY, JULY 11, the convoy set off for Pittsburgh at seven in the morning. Fifteen minutes later, the Militor reached Greensburg. Towing three disabled vehicles, all fully loaded, Sergeant First Class Theodore Wood had driven over the mountains all through the night. He had been at the wheel over nineteen hours straight.

Jackson doesn't say who took over from the stalwart Wood; he was too busy down the road noting fouled spark plugs and broken clutch discs. The machine shops carried a $75,000 stock of spare parts, and if possible, any vehicle that fell out of line was patched up straightaway by the roadside. If not, the Militor towed it until they could catch up and fix the problem in camp. Regarding breakdowns, McClure's road drill was crisp and brutal: "Keep the convoy rolling—cut out the cripples."

He'd changed the day's schedule. In theory, they were due to parade through Pittsburgh, then press on along the Lincoln Highway to the Ohio line at East Liverpool. Claiming that rain and roadworks had rendered the road that way impassable, however, he now telegrammed Washington to propose a jog north through East Palestine, Ohio, instead. As it turned out, they wouldn't reach either of those places.

The road into Pittsburgh described an awkward route west to McKeesport, north around the right bank of the Monongahela, then west again through the suburb of Wilkinsburg. Straightened out somewhat, and since then bypassed by Interstate 76, the same road today is a weary strip of uninviting lounges, exotic-pet stores, used-car lots, and peeling cabin motels. It has the look of a place whose future has been and gone already—but in 1919 it was a highway at the cutting edge of progress, and Pittsburgh meant to welcome the representatives of that progress in style.

To mark the convoy's passage, the city was holding "Transport Day." Above copious spreads of advertising from truck dealers and manufacturers, the *Gazette Times* and the *Chronicle Telegraph* both declared in bold type that this was "A Day of Vital Interest to Every Business Man and Firm in Pittsburgh. A Day Given to the Nation's Right Arm—THE MOTOR TRUCK."

While its commercial brethren banged the drum for motor transport, the convoy was met at one o'clock in East Liberty by an escort of police on motorbikes. They came into the city on Penn Avenue, parading through downtown before they passed in review before Colonel McClure, Mayor Babcock, and the chamber of commerce at the City-County Building.

As the vehicles looped around the building, thousands lined the streets to cheer their passage, and the soldiers responded in kind. Mascots rode along with them. A raccoon captured in the mountains graced one truck, the medical detachment sported a fighting rooster riding on the radiator of another, and several bull-dogs were spotted sitting beside the drivers. The trucks carried bright banners as well. One proclaimed, MEN WANTED FOR THE UNITED STATES ARMY, while another cheerfully declared, NEW YORK TO FRISCO WITH THE GAS HOUNDS.

The mayor rode in the parade with McClure and wished him luck. McClure responded with the stern catchphrase that he'd use all the way across America. He said, "We're going to get there; that's all."

The *Dispatch* reported him to be "radiating confidence"— and McClure kept the difficulties of the exercise to himself. He made light of the accident in the mountains; he said nothing about the fact that the kitchen trailers were so weakly constructed that the road was starting to break them apart. He had to retire one of the two-wheelers in Pittsburgh and ship it back to Camp Meigs; it had lasted four days. Nor did he say anything about the daily roster of mechanical hiccups, which accounted, today, for the Militor and its towed retinue of patched and mended vehicles passing through the city two hours behind the rest of the convoy.

In short, McClure kept quiet and did his job. Had he and his men been in the city two days later, however, they would surely have shared a dry smile over a cartoon in the *Gazette Times*. It showed a gaggle of men gathered around a car with a busted rear axle. "Human beings used to run without doctors," said one of them glumly, "wonder if cars'll ever run without mechanics?"

CALIFORNIA (IT HAD to happen in California) reported a dramatic development: the first arrest of a speeding motorist by an airplane. It had taken place near Los Angeles, and the speedster was doing sixty. The motorbike cop in pursuit had engine trouble, so he pulled in at an aviation field and went after the miscreant in a plane instead. When he landed on the road ahead of him, the driver stopped—naturally assuming the pilot needed assistance—and was duly arrested.

Pittsburgh, compared to the far-off and palm-fringed paradise that was California, offered less of a model for the future. A city of nearly 600,000 people, it was a smog-clogged warren where the air was so foul that white shirts turned black in minutes. This was a place where America had good reason to fear socialism, and where the workforce (one in five of whom was foreign-born) might well feel they had good reason to embrace it. With production in heavy industry cut back after the end of the war, in 1919 the city had a series of violent strikes—by miners, steelworkers, streetcar motor-men and conductors—in which lockouts, riots, shootings, and bombings were all too common.

No surprise, then, that McClure didn't want to stay there. On the other hand, he couldn't make it to East Palestine either. Between the congested traffic in the city, the length of time spent on civic courtesies during the parade, and the damaged vehicles still lagging behind with the Militor, the day was dragging on.

They crossed the Allegheny over the Sixth Street bridge; they made fifteen miles up the east bank of the Ohio to Sewickley. There, at five in the afternoon, with East Palestine still over thirty miles ahead, McClure called a halt.

SEWICKLEY WAS, AND remains, an upscale village suburb. From the late nineteenth century, Pittsburgh's wealthy had been building summer homes at Sewickley Hills, above the river; the Allegheny Country Club was built there in 1902. Five years later, Pittsburgh annexed Allegheny City—the north shore where the ballparks are now—because it liked the look of the property values. Disinclined to pay city taxes, the rich moved up the river for good.

Wealthy as they were, they were early buyers of automobiles. Sewickley's first three cars had appeared in 1899, and all three were steam-powered. The first "explosive motor" in the area (as gas-fueled cars were known) was a DeDion-Bouton Motorette owned by Percy V. Stowe of Edgeworth. In these genteel surrounds, the noise it made provoked "a great storm of angry remarks and strong language. . . . He reluctantly disposed of it to purchase a steamer."

Electric and steam-powered vehicles vied with gasoline well into the second decade of the twentieth century. Electric cars had three advantages: they were easy to start, they weren't smelly or noisy, and they weren't likely to explode. Steam wasn't noisy or smelly either, but it had the signal disadvantage that it took a while to get the water boiling—hence the word *chauffeur,* from the French verb *chauffer,* "to heat up." When the well-to-do of France took to motoring in their early steam-driven cars, passing pedestrians, delighted at the spectacle of their betters perspiring by the roadside as they fed their ungainly boilers, would jeer, *"Chauffeur! Chauffeur!"*—"Stoker! Stoker!"

By 1919, when Sewickley found a large number of military vehicles parking for the night along Beaver Road, gasoline had won. The first trucks showed up about three-thirty in the afternoon, and they kept on coming in disorderly batches through the next few hours. The Red Cross Canteen Committee swung into action and served the soldiers coffee, cakes, and sandwiches; private citizens opened their homes to help with that effort. The *Sewickley Herald* noted that the convoy was meant to be reaching East Palestine that night "but decided this was far enough."

In his telegrams to Washington, the reason given by McClure for not sticking to the Lincoln Highway to East Liverpool and heading north to East Palestine instead was doubtless true enough. A fourteen-mile stretch along the official route to East Liverpool was the highway's last piece of dirt road in Pennsylvania. The state was working to correct that, and detouring through rain-soaked mud around the roadworks might well have been awkward.

What McClure didn't mention—while the ladies of the Red Cross fed his men and the people of Sewickley ambled down Beaver Road to inspect his "monster trucks"—was that he had another reason for going to East Palestine. The convoy had been invited to lunch by Harvey Firestone.

CHAPTER FOUR

A Revolution in Movement

FOR THIRTY MILES north of Pittsburgh, hugging the riverbank under the jumbled hills, the Ohio River Boulevard is an almost uninterrupted strand of half-hidden heavy industry and, in some cases, industrial remains. Vast plants and freight yards loom among the trees, interspersed with the imposing spans of mighty steel bridges painted black and blue, looking bruised and rugged like the hard-worked landscape.

Leaving Sewickley at six-thirty in the morning, the convoy passed along here on Saturday, July 12, 1919. They left the river where it bends around to the west at Rochester and headed north into wooded hills toward East Palestine. On the chucky, rutted roads brackets shifted, bearings broke up, and mechanics hurried to get lamed vehicles running again. "All tools furnished with trucks," Elwell Jackson noted impatiently, "are of inferior quality and construction."

They made thirty-five miles in seven and a half hours. At two o'clock factory whistles, church bells, and cheering crowds greeted them along Unity Road into "the city of industry." They passed through streets elaborately decked out in red, white, and blue to make camp at the fairgrounds and were soon surrounded by hundreds of curious onlookers.

East Palestine was a busy little town whose population had grown from 3,537 in 1910 to 5,750 by the end of the decade—and the reason for this expansion was car tires. In 1910, Edwin McGraw's tire company made eight tires a day; by 1919, it was making 5,000 a day. That year the company put up an electric sign four stories tall on Forty-sixth Street and Broadway in New York.

On red it said, STOP STOP FOR 30 SECONDS; on green it read, GO GO ON MCGRAW TIRES, EAST PALESTINE, OHIO.

Getting the convoy to leave the Lincoln Highway and come to East Palestine, said the *Columbiana Ledger,* was a "neat little coup . . . maneuvered by the East Palestine Chamber of Commerce. Incidentally, it has thrown East Liverpool and Lisbon into dismay." The latter towns were aghast that the convoy had taken another road. To soothe their ruffled feathers, Henry Ostermann went to East Liverpool to speak at a hastily arranged good roads meeting. Since the convoy's newly widowed pilot had a lover there, it would have been no great sacrifice.

Doubtless well satisfied at the discomfiture of their neighbors to the south, the East Palestine chamber of commerce gave a dinner for the officers and journalists at the Rubber Club. The clubhouse was opened for the enlisted men to play pool and billiards; the McGraw plant's shower baths were made available for them too. On Sunday morning the Red Cross opened a canteen at the fairgrounds, and through the convoy's rest day they served seventy gallons of lemonade, thirty-five of ice cream, four hundred chocolate bars, five hundred packs of cigarettes, and such other handy items as matches and writing paper.

Disputes over the right to play host to the convoy like this and, more generally, over the routing of the highway along which they drove would recur the whole way across the country. In East Palestine's case, however, it certainly helped that Harvey Firestone's country homestead Harbel Manor was just down the road. Indeed, it was surely decisive in the matter.

Like that other tire magnate Frank Seiberling at Goodyear, Firestone was heavily involved in this venture. He had a tire truck keeping pace with the convoy to supply them with spares; his Ship-by-Truck bureau used the convoy's passage to promote motor transportation in every town and city it called at. Farther west in Ohio, a truck carrying a shipment of Firestone tires for the Yellow Taxicab Company of Chicago would travel alongside the convoy. It had painted on its sides, "Akron to Chicago—26 hours by motor truck—5 days by railroad."

The army film crew was busy too. They filmed the men in their camp, with the Stars and Stripes fluttering on their vehicles. On

Sunday morning, they filmed a fleet of local cars ferrying three hundred men to a chicken dinner at Harbel Manor. They filmed Firestone chatting in his white linen suit with McClure and his officers; Eisenhower, lean and blond, stood a head taller than most of those around him. The men ate off fine crockery on tablecloths dressed with flowers beneath a huge tent. There were nearly five hundred at the dinner in all, among them leading industrialists from Akron, Alliance, Lisbon, and Salem. A band played, a male trio sang, eight speeches were given, and the cameras rolled.

In jerky black and white, with that quaint, slightly speeded up gait of old movies, the soldiers stroll busily about the lawn. All are smoking ferociously, with thick clouds of smoke drifting about them in the sunshine. One of the convoy's star turns performs for the movie crew, two men nicknamed Mutt and Jeff, after the comic strip. They claimed to be the army's tallest soldier and its shortest; the small man shows how tiny he is by curling himself up inside a truck tire.

Tires made money for northeast Ohio for decades. Though the corporate relationship has now spectacularly soured, in those days Harvey Firestone was close with Henry Ford. The two men went on much publicized luxury camping trips, along with Thomas Edison and the biblically bearded naturalist John Burroughs. Catered to by Ford's Japanese chef Harold Sato and calling themselves the Vagabonds, they reflected Burroughs's desire "to touch naked reality once more."

Naked reality, in northeast Ohio today, is that much of the work rubber made for so many thousands of people has gone. Like the old industry, the Firestone homestead is gone too; Henry Ford took it down and rebuilt it at Greenfield Village, his eccentric museum-cum-attraction in Dearborn, Michigan. It had stood seven miles to the west by Columbiana, where Highways 7 and 14 meet today. At this now dismantled spot, the men of the convoy had their luxury break from the road.

"Equipment thoroughly inspected adjusted and repaired," McClure cabled Washington, "personnel ready for good start in morning. Weather clear and slightly warm."

THE REST DAY had little effect on either the convoy's road discipline or its occasionally ham-handed public relations. Leaving East Palestine at six-thirty on Monday morning, they were out of shape within a few miles. The *Columbiana Ledger* described the convoy's passage: "It did not travel in close column but was scattered out at long intervals. It began to pass at an early hour and kept coming in detachments and by single cars for about three hours." At least the soldiers, said the paper, "looked bronzed and business like."

Along the road in Alliance, they hadn't known over the weekend what the convoy was doing. The *Review & Leader* said on Saturday evening, "An effort to determine the route through the city has failed as no one in authority with the train seems to be in authority to answer such questions."

Colonel William Henry Morgan sorted it out. The military title came from four years on the Ohio governor's staff, but he was much more a businessman than a soldier. The inventor of the electric overhead traveling crane, he'd succeeded his father in 1897 as president of Morgan Engineering. It was Alliance's largest enterprise, and Morgan was the man of the town.

Morgan "always went with large scales of everything he did." His home was a castle of Vermont marble called Glamorgan; it was built in 1905 on a fifty-acre estate on South Union Avenue for $400,000. Inside, it was a deranged mix of Italian Renaissance, Louis XIV, Elizabethan, and Japanese. Unlike Harbel Manor it is, happily, still there, though the decor is a little more restrained. Morgan's widow sold it for $25,000 in the Depression, and in 1973 it became the headquarters for Alliance City Schools.

Morgan was one of the speakers at Firestone's dinner. Presumably aware of the uncertainty over the convoy's plans in Alliance, he leaned on McClure to make sure they stopped in his town. Ordinarily, McClure didn't stop more than he had to for anybody anywhere, but plainly Morgan wasn't a man whose invitation you turned down.

Ostermann in his Packard and a vanguard of officers' cars pulled up at Glamorgan at about nine o'clock—the local reporter noting their "superior make and upholstering"—and the bulk of the convoy came in an hour or so later. Morgan had his company band playing, and he served out thirty cases of soft drinks, six hundred packs of cigarettes, twelve hundred cigars, and five hundred boxes of matches. It was beginning to be apparent that, whatever else this cavalcade might lack, they weren't going to go short of nicotine.

THE CONVOY REJOINED the Lincoln Highway at Canton, a thriving city of eighty thousand that was doing very nicely as a result of the Good Roads Movement. As in Pennsylvania, by 1919 much of the highway through Ohio was paved. For the most part, the work was done in brick, and many of the bricks were made in Canton.

Just east of the city, you can still see today how the Lincoln Highway looked. At Cindell, north of U.S. 30 and running parallel to it, there's a one-mile stretch of original brick-paved road. It's fifteen feet wide, with no shoulders. A little farther east, there's a 2.7-mile stretch that used to be Route 30, until 1935. It runs from the village of Robertsville, on Apple Hill Road, and empties out onto today's U.S. 30 at Paris Avenue in Paris township. It's not perfectly preserved—it's been patched and filled with asphalt along the way—but you can still stand on this matte-red brick paving and see what kind of highway the army drove on through Ohio over eighty years ago.

The road followed the contours of the land, snaking through the lush green farmland, sloping and curling over gently rolling hills. When they built a road then, they didn't cut and fill the landscape so the way would be straighter, wider, or safer; the budget didn't allow it. Oftentimes the road would have one right-angle turn after another, jogging left and right along the course of the section lines. In so doing, it would cross and recross the railroad tracks; in consequence, cars would be struck and their occupants killed on grade crossings with depressing regularity.

Ohio used brick for this slender, sometimes perilous highway because Canton—as well as Waynesburg, Wooster, Malvern, and Alliance—had been making bricks for over a hundred years. The area had high-quality shale and clay; with the canals and then the railroads, it had shipping routes too. The state's first paved street was laid in Steubenville in 1884, and mass production of paving brick began in Canton the following year.

It takes half a million bricks to pave a mile of road twenty-five feet wide. When Ohio and other eastern states started giving their roads hard surfaces, Canton's Metropolitan Brick Company became the biggest in America. The company's Ironrock Street Paver was used in New York's Queens-Midtown and Holland Tunnels, on Carl Fisher's Indianapolis Speedway, and along stretches of the Lincoln Highway as well. In 1912, the firm's owner, Harry Renkert, put up Canton's first "skyscraper," an eleven-story office building on Market and Third—built with bricks, obviously—and it still stands today.

The demand died when road building moved on to concrete, asphalt, and blacktop. There are no brick companies left in Canton now; you go to Canton today to visit the Classic Car Museum instead. Many of the cars preserved here are objects of great beauty, and they're lovingly tended. A sign says, DO NOT TOUCH CARS. BOB SHOOTS EVERY 10TH TOUCHER AND THE 9TH ONE JUST LEFT. THANK YOU.

Bob is Bob Lichty, the museum's director. Lichty says of the Lincoln Highway that used to run through his town, "It's one of the most significant events in United States history. It impacted the whole country, both sociologically and commercially. The Lincoln Highway came first, when the U.S.A. was still this vast muddy wilderness between cities. At that time, a truck on solid tires, that's ten miles an hour if the weather's good. But a truck on pneumatics on a good paved road, that's forty-five miles an hour. That's intercity and interstate transport, and it's the death of the railroad.

"So the convoy's a defining moment. You have the existence of the road itself, and then the convoy crystallizes what it's all about. It's a revolution in movement."

"A FEW YEARS ago," says Lichty, "in downtown Akron, I heard an old Mack chain drive coming on solids. The tires are kind of crunchy, you get rocks popping out from under them, and the engine's loud, with a minimal exhaust system. It's a totally distinctive, singing sort of sound. I heard it *blocks* away."

Lichty's driven a 1914 Four Wheel Drive, and a 1919 Mack; he knows the scale of the task the men of the convoy were tackling. He says simply, "They steer *horrible*. It's a big, big wheel to get leverage. It's very, very heavy."

Another Lincoln Highway historian, Drake Hokansen, says the combination of solid tires and poor roads would have produced a constant, bone-jolting rattle and shudder. It would have been so bad that if the driver attempted any speed higher than ten miles an hour, it would have taken the sum of his effort just to hang on to the wheel and not be flung from his seat.

Whether it was the ungainliness of the steering, the inexperience of the driver, or whether the accident was in fact the other man's fault, isn't clear—but after lunch and a parade through Canton, at three in the afternoon a Standard Class B collided with a civilian Ford truck four miles west of the city. The Ford was wrecked; luckily, its driver wasn't hurt.

McClure's adjutant Captain William C. Greany (also the convoy's statistical officer) would later report that they had a total of 230 accidents. One assumes he was including even the most minor incident—but if the figure seems a big one, the real miracle is that they didn't have more.

They pressed on for Wooster. The road was good brick paving nearly all that day; they made eighty-three miles in nine hours. Magnetos and carburetors acted up, a steering arm worked loose, a radiator sprang a leak, a cylinder head blew out in one of the Dodges, two Garfords were lamed, and the Militor towed one of the machine shops the last thirty miles. "Only minor mechanical difficulties today," reported McClure.

Wooster was a town of some eight thousand people; the trucks started arriving there about three-thirty in the afternoon. The fire bell rang to welcome them in, and as they passed down Liberty Street young women handed out more cigarettes and chocolate for the soldiers. The driving was tiring, thirsty work. One truck crew stopped on Pittsburgh Avenue and asked Mrs. Karl Fisher if they could drink at her well, and she told them they could drink all they liked. She told the local paper, "They drank it up like camels."

The convoy camped at the fairgrounds, where a ring had been set up by the grandstand for boxing and wrestling matches that evening. The men had cheese sandwiches for supper, while the spectacle of their encampment and the bouts in the ring drew a big crowd to fill the stand. The convoy's equipment was "the occasion of many an exclamation of surprise and wonder"; the boxing included a comedy bout between Mutt and Jeff.

With his audience thus assured, "official speaker" Dr. Johnson gave his daily oration. He's a hard man to pin down, this Johnson; he's reported by different sources to be a native of Allen County, Indiana; a New Mexico rancher; a Presbyterian preacher; a Good Roads lobbyist based in Washington; a philanthropist of national repute; and a member of at least three different highway associations. Whatever his precise background or affiliation, he clearly wasn't shy of the lectern.

"We are at the beginning of a new era of American progress and history," he told the people of Wooster. "Now that we have finished the job on the other side, the next great job will be the improvement of the highways so that automobiles and motor trucks can be operated on them economically."

Presumably having heard Dr. Johnson's address once too often already, the searchlight crew broke his rhythm when they started playing their beam across the evening sky. Unperturbable, Dr. Johnson plowed on. "We are speaking to the entire family of the nation," he declared.

Colonel McClure proclaimed, "We are attempting and we are going to cross the continent."

DURING THE NIGHT it rained. In the morning they had trouble getting out of the campground, never mind getting to California. It carried on raining until, in detours around roadworks, the mud was eight to ten inches deep. Sixty-three miles through Ashland, Mansfield, and Galion to Bucyrus took nearly twelve hours. One of the tankers' rear wheels went through the floor of a wooden bridge. The tanker was towed out, and the engineers spent three hours rebuilding the bridge so the rest of the convoy could pass over it. Behind the train, with the stalwart Sergeant Wood at the wheel, the Militor towed the broken-down machine shop all day.

The convoy lurched through the sodden farmlands of central Ohio. Between rain and roadworks, the Lincoln Highway between

Ashland and Mansfield was deemed impassable; they looped around to the north through Olivesburg. The *Mansfield News* ruefully admitted that Richland County's stretch of the highway "must be given much attention before the full purpose of the great ocean to ocean trail is fully met," and that the truck train's discomfort had proved it.

Going ahead in his Packard, the man working out the detours and consulting with local officials and auto club members was the convoy's pilot, Henry Ostermann. The possibility was raised of them giving up for the day and stopping in Mansfield, twenty-five miles short of their objective in Bucyrus; McClure decided to push on. Despite the rain, the streets of Mansfield were lined with onlookers, but few could have seen the whole train. The convoy was so disarrayed by mud and breakdowns that although the first trucks came through at four o'clock, the last of them didn't appear until ten in the evening.

McCLURE SAID LATER that his "most perplexing problem" wasn't bad roads or breakdowns; it was feeding the men. He didn't realize this at first, but as the convoy progressed, "its extreme importance became daily more and more evident." In essence, you can't get across America on a diet of cheese sandwiches.

He had seen in the first couple of days that keeping the kitchen trailers with the convoy didn't work. It held the whole train back while lunch was prepared, and it meant a long wait for supper when they made camp at night. From the third day, he therefore had the mess unit stay back in camp preparing lunch while the rest of the convoy set off after breakfast.

The mess unit was six ration trucks towing the kitchen trailers, which the men had dubbed "goulash cannons." When they were ready they chased after the convoy, and when they caught up, it pulled aside to let them pass. Once ahead of the train they stopped at about eleven in the morning, and they had sandwiches and coffee ready for noon. The main train caught up to them and ate; the vehicles were oiled, gassed, and watered; and the mess unit went on ahead again to have a hot meal ready in camp at the end of the day's run.

That, at least, was the theory; the practice could be a lot more awkward. On this difficult day, for example, a welcome party from Bucyrus—the mayor, the police chief, the secretary of the chamber of commerce, and a reporter from the *Bucyrus Journal*—was naturally keen to know the convoy's plans as it approached the town. In the event, finding Colonel McClure at all proved problematic.

That afternoon the would-be welcomers drove to Mansfield, watched forty vehicles pass, and saw no sign of the convoy commander's Cadillac. Assuming they'd missed him, they raced back toward Bucyrus, overtaking the convoy on the road. They stopped in Galion and called Bucyrus to see if McClure had arrived there yet.

Their driver was a man named Walter Michel; their car was Michel's Marmon. While they were on the phone Michel rushed in and said a Cadillac with four officers in it had just gone by.

"The long lost colonel was found," wrote the *Journal* reporter breathlessly, "but he was on the road to Bucyrus at a forty-mile clip. The question was asked of Walter Michel: 'Can you catch him?'

" 'Catch him,' said Walter. 'If you're not afraid of speed, there's nothing to it.'

"He was told that it was absolutely necessary to pass the colonel before we reached Bucyrus.

" 'What's Bucyrus got to do with it?' said Michel, as he opened her up, 'don't need half that distance.' "

A few miles to the west, they spotted McClure half a mile out ahead of them. Michel was doing sixty now, hanging close on the Cadillac's tail, leaning on the horn to get McClure's car to stop. Eventually, not getting through to them that way, Michel roared past and pulled over in the road ahead of them. The Bucyrus delegation got out and waved the convoy commander down; McClure and the welcome party started talking. Meanwhile, McClure's driver was out of his seat and running forward to the Marmon; he jumped in and started looking it over. He said, "Great guns, what a car."

Once pleasantries and mutual automotive admiration had been exchanged, the mayor and his party escorted McClure on the last stretch into Bucyrus. The mayor was eager to have the convoy parade around the town before they went into camp at the fairgrounds.

Plainly fretful after a demanding day—"frequently glancing at his wrist watch, and looking anxiously toward the east"—McClure asked first that he be shown directly to the camp.

Having assured himself that the kitchen unit had arrived there and that the trucks wouldn't mire in the ground, he consented to be shown the mayor's proposed route around the town. He was torn between concern for his men and his wish not to spurn Bucyrus's hospitality. At six-fifteen, as the first trucks lumbered into view under threatening weather, he said the men had been up since five-thirty in the morning, and that with all the delays they'd had no food on the road. He suggested that maybe a dozen trucks could split off and tour the town; but with dark clouds gathering and no one on the streets, he was relieved when the mayor decided that, "in justice to the tired men," they had best go directly to camp.

TOILING FAR BEHIND with the breakdowns in tow, for the second time Sergeant Theodore Wood did stout duty with the Militor. A small, wiry man with a pencil mustache, he was at the wheel without sleep or food nearly nineteen hours, finally making camp in Bucyrus at two-fifty in the morning. For the second time, Elwell Jackson commended Wood's endeavors to his superiors in Washington—sharply noting that no rations had been sent back to him—while McClure, for the second time, didn't see fit to comment.

That aside, the remaining two days in Ohio went well. They left Bucyrus with every vehicle rolling under its own power. The land flattened out, the weather improved, and so did the roads. They passed through Upper Sandusky, then made due west through Williamstown and Beaverdam to their night stop in Delphos. Feted by mayors and reception committees as they went, passing through streets lined with crowds and decked with flags and bunting, they made seventy miles in nine hours. Jackson reported contentedly, "No maintenance difficulties of any consequence . . . every phase of the convoy is functioning better as experience is accumulating."

In Upper Sandusky, Henry Ostermann told the *Daily Chief* that the Lincoln Highway would be hard-surfaced all the way to the Mississippi by 1920. Then he quit the line of march and detoured north to Toledo for a meeting with officials of the Lincoln Highway Association. Toledo was halfway between Detroit and Upper Sandusky. Ostermann would have reported there on the progress of the convoy so far and on its impact on the Good Roads issue. More specifically, he would have reported on the crisis they had provoked in the city of Lima.

Planning the convoy's itinerary, the route's navigators had changed the course of the highway to the line the army had followed that day, due west from Upper Sandusky. It was a straighter route, and a shorter one by eleven miles—it ran nearer to the line that U.S. 30 follows today—but Lima was south of that line, and now it was cut out of the action.

Later, as towns clogged with through traffic, they would clamor for bypasses—or at least they would until, all too often, they got one and their town center died. At the dawn of the paved road, however, everyone wanted it bringing business down Main Street, so Lima, after six years on the original line of the Lincoln Highway, was now horrified to find itself abandoned.

Town officials planned to send a delegation to Detroit. Representatives of the chamber of commerce, the Rotary Club, the Lima Automobile Club, the Merchants' Association, and the county commissioners decided to travel to the Motor City and protest in the strongest manner. They were bluntly informed, however, that all the directors of the Lincoln Highway Association were out of the city, and that there would be no board meeting until August. Moreover, regrettable though it might be, "the obvious inefficiency" of the route through Lima had "made this change finally essential." There was nothing Lima could do. Following the new line drawn by Ostermann, the road and the convoy passed them by.

DELPHOS NOW PROCLAIMS itself "America's Friendliest City." During that Wednesday afternoon and evening, it did its best to earn that name. The convoy's visit, said the *Delphos Daily Herald,* was "one of the largest and most successful affairs ever conducted in this city."

The first trucks arrived at three-thirty and were piloted

through crowds along Main Street to Waterworks Park. The park was six and a half acres that had been planted with trees by the townspeople in 1899. The only trouble, said one of the officers, "was the fact that [the convoy] would not get to remain there long enough."

As soon as the men had pitched camp, Mayor George N. Lea-Sure gave a brief speech of welcome from the bandstand. He handed McClure the key to the city, invited the entire complement of men to supper at St. John's auditorium, announced that dances would be held at city hall and in the Knights of Columbus Hall, and set the town busy with festivities that lasted into the small hours.

Local cars ferried forty of the soldiers for a swim in the Auglaize River. Once darkness had fallen, the searchlight played, and flares and signal rockets were launched from the corner of Third and Main. The dance halls were packed, about two hundred of the men went to supper, and meals were sent to those whose duties required them to stay with the trucks in the park. The town's slogan for the night was "everything free," and it was. The Knights of Columbus had postcards and writing paper set out on tables in their hall with pen and ink at the ready; the men of the convoy dropped 465 postcards and 75 letters in the box provided, and the Knights of Columbus stamped and mailed them.

One of the soldiers had earlier noted in his diary, "The difference between the spirit of the people in Pennsylvania and Ohio has been very marked. In Pennsylvania, the people were almost cold in the reception they gave us, while in Ohio they have received us with open arms." Returning the compliment, toward the end of the night's dancing, those soldiers still present insisted that the rule whereby only men in uniform could dance with the local girls be waived. Throughout the evening, said the *Daily Herald,* "they conducted themselves as gentlemen."

They had trouble starting some of the vehicles the next morning—Jackson blamed poor-quality gas—but by the sounds of it, when reveille was called at four-fifty, more than a few probably had trouble starting themselves. One soldier received "a severe injury to his hand and arm," presumably from a crankpin backfiring on him; apart from that, the convoy left Ohio without incident, passing through Van Wert toward the state line and Fort Wayne, Indiana.

The *Van Wert Times* called this transcontinental trip "one of the greatest publicity stunts attempted in the history of the country." The *Twice-a-Week Bulletin* was more precise. "For many years," it said, "the Lincoln Highway Association has endeavored to secure the backing of the government in its project. . . . [The convoy] is the first assistance that it has received."

It seemed to be working. In his daily telegram to Washington, McClure reported that as they'd crossed Ohio, he'd been unofficially advised that the state was in the process of awarding road contracts worth $9 million—and that the legislature had passed a $45 million road-improvement program.

They had spread the word in three states. Eight more still lay ahead.

CHAPTER FIVE

★ ★ ★

Soldier Weds in Hurry

IN 1919, INDIANA was 103 years old. Its highway commission, by contrast, was two years old. Despite that seeming tardiness at state level, however, the counties along the Lincoln Highway—spurred by Detroit, by seedling miles, and by Henry Ostermann—had been eagerly improving their stretches of the transcontinental road. Here and elsewhere, work on the highway had become a point of local pride. In the absence of any federal highway system, Americans were building this road for themselves.

The Lincoln Highway Association's 1918 guidebook said that 71 of 169 miles through Indiana were now brick or concrete, with nearly all the rest graded and graveled; only five miles of dirt remained unimproved. Even allowing for the guidebook's tendency to take a rosy view, in the five years since the founding of the highway—and with the country at war for eighteen months of that time—this was no small advance. Jackson and McClure reported "considerable inconvenience" caused by clouds of dust; otherwise, their passage through the state was for the most part relatively comfortable.

Leaving Ohio on the eleventh day of the journey, they made the fifty-one miles to Fort Wayne in six hours. McClure arrived at ten o'clock, two and a half hours ahead of the convoy. He was met with the suggestion that the trucks might park along East Berry Street so the public could have a good look at them. He demurred and asked that they be permitted to go directly to camp in Lawton Park. He had fast come to the view that civic courtesies had to wait until the trucks had been checked over at the end of the day's run. Working to assert a more disciplined regime, he wanted every bracket and bearing, every gas line and grease cup immaculate before the swimming and dancing began.

A reception committee led by the mayor, the postmaster, and the chamber of commerce escorted the convoy into town. It had been an easy day; the soldiers were "a great gang of happy Yanks." After chow and inspection, they headed for a swim in the pool in the park. When it turned out they didn't have enough swimming trunks, the Wolf Tent & Awning Company erected a canvas screen around the pool, so the soldiers "could revert to the good old swimmin' hole costume with perfect propriety."

The Rotary Club presented dinner and speeches for the officers in the Wolf and Dessauer Auditorium. The convoy's orator, Dr. Johnson, spoke after the meal, and again to the crowds in the park from the bandstand. When his grandparents had traveled to Fort Wayne in 1832, he said, they'd made ten miles a day. Now you could go twice that distance in an hour. Already, more people were traveling by car than by train. Already, the nation had 500,000 trucks on the road. Soon, he prophesied, it would be ten times that many. They had to come, and there had to be good roads for them, because "the railway is no longer capable of meeting the transportation needs of the country." So the Townsend Bill had to pass. It would, he said, mean $20 million from Washington for Indiana's roads.

Interviewed in the *News & Sentinel,* George Dewald of Firestone's Fort Wayne branch backed Johnson up with another telling argument. While America reeled from one pay dispute to another—100,000 men had just been locked out from their jobs in Chicago—Dewald said the economies offered by truck transportation would bear down hard on that bane of the times, the high cost of living. This prospect was, he said, "a bright ray . . . in the dawn of new things."

In Lawton Park, the convoy's searchlight shone its own bright ray, and the General Electric band played between speeches. The weather, reported Jackson, was fair and warm.

SOUTH BEND WAS seventy-six miles along the Lincoln Highway from Fort Wayne. It had started life as a remote fur trappers' camp amid untamed flatlands of marsh, forest, and prairie. By 1850, the population of the infant city was 1,652. That year two brothers, Clem and Henry Studebaker, came west from Pennsylvania to start a business there.

Their father was a blacksmith and wagon builder named John Studebaker; he had five daughters and five sons. In South Bend, Clem and Henry followed in the family trade. They began work with two forges and a capital sum of sixty-eight dollars. When they opened for business on February 6, 1852, their gross sales that day totaled twenty-five cents for putting two shoes on a horse.

In their first year, they built two wagons. Their nineteen-year-old brother John came to join them, but he was soon off to California with the Gold Rush. In South Bend, Clem and Henry struggled along—often bartering wagons for livestock, too rarely seeing cash—and they appealed to John to come back and help them.

After five years in the West, John agreed. He hadn't struck gold, but he'd done well enough making wheelbarrows for the miners. The story has it that in 1858 he sailed back from San Francisco to New York, crossing the Isthmus of Panama on the way, with $8,000 in gold nuggets sewn into a leather belt around his waist. Whatever the detail, he brought back enough to put them on a sounder footing.

Ten years later, when the business was reorganized as the Studebaker Brothers Manufacturing Company, they had 140 mechanics in a four-acre plant, with enough inventory to make six thousand wagons. The remaining two brothers had joined the firm; in 1870 one of them went to St. Joseph, Missouri, to open a branch selling wagons to pioneers. Before long they had outlets from Dallas to Denver, and from New York to San Francisco.

They became the world's largest producers of horse-drawn vehicles; they made carriages for presidents. As sons and sons-in-law took over the business and the British army bought Studebaker wagons to help fight the Boer War, it was inevitable that they would start experimenting with horseless carriages. Like many others they wavered at first between electric and gas-fueled cars, but they soon saw which way the future lay.

In 1908, they went into business with a Detroit firm called Everett-Metzger-Flanders. It wasn't a great success at first; E.M.F.

came to stand for Every Morning Fixit, Every Mechanical Fault, and Every Mark's Favorite. The larger part of their profits came from horse-drawn vehicles as late as 1911—but, overcoming these teething troubles, they pushed on and built car plants in Detroit, Chicago, and Walkerville, Ontario.

By 1917, the business that had started out putting shoes on a horse employed 250 women in South Bend just to stitch the mohair canopies for their touring cars. Two years later, as the convoy neared the city, two Studebaker sons lived in houses worth $750,000, while the home of a third was valued at a round million—but they planned to make themselves and their city plenty richer yet.

South Bend was already growing fast, from 53,684 people in 1910 to 70,983 in 1920. No small contributor to that growth were Studebaker's sales of wagons, artillery harnesses, and other equipment to the Allied armies worth $37 million. Now, with the war ended and automobile sales set to soar, they planned to shift production from Detroit and open their biggest plant yet in their home city. Twenty thousand people would celebrate its opening in 1920; within a few years, it would employ that many.

The day before the convoy arrived, the chamber of commerce announced that this expansion would likely see South Bend's population grow past 100,000 people, and that the city needed eight thousand new homes to cope with the increase over the next five years. It estimated a cost of around $4,000 per house—coincidentally, about the price of a top-end car at that time. It was no surprise, then, that when the convoy came to town, the Studebaker Corporation invited the officers to dinner.

THEY CHOKED ON dust, and so did their carburetors. They stopped for lemonade in Churubusco, then pressed on through level farmland up what's now U.S. 33 through Merriam and Wolflake, Kimmell and Ligonier, Benton and Goshen and Elkhart. Tire firms and garages hung maps of the convoy's route in their offices. Postmasters in each town called ahead to the next, and factory whistles blew as they approached to bring excited and expectant people onto flag-decked streets.

In South Bend, Henry Ostermann and Lieutenant Doron arrived early, and were given lunch by the local Firestone branch at the Oliver Hotel. The hotel was "best in the West"; it had 250 rooms, "unsurpassed in appointments and service," and it announced in the guidebook that it catered "especially for automobile parties." Studebaker had booked blocks of rooms here for twenty of the convoy's officers that night.

McClure arrived at three o'clock. The trucks started coming in soon afterward, after nine hot and dusty hours on the road. Firestone and the Republic Truck Company had sandwiches and cigarettes waiting for them outside the city limits. Mayor Carson, Chief of Police Kline, and Fire Chief Serbell led them into town with an escort of fire trucks. Overhead, an army airplane—promoting the air service on a recruitment tour of its own—added the buzz of its Liberty engine to the festive blaring of the fire sirens. They came in on Lincolnway East—it's still called that today—and they passed through crowds drawn by all the hype and noise to the city center streets.

Presumably McClure must have had a quiet word with someone, because the line of parade was soon abandoned. Plainly exhausted, the men were allowed to retreat to Springbrook Park. The kitchen trailers were there with a meal already, and so was a truckload of lemonade from the chamber of commerce. It was emptied fast "before the combined attack of the thirsty Yanks."

A local band had joined the parade, and then another band turned up—a fifteen-piece affair sent by Goodyear president Frank Seiberling from Akron. They played all evening, and they would play all the way to San Francisco. The big five-ton Packard they rode on had Goodyear's latest forty-four-inch pneumatic tires, and it had driven across the continent once already to prove what a truck thus equipped could do. These tires would be an object of constant wonder; one of them alone cost more than most men made in a month.

While the soldiers ate and danced in the park, the officers went to the Chain-o'-Lakes Country Club for a dinner given by Studebaker. Dr. Johnson spoke, praising the good roads of St. Joseph County; McClure thanked the people of South Bend for their hospitality.

They were in good shape, with all vehicles rolling under their own power, and they were tightening up their drill. In the morning, it took less than half an hour for the convoy to leave the park in close formation. Soon they would be in Illinois.

THEY PASSED THROUGH New Carlisle and La Porte, Valparaiso and Merrillville, Schererville and Dyer to the state line. The *La Porte Daily Herald* had warned its readers ten days earlier that the aim of the exercise was "to impress upon communities along the Lincoln Highway the need of keeping the big transcontinental route in good shape."

If they didn't do that in La Porte, said the paper, Michigan City was making "strenuous efforts" to have the route pass through there instead. It urged readers earnestly to pay their five dollars and join the association. If you did, you'd get a radiator emblem. More important, you'd stay on the road.

Welcome banners were hung, and courthouse bells rung; mayors and businessmen lined up to greet this "momentous trial of the motor vehicle." Again the *Daily Herald* noted nervously that the army was studying the condition of the road with a beady eye. "It has been hinted," said their reporter, "that counties too backward to keep their portion of the highway in repair will lose the road."

Keen participants in Henry Joy's "great patriotic work"—and more than keen to avoid being dropped from it—turned out in numbers in town after town. Amid the push and jostle a railroad watchman named Crawford Miller was run down in Valparaiso by one of the army trucks. Luckily, the worst he suffered was a broken collarbone. A little farther on an ambulance left the road and turned turtle in the ditch, knocking its frame awry. Elwell Jackson blamed the driver's carelessness, not the state of the highway.

The roads were stone and dirt; they were "fair to poor." The convoy made eighty miles in a little under nine hours and reached Chicago Heights at about three in the afternoon.

THE MEMBERS OF the Chicago Heights Automobile Club were an active crew. They had an attorney on permanent retainer to defend their members free of charge "when innocently arrested for violating any law regulating the use of automobiles."

They anticipated the convoy eagerly; the town had been "on the qui vive" for days. Back when the expedition had departed from Washington, the *Chicago Heights Star* had fretted, "Is Ostermann lost?" The highway's local consul hadn't heard from him. The town's citizens, said the paper, "want to give the convoy a proper reception, but are at a loss to know when it will arrive." Now it turned out they were going to have them all through the Sunday rest day.

Too much of this town today is bleak and alarming, charred and litter-strewn, but in 1919 it was packed and busy. Twenty-seven miles south of Chicago, it proclaimed itself "the crossroads of the nation" because the Lincoln Highway intersected here with a branch of the Dixie Highway to Florida. First laid out in 1865 with a population a little above a thousand, by 1919 it was twenty times that size.

Growth had started with the railroad, back when the site was called Thorn Grove. (Thorn Grove later turned appealingly into Bloom; today's name wasn't adopted until 1892.) The Joliet and Northern Indiana came first, in 1853. Others followed until the area was "webbed with rails, switches, crossings, stations, depots, yards and water tanks." Before all this, a round-trip to Chicago took two days, four if the weather was poor. Now it took a few hours.

Bloom boomed—and got its permanent name—after a group of real estate merchants formed the Chicago Heights Land Association in 1891, spotting industrial gold in that mesh of rails. Acquiring four thousand acres, they offered free water and free factory sites; they drew twenty-five hundred people in crowded trains to view their open prairie. With lower taxes than Chicago, by the turn of the century the town had sixty-seven factories employing fifteen hundred men, along with stately houses on wide avenues with electric lights.

By 1910, the workforce had grown past four thousand. The Hamilton Piano plant turned out seven thousand pianos a year; the town made steel, aluminum, machine tools, packing crates, bricks, bottles, batteries, paint, fertilizer, chemicals, and rail tracks.

Thirty-eight different rail lines had shipping facilities here. East of the tracks (downwind of the industry) immigrant laborers speaking several dozen languages crowded into dismal housing. Downtown, Illinois Street from Halsted to Chicago Road teemed with stores and businesses. Past Thorn Creek to the west, the wealthy lived among landscaped lawns and parks; the country club went up in 1912.

In the years before the arrival of the convoy, Mayor Hood had invested in extensive street paving. It was said that "he made a city out of a mud-hole." Real estate dealers used the paving to promote their lots. You could buy a plot of land with your Liberty bonds, said L. B. Schilling, "and watch your investment grow. My beautiful subdivisions invite you."

The banks of the town proclaimed the robust health of their finances; other businesses spoke of the newness of the age. You could own "Mr. Edison's Wonderful Phonograph" and pay for it in installments. Five dollars down got you a Federal Electric Washing Machine. "Just figure the wages of a washwoman—if you can get one," the company's ad cajoled.

For your next auto trip, you could drop by the Stolte Drugstore and get thermoses, lunch kits, flashlights, goggles, and air cushions. You could pick up a roll of Kodak while you were at it—because "The Film in the Yellow Box . . . Will Bring Your Trip Home With You."

On Chicago Road, the Lincoln-Dixie Tire Repair Company and the Lincoln Highway Tire Repair Shop vied for your business. "Let us serve you," urged the latter. "We will convince you of the truth of our statements."

Like the highway itself, all that is gone now. U.S. 30 today is a four-lane road through a plastic eternity of malls and tower signs and chain motels. The name Lincoln flickers alongside it—appended to a retail court, a school, a body shop—like the distant memory of another world, a world long ago bypassed. But as with your holiday snapshots or the down payment on your washing machine, the seeds of the way we live now were planted then. They were planted in concrete, and they were delivered by truck.

THE LINCOLN HIGHWAY consul for Chicago Heights was a druggist named B. H. "Snow" Vannatta. As the convoy drew near he cleaned out his store's front window and built a display map in it showing the central section of the United States. Mountains were represented by piles of dirt, farmland by sawdust dyed green, and the highway itself by a trail of sand drawn clear across it. Vannatta made a miniature telegraph line running alongside the sand highway and set down toy automobiles to drive along his dream of the road.

The town was so keen on the convoy and its message that its leading citizens—Mayor Klingler, Postmaster Stolte, Consul Vannatta, and a fair number of others—drove all the way to Valparaiso, Indiana, to greet them. They returned with the lead vehicles at about three o'clock and pulled up on Fourteenth and Wentworth to let the rest of the train catch up. It took over an hour to assemble the whole parade.

The fire whistle blew, and the Goodyear band led the army into town down West End Avenue. They made up "a dust-blown, hard-looking crowd." They were escorted to a shady grove on a hill south of Sixteenth Street, just west of Thorn Creek—in the upscale part of town—and before long the place "looked like a miniature city that had sprung up in a few hours."

The camp teemed with visitors. Many interested parties had come from Chicago, and McClure was soon surrounded. The *Star* described the scene: "The gas and oil men, the tire men, the auto supply men swooped down on him by the score, and there were newspaper men, moving picture operators, camera fiends, and good roads advocates, all anxious to speak with the man who was doing this big thing for the government." McClure was, said the paper, "An efficient officer and a courteous gentleman, who met the numerous demands on his time with unfailing cheerfulness." He offered his mantra to all those around him—"We're going to get there; that's all"—while the ladies of the town served coffee and doughnuts.

After supper the men were at liberty, and the streets filled with young women come to eye the soldiers. Many of the officers left them to it. Elwell Jackson was driven up to Chicago, where he stayed at the Chicago Automobile Club as a guest of the Four Wheel Drive Auto Company.

Back in Chicago Heights on Sunday morning, the Goodyear band gave a concert from the balcony of the Victoria Hotel. In camp the men shaved and did their laundry, watched all the while by curious onlookers. For lunch, many homes were thrown open for them to eat with the townspeople, while the officers dined at the country club. The Knights of Columbus organized a baseball game, in which the local team roundly trounced the army men. The Elks held a dance, and the American Manganese Steel Company opened its shower baths.

Flies swarmed about the kitchen trailers. The movie men filmed Sergeant Wood doing stunts with the Militor. The men strolled in the sun, glad not to be having their insides rearranged on the jolting trucks for a day. They played cards, wrote home, or paired off to promenade with the local girls. More hectically amorous than the rest, one of them "improved the golden hour" by borrowing five dollars and getting married.

The *Star* was enchanted. The soldier's name was Private Philip Fred Gollick. He had, said the paper, met Miss Mabel Ruth Kelley on Saturday evening, and it was love at first sight. Unfortunately for local pride, she wasn't a Chicago Heights girl—she was thought to be eighteen years old, and came from Muskegon, Michigan—but this minor lapse on her part could be overlooked in the romance of the moment. She had a local connection, after all; she was staying with her aunt, Miss Gazy of School Street.

Gollick wooed her that Saturday night with a passion, until his pass from camp ran out; he renewed his suit in the morning. Once she'd agreed to his proposal, he borrowed the money for a marriage license. Frantic telephone calls ensued to Chicago and Joliet, until a county clerk willing to issue one on a Sunday could be found. A local man with a motorbike roared off to get it; an Episcopalian minister was sent for, and the ceremony was performed under the trees. SOLDIER WEDS IN HURRY, said the *Star*.

But perhaps there was more to it. Perhaps the *Star*, starry-eyed, had gotten it wrong. A sharp-eared fellow from the *Chicago Evening Post* had heard a different version. He reported Colonel McClure, naturally concerned for the young couple's welfare, asking Gollick, "Isn't this rather sudden? You've only known the girl an hour."

Not at all, the ardent Gollick apparently replied. He said that (far from rushing into anything here) he'd met Miss Kelley in Bucyrus back on Tuesday, and these past five days she'd been following the convoy by train. Once they were married, he said, she'd keep on following them all the way to the Pacific—after all, Gollick came from Los Angeles—and the ride into the West would be their honeymoon.

THE HIGHWAY SKIRTED south and west of Chicago, through Joliet and Aurora and the little settlement of Mooseheart. This last was headquarters to the Loyal Order of Moose of the World, along with a home for their widows and orphans; they even had their own radio station. Thanks to the Moose, it was also the site of the first concrete paving in rural Illinois. Beating the seedling miles to it, they'd welcomed their stretch of the Lincoln Highway into being with a Good Roads Day on April 15, 1914. Men came from miles around in straw hats and white shirts to give their labor for free; Governor Dunne wielded a silver shovel to help shift the first cement.

The men were all given a Good Roads paycheck, a certificate that said, "Because he labored willingly with his hands. As he works successfully with his brains. Because he showed by such work that he believed in THE GOOD ROAD—the road which bears the product to market, the worker to his pay, the physician to his patient, and the dullard to understanding—and because his motive in this work was not selfish gain, but rather to the end that we all enjoy a BETTER TOWNSHIP, a RICHER COUNTY, a HAPPIER STATE, and a GREATER NATION."

Four and a half years years later, on November 6, 1918, Illinois voters approved a $60 million bond issue for forty-eight hundred miles of hard-surfaced road. Before the vote, for sixteen months the proposal's backers had waged "the most strenuous campaign ever carried on in the state on a public utility question."

Illinois was getting there, at least in principle. In practice, wartime conditions made labor and materials both rare and costly, and voting in favor of roads wasn't at all the same as actually seeing them built. Besides, a lawsuit questioning whether the road act was constitutional bogged it down in the courts for months, and the Supreme Court didn't uphold the state's right to fund road building in this way until April 1919.

In the meantime, patchy improvements that had already been made helped the convoy cover 172 miles through Illinois in two days—but it was far from comfortable. The highway was a random mix of concrete, brick, gravel, and dirt; on the worst stretches, the trucks kicked up a dust cloud so thick that visibility fell to twenty yards.

On the first day, from Chicago Heights to De Kalb, they were ten and a half hours on the road. The Militor towed a Garford with a holed radiator for much of the day; the cooking range fell off one of the kitchen trailers in the middle of the street in Joliet. It was the second time this had happened in three days. McClure reported that morale was still good, except for these continuing problems with the mess arrangements. It was hot, hard work, and too often the men were hungry.

The local people made up for it where they could. Joliet served cold drinks; Aurora handed out sandwiches, cakes, and ice cream. The convoy stopped there for only an hour, for lunch in Lincoln Park, but thousands came to see them all the same. Flags flew from homes and businesses all along their route; the highway in Illinois was a festival in red, white, and blue. When the men spent the night at Annie's Woods in De Kalb, the Red Cross served several hundred gallons of lemonade, and Colonel McClure was first in line.

Three thousand people came to look at the convoy, and to hear Dr. Johnson speaking for the Townsend Bill. That was nearly one in three of De Kalb's entire population. The crowd stayed in and around the camp until past eleven that evening; the men were running on six hours' sleep a night, if they were lucky.

ON THE DAY after the convoy's departure, the *De Kalb Daily Chronicle* reported that the county's Good Roads Movement "is now under way . . . people the state over, regardless of whether they own a car or not, are beginning to see the benefits possible from good roads." Evidently they needed to. Tourists complained to the townspeople that the Lincoln Highway was "full of detours . . . in such condition that no car could stand up under such wear and tear." The paper looked on the bright side, arguing that the detours were there because of roadwork. "Think of the pleasure that will be possible," it said happily, "when the cement road has been built from coast to coast."

McClure must have dreamed of that day. He must have wondered if he'd ever see it in his lifetime as well. He reported to Washington that ninety miles of the highway between De Kalb and the Mississippi were little more than a dirt track, and he described the condition of it bluntly as "deplorable."

The clouds of choking dust they kicked up were so dense that the driving became dangerous; he had to space the vehicles wide apart so they didn't cannon into each other. Between the dust and the day's litany of accidents and breakdowns, they ended up so strung out into broken sections that the towns they passed through were disappointed at the intermittence of the spectacle; the last vehicles were stranded many hours behind the first.

Two plank bridges gave way beneath the weight of the trucks. Engineers toiled to repair them in the grit-clogged heat. In Morrison one of the motorbike riders, trying to avoid a civilian auto, careered into a hitching post and was flung from his machine. Riderless, the bike carried on down East Main Street, finally crashing into the curb outside city hall.

The Militor started an hour behind the main train, towing a disabled Garford. A Mack towing the pontoon trailer couldn't haul the load up a sandy grade and stalled in the dirt. They had to unhitch it, then drag the trailer by hand up the hill on ropes. A Riker three-ton slipped down a twelve-foot embankment and rolled at the base of it. The six men riding it managed to jump clear, and the truck, once righted, was fit to go on. Other trucks broke down and needed tows from the Four Wheel Drives and the Militor. Finally, as they neared their camp across the river in Iowa, five trucks mired in soft earth and had to be dragged out one by one. For the second day running, they were on the road nearly eleven hours. It was, McClure grimaced, "The most tedious day of the expedition."

They'd been through Rochelle, Franklin Grove, Dixon, and Sterling. They crossed the Mississippi late in the afternoon over the leaping, spindly frame of the Fulton High Bridge into Clinton, Iowa. If the day had seemed rough, however, it had been a boulevard cruise compared to the trials that lay ahead.

Did the men sense that the great river was a landmark moment? Did they know that before long they'd be looking back fondly on the Illinois dust? One man at least knew all too well what the road would be like in the West. When he'd arrived in Chicago Heights ahead of the convoy, the first thing Henry Ostermann had done was take his Twin Six up to Chicago to have it thoroughly overhauled.

In sixteen days, they'd gone 906 miles. This distance was already as far as any truck convoy had ever managed in the past—but they hadn't completed even one-third of their journey yet.

CHAPTER SIX

★ ★ ★

The Mud Column

IOWA IS A farm 350 miles wide, and a wonderfully attractive one; in 1919, it was also a highly prosperous one. The war had sent prices for farm produce soaring to unprecedented levels, and land prices with them. It was the golden age of American agriculture, and—as long as you hadn't lost a son to the fighting, or loved ones to the flu—the Midwest was a blessed place to be.

High prices for food and low prices for Model T's meant that one in seven Iowans now had an automobile; it was the highest per capita car ownership of any state in the Union. The traditional resistance of farmers to paying taxes for road building, however, meant that virtually nowhere in the state was there a paved surface on which to drive these cars. Such roads, said rural people, were "peacock alleys" for the city rich.

So Iowa still had dirt roads. They spewed dust when it was dry, and when it rained, the rich black soil that produced such a bounty of corn and hogs became a fathomless quagmire.

In 1915, driving from Detroit to San Francisco during a particularly wet spring, Henry Joy had seen for himself how bad the mud could be. The following year he stirred fierce controversy when he wrote indignantly in *Collier's* about what happened to Iowa in the rain. "Not a wheel turns," he declaimed, "every farm is isolated. Social intercourse ceases. School attendance is impossible. Transportation is at a standstill. Millions of dollars' worth of wheeled vehicles become . . . worthless."

Iowans were incensed at this bad publicity, but Joy was right and many of them knew it. As farmers bought vehicles—trucks and tractors as well as cars—they became more inclined to accept the need for good roads. In April 1919, the state finally passed a law creating a primary road system. It was touch-and-go, with campaigners against the measure arguing that it implied the end of local government. One historian has said that if the system's name had suggested "either state control or paving, it probably would not have been approved."

Campaigning was fierce on both sides. Joe Lang wrote in the the *Iowa Magazine* that if people wanted greater farm production, better educational facilities and opportunities, a decent social life, and a healthy community spirit, "the solution of all these problems, the one final answer to them, the one thing that leaves but details to be arranged, is a passable system of all the year roads."

It would take money to build such roads, Lang continued, but that was only common sense. "You cannot live in an eight or ten room house with electric lights, hot water and other modern conveniences for the same outlay that you can live in a cave or a shack, but the question is simply whether it is worth it."

Opponents had to be mollified nonetheless, so the new law included a provision that individual counties had to vote in favor of raising the money before the road improvements the bill envisaged could proceed in their domain. The convoy was therefore a major spur to help this change along; counties were voting on bond issues for paved roads all across the state even as the motor train passed through. Seventeen counties had already declared themselves in favor of spending the money, while those four that had so far voted against (Franklin, Hardin, Story, and Tama) were chided for being "in the mud column."

The men of the convoy were fortunate. They did not have to find out the hard way what being in the mud column could mean. In the six days it took them to cross the state the weather stayed fair, and their worst discomfort came with the choking dust. Otherwise, running through the middle of the state along the line of what's since become U.S. 30, their passage was one long promotional party.

THEIR FIRST STOP was Clinton—and Clinton was an exception to the local rule in two ways. In a rural environment spilling over with money, it was an industrial town, and it was broke.

It had started life as a ferry crossing on a narrow stretch of the Mississippi. In 1855, a consortium of eastern bankers and railroad men bought five hundred acres on the west bank. They reckoned it looked a good spot to build a bridge, and the river was spanned ten years later. Meanwhile, the steam-driven circular saw had been invented. Clinton turned out to be ideally placed to process the pine brought downriver from Wisconsin and Minnesota. The river brought the lumber, and the railroad took it west for the settlers to build their houses. For three decades Clinton thrived on the back of its enormous sawmills until, in the early 1890s, the town had a population of around thirty thousand.

Then the business dried up. New sources of lumber supplied new settlers farther west until, by 1897, all but two of Clinton's mills had closed. Four thousand people upped and left. Store owners were ruined, all the savings and loans went into receivership, and for two years the city's police and firemen got their monthly wages of fifty dollars in worthless warrants that the town had no money to redeem. If they were lucky, they could sell them for five dollars; in a bad month they were worth fifty cents.

One way Clinton tried to keep the mills going was to surface its roads in creosoted wood blocks. The result, in summer, was a street that buckled and stank.

When the convoy came through twenty years later, the town hadn't really recovered. The population was still shrinking, now below twenty-five thousand. In this context, being on the Lincoln Highway meant worlds to these people. It was the artery that would bring them new business, and it meant so much to them that they'd even called their baseball team after it; Clinton was represented by the Lincoln Highway Athletic Club.

The highway's local consul was a garage owner named A. A. Daehler. On the eve of the convoy's arrival, he organized twenty-five local businesses to take out a half-page ad in the *Clinton Herald* urging people to come and see it. It was, said the ad, an "epoch-making tour."

Ostermann got to town with Lieutenant Doron the night before the motor train and put up at the Lafayette. From the way his arrival was reported, here and elsewhere—Ostermann driving his Lincoln Highway Packard Twin Six, "the red, white and blue car well known to tourists from coast to coast"—it's plain the man was a celebrity. He told the local papers that the convoy "is really as important as the first transatlantic flight."

Certainly, he pointed out, people who weren't on the highway knew how significant it was. Davenport, Des Moines, and many other places were all trying to get the convoy (and the road) diverted their way. Ostermann spoke to the board of the Clinton Commercial Club and reassured them that, whatever these other towns might say, there was no chance of the highway being taken from Clinton. After all, in proportion to its population, more people in this town had joined the association than anywhere else along the entire length of the road.

The convoy crossed High Bridge between Fulton, Illinois, and Lyons, just north of Clinton, late on the afternoon of Tuesday, July 22. Built to carry wagons in 1891, it was a vertiginous, rickety structure, with four steel trusses resting on stone islands and steel pylons; now its planking was coming loose under the pounding meted out by the ever increasing weight of motor traffic. Nails and spikes stuck out of it everywhere, menacing tires; in a five-ton truck it would have been a jolting, unnerving ride.

The vehicles crept over the river in relay, three or four at a time, moving at a snail's pace. Soldiers hauled the trailers by hand, not trusting them to stay straight on the unsteady bridge. Dozens of cars pulled aside at either end, giving the trucks right of way. Hundreds of people lined the banks of the river to watch, or stood in cheering groups along the three miles of roadside from Lyons into Clinton.

They camped in River Front Park. That afternoon and evening, a crowd estimated at between fifteen and twenty thousand turned out to see them. Among the milling throngs one mechanic, too busy fixing an engine to sit down for his meal, ate an oil-smeared egg sandwich as he worked; others wolfed down great wedges of watermelon. One lad wrote home, resting his paper on the back of a frying pan; another stood scratching his head, wondering whether to change his dust-coated clothes before or after he'd been to the pool at the YMCA.

A few of the soldiers weren't able to enjoy Clinton's hospitality. They'd been given typhoid shots by the medical unit and were lying on stretchers looking sorry for themselves. The major in charge of the unit told fretful women with sons in the army not to worry too much about it. He said, "Wait until they've had their second shot before you sympathize with them."

Machine guns were fired across the river from the Clinton Boat Club, the Citizens' Band played in the park, and Shean's Jazz Orchestra entertained at the Coliseum. The dancing went on past midnight; with reveille sounded at five in the morning, it would be another long day before they got to Cedar Rapids.

THEY HAD ALL their daily little glitches to contend with. Elwell Jackson meticulously noted blocked gas lines and oil-soaked magnetos, cruising up and down the cavalcade through the drifting clouds of dust. One of the spare-parts trucks couldn't make it up the least hint of a hill, and the Militor had to tow it. A machine-shop truck went through a culvert; the Militor had to rescue that too. A fender fell off one of the kitchen trailers, the fog of grit kicked up by the vehicles' passage clogged their ball bearings, and at least a dozen trucks choked and stalled.

The soldiers patched and mended as they went—but it could have been worse. The sun shone, at least some of the time a wind from the south blew the dust from their path, and the Iowa Highway Department had dragged the road smooth to ease their journey. Moreover, as McClure contentedly reported, their progress throughout the day "amounted to an ovation."

The Lincoln Highway didn't bypass towns the way U.S. 30 does now. Here in Iowa, and all across America, it went from one Main Street to the next. Through De Witt and Wheatland, through Mechanicsville and Mount Vernon, through the green fields and the gently folded land at the heart of America, the convoy was cheered from one town to the next.

It was threshing season, and an army of men sixty thousand strong was working its way north toward Minnesota and the Dakotas to bring in the wheat and barley. As the trucks passed among them they quit their fieldwork and gathered at every crossroads to hail the soldiers on their way. Exultantly McClure reported, "Entire state enthusiastic for good roads."

The *Mount Vernon Record* compared the trucks to the wagon trains that had brought the founders of these little towns into Iowa, the grandparents of the people now watching the convoy pass. "The world has been moving since those days," said the paper, "and the pace of the past ten years surpasses that of all the preceding years. And we are still speeding up. People have not even stopped to get their second wind. By the time they stop for their third, fourth, and even fifth wind, it will be necessary to have brick pavement from coast to coast on the Lincoln Highway."

Anyone who looked into the future could see that it was paved. The towns of Cedar Rapids and Marion, for example, were five miles apart, and had been engaged in a fierce battle ever since the 1850s as to which of them should be the seat of Linn County. When the Lincoln Highway was first laid out, Marion owned that honor; in 1919, the convoy duly passed through there on its way to making camp in the larger town.

Going through Marion was, however, an awkward jog north for the road to make. Cedar Rapids therefore settled the question by paving the road due east toward Mount Vernon, cutting Marion out as a fait accompli on the ground. The traffic naturally followed the pavement; Marion soon lost its role as the county seat, and within a couple of years it was no longer on the Lincoln Highway either. Pavement, in other words, wasn't just the future; pavement was power.

You had to have pavement, or someone else would lay it and you'd lose out. What if tourists didn't enter the state at Clinton and drive to Cedar Rapids, but made their way via Davenport to Iowa City and Des Moines instead?

By way of admonition, the *Cedar Rapids Evening Gazette* reprinted this threat from the *Davenport Democrat:* "The fact that automobile travel will follow the hard roads, whether we name them Lincoln Highway or what not, makes it plain that Davenport will be the principal entry to the state from the east if we are prompt in offering a hard road across the state from this point."

Cedar Rapids wasn't having that. The *Evening Gazette*'s publisher, Clarence Miller, had owned Linn County's first gas-fueled car; the paper liked to believe that both itself and its city were up-to-date. On July 7, the day the convoy set off from Washington, it had proudly announced the first delivery in Iowa of a newspaper by airplane. The *Evening Gazette* would be flown to surrounding towns by the McCook-Doty Aeroplane Company and (somewhat unnervingly) "dropped from the sky."

The paper was produced in a city that had grown in seventy years from one log cabin selling lodging and liquor to a burg of forty-five thousand souls; as Iowa thrived, so Cedar Rapids now boasted the largest cereal mills in the world. It was certainly not a place to be outdone in the hospitality stakes. In Greene Square they served a chicken dinner for 350 people, with the tables arranged in the shape of a wheel. The men were set around the rim, while the officers and their hosts sat along the spokes. "We have had many things done for us," declared McClure, "but this outshines them all."

It was his thirty-sixth birthday. Ostermann organized a surprise party at the Hotel Montrose and presented him with a purse holding fifty dollars in gold. "No mechanical breakage to report," McClure blithely wired Washington—not troubling to mention that about ten of his vehicles missed some or all of the festivities, struggling into the city late through the night after they'd fixed themselves up along the road.

He didn't mention the accident that befell dispatch rider Sergeant Harold Moliter either. Moliter's legs were injured when he was knocked off his bike at First Avenue and Twenty-eighth Street by a careless civilian driver who suddenly turned without signaling. At least a few of the men must have wondered, if this was a good day, then what would a bad one be like?

THE MODERN WORLD went on about its business. New York City appointed its first female deputy district attorney; the first ever strike of airmail pilots began on the New York–Chicago run, after two pilots were sacked for refusing to fly in fog. The men who went out in sympathy with them charged tartly that their planes "were poorly equipped for flying even in good weather."

The *Evening Gazette* reported that John McKellar of Newark, New Jersey, had come to town, a human fly who planned "to walk up the side of several buildings between now and Saturday." His first targets for "the monkeyshine" were the Allison Hotel and the Killian Building. If they'd bear his weight, he said, he'd do handstands on their flagpoles.

The world was full of new entertainments; life was more lively by the day. As the convoy left town, go-ahead Cedar Rapids raised the speed limit outside the business district from fifteen to twenty-five miles an hour. As you put your pedal to the metal you were, perhaps, running on Red Ball Gasoline from the Hawkeye Oil Company—because, as the advertising encouragingly put it, "It ALL explodes EVERY time."

Amid this heady acceleration of things fun and things reckless, doubtless few listened to the killjoy bankers of Des Moines. They said $350 an acre for Iowa land was too much and warned ominously, "If the present boom continues there are going to be a number of heads bumped when settlement day comes around next spring."

Things were certainly booming back in Akron. Goodyear president Frank Seiberling was ordering up inventory anywhere and everywhere he could get it, building a huge factory in Los Angeles, and tapping rubber on a new twenty-thousand-acre plantation in Sumatra. It seemed you couldn't build enough tires for America. Seiberling was at the peak of his success; he was also, since the retirement of Henry Joy, the president of the Lincoln Highway Association.

In Iowa the Goodyear band played on, and the convoy followed it down the road to the west.

THE HIGHWAY RAN south of where U.S. 30 lies now, through the soft rise and fall of the rich green land along the north bank of the Iowa River, through Belle Plaine and Chelsea and Tama. The latter, a town of some three thousand people, was home to a banker named David E. Goodell, who was also Iowa's state consul for the Lincoln Highway. Thanks to Goodell, Tama is the site of a little gem of a bridge.

It was built in 1915 where the original road ran into town from the east; it stands today where East Fifth Street forks away from U.S. 30. It spans only a few yards over a small creek, but the span is enough for the two rails to spell out LINCOLN in white concrete letters on one side, and HIGHWAY on the other. The bridge was placed on the National Register of Historic Sites in 1976 and restored in 1987 with $15,000 of community donations. Back in 1919, the convoy rumbled across it before stopping along Third Street for lunch; then they pushed on to Marshalltown.

They arrived at about four in the afternoon and made camp in Riverview Park, which had a rock garden with waterfalls, a modest zoo, a bandstand, and a dancing pavilion. That night the local Red Cross served dinner there, saving the men from the dire produce of their battered mess kitchens with homemade meat loaf, potato salad, deviled eggs, cake, and ice cream. The people of Marshalltown were thoughtful in another way, too; they had the good sense to finish the music at ten in the evening.

On the road the next morning, Martin Berend displayed rather less sense. With the trucks strung out past State Center along what's now County Road E41, running at a steady eight miles an hour, Berend overtook them at speed through dense clouds of dust—and ran up the back of a Ford that was overtaking the convoy more sedately. Luckily no one was hurt, though the Ford was badly damaged; again, one has to wonder that there weren't more such mishaps.

Iowans had the choice of cloying mud in wet weather or blinding dust in dry; they also had the choice of doing something about it or staying in the mud column. Just east of Ames, the editor of the *Nevada Representative* took time out from his own local difficulties (BARKER BROTHERS WANT TO BEAT UP THE EDITOR) to spell it out on the front page that counties voting yes would get money for their roads, while counties voting no would not. It was the issue of the moment, and the slogan was blunt: "Get Iowa out of the Mud!" Even in good weather, the convoy was vivid proof of "what a dirty ride such a trip is."

The trucks rolled on through Ames—which, unusually, had not been wide awake to their coming. No one had prepared a welcome; no one had been in touch with McClure. Ames was also unusual in that the Lincoln Highway didn't run down Main Street, so local auto dealer Lisle Minert went east of town to Nevada with a journalist from the *Ames Daily Tribune*. They tried to find someone whom they might persuade to change the convoy's route; they wanted it to drive through downtown.

They came on the mess unit, running two hours ahead of the main train to get lunch ready in Boone. To their chagrin they were told that the scouts had been ahead and marked the route, and that the trucks could not now deviate from it. They did manage to get one of the kitchen trailers to pass down Main Street (luckily, for once, no parts fell off it) and when they finally found McClure, he consented to take a detour with them through the business district, and through the Iowa State College grounds as well.

There were crowds of people out, all lining the wrong street. "I am sorry Ames people did not get in touch with me at Marshall-town last night," said McClure. "I want the boys to see all that is to be seen, and to make it as easy for the public as possible."

The *Daily Tribune*'s man noted how big a fuss had been made of the convoy in Marshalltown, and how all Boone turned out like-wise to greet them for lunch. "It is to be regretted," he said sharply, "that for lack of organization or someone to do something, Ames passed up an opportunity."

THERE'S A SMALL irony that this should have happened in Ames, because the college through which McClure took his detour had educated one of the most important men in the history of Ameri-can transport.

Thomas Harris MacDonald was born in a log cabin in Leadville, Colorado, in 1881; soon afterward the family moved to Montezuma, Iowa. MacDonald studied civil engineering at Iowa State and graduated in 1904—the same year that Iowa awarded a grant of $3,500 to his college for a commission to study the road problem.

MacDonald had been taught by Anson Marston, the dean of engineering, who became the new commission's chief engineer. Marston said bluntly, "It seems absurd that in a state so wealthy and prosperous, so advanced in education and intelligence, that the entire agricultural economy and the basis for practically all busi-ness activity should be left to the mercy of bad weather on account of roads which would be a disgrace even to a barbarian."

MacDonald went to work for Marston, succeeding him as chief engineer in 1913. He had to work in the face of Iowan reluctance to pay for good roads; he could grade them, he could drain them and drag them, but he couldn't pave them. In 1916, before the tide of sentiment turned on the issue, the state elected Governor William L. Harding on a "mud road platform"—Harding being opposed to bond issues for the highways of Iowa.

Three years later, while the convoy was on the road through his state, MacDonald moved to a post where he could get more done; he was appointed chief of the Bureau of Public Roads in the Department of Agriculture. He was a man who knew his worth— before taking the job, he haggled his annual salary from $1,500 in Iowa to $6,000 in Washington—and he was also a man of unbending rigor.

Reserved and austere, he'd take off his coat and tie only when he needed to get down in a ditch to show his workmen what he wanted done. He was always "Mr. MacDonald," even to his wife, or simply "Chief." Only the greenest employee would dare to try to share an elevator with him; everyone else knew that his secretary, Miss Fuller, was the sole person accorded that privilege.

Road building for this man was a mission, plain and simple. "Next to the education of the child," he said, it was "the greatest public responsibility." He was "the father of the nation's highway system," and he was the nemesis of the Lincoln Highway too. He lasted thirty-four years in charge of the roads of the United States, from Wilson to Eisenhower—and there's another small irony in the fact that the president who finally sacked him had, in 1919, driven coast to coast along the road that Thomas MacDonald would later kill.

EISENHOWER HAD MET Mamie Geneva Doud in the fall of 1915 at Fort Sam Houston in Texas, and they had married the following summer. Mamie had spent her childhood in Boone, Iowa; it was then and still is a fetching, tree-shaded town of around thirteen thousand, and today you can visit her house at 709 Carroll Street. Given that her father became a millionaire, it's a pleasant but surprisingly modest one-story place of pale yellow clapboard.

Because of this the Lincoln Highway here is no longer the Lincoln Highway but Mamie Eisenhower Avenue. In 1919 her favorite aunt and uncle, Joel and Eda Carlson, still lived in the town; for a while, as Ike was posted to one camp and then another, they had looked after his and Mamie's baby son Doud Dwight.

When the convoy pulled into Boone, Eisenhower hadn't seen his wife and child for over eight months. At the time of the Armistice the previous November, Mamie had been on her way back from Camp Colt to Denver, where one of her sisters was dying. Ike's different postings, and then the absence of married quarters at Camp Meade, had kept them apart ever since. Visiting the Carlsons, he must have felt their separation anew.

Boone knew he was coming; its citizens planned to make the most of the convoy altogether, even if they only had it for an hour. It was, said the local *News Republican,* "one of the biggest things in the history of Boone," and the paper urged all those who could possibly make it to get downtown "to give the visitors the glad hand."

Ike and Sereno Brett came in ahead of the main train, and the town's adopted son was cautiously politic about the road. He told the paper, "I can't say too much about the condition of the Lincoln Highway," a noncommittal offering that might be taken several ways. Characteristically, Henry Ostermann was more fulsome. The road, he said, "is the best I have ever seen it in Iowa."

Given the true condition of it—a graded dirt track dotted with inadequate bridges—this didn't say much for what it had been like before, and the *News Republican* knew it. Now that Tama and Story Counties along the highway had voted to stay in the mud column, the paper was in a high funk of paranoia about the threat of the route being shifted south, and running through Des Moines instead.

"Many people along this line," it warned,

seem to think the location is fixed for all time. Unfortunately, this is not true. . . . The Lincoln Highway will follow the line of "least resistance"—a paved highway is that line, a mud road is not. . . . The Lincoln Highway officials are practical men of large business foresight. How long can it be expected that such men will stand behind a community that refuses to get out of the mud? . . . Are we, living on the Lincoln Highway—the greatest asset in Iowa—to remain asleep at the switch? . . . It is time there was concerted action all along this highway, to save it from the junk pile. Will we take it?

Ostermann and Consul Goodell sought to reassure them that the road would not be taken elsewhere; any talk to that effect from Des Moines was "a lot of bunk." From the tone of the debate, however, it's abundantly clear how much this meant. A town on the Lincoln Highway was a town on the road to the future; a town that lost it risked commercial death in the mud.

THE CONVOY PASSED through Ogden and Grand Junction, reaching Jefferson at about five in the afternoon. Jefferson, a town of some thirty-four hundred people, was the seat of Greene County; it was strong for good roads, and it was strong for the highway. On September 22 the previous year, thousands had gathered outside the courthouse to dedicate a new statue of Lincoln; the intense patriotism sparked by the war had only heightened the reverence many northerners still felt for Honest Abe.

James E. Moss was a local farmer and a member of the Lincoln Highway Association. Sending in his membership fee in 1921 he wrote to Detroit, "I am glad to be able to pay [my annual dues] as the Lincoln Highway will be the greatest memorial in the world in memory of one of our greatest citizens, and of the greatest world power. I am one of the Civil War soldiers. Lost a foot at Mission Ridge—glad to be yet alive. Will be one, if not the heaviest tax payer towards paving the Lincoln Highway, having two miles of the route through my farm in Greene County."

Today, the road through his land is County Road E39. West of Jefferson and just north of Scranton, on two corners of a field by the highway, Moss put up two markers—busts of Lincoln on simple white pedestals. But time went by, and memory faded as to why they were there, and then vandals knocked Lincoln's visage to the ground.

Now local people have had new busts made, and in May 2001 they were preparing to remount them on the plinths James Moss had built eighty years before. Two of those involved were Bob and Joyce Ausberger, farmers north of Jefferson. Joyce had come here in 1960 to teach fourth grade, and the year she started work, the Lincoln Highway was in one of her textbooks.

It was a geography book called *Journeys Through Many Lands*, published in 1950. After an introductory piece entitled "Our Air-Age World," each chapter was a different slice of educational travel—and the first of them was "Across the United States on the Lincoln Highway." The book went out of use soon after Joyce started teaching. She said, "It wasn't done real well, but it said it was the first transcontinental road and it went through these states, and we'd show kids how people lived then. But it was the last schoolbook I've seen on that—and kids should know about this. It's an integral part of modern United States history. That change from the railroad to the road—*everything* boils down to that."

Greene County had been keen to spruce up its piece of the highway from the moment the project was launched. In 1914, the board of supervisors put up $15,000 to get it graded and graveled, and board members went knocking door to door to raise $5,000 more to help finish the job.

Two big boosters for the road were Paul Stillman and Victor Lovejoy, respectively the publisher and editor of the weekly *Jefferson Bee*. Stillman was the highway's county consul; his paper campaigned for paving with a passion. On Monday, July 28, 1919—two days after the convoy came through—the county was due to vote on a $1 million bond issue. For weeks before the election, the *Bee* hammered home the message. On July 9 it carried a front-page picture of a car stuck in gumbo and captioned it, "A familiar sight last winter and spring. . . . The only permanent solution is paving."

Vote yes, and there'd be sixty-five miles of paved road in the county within four or five years. Vote no, and you'd wait twelve or fifteen years before you were out of the mud. The paper stressed that the bonds wouldn't be retired out of general taxation; they'd be paid off with federal aid money under the 1916 Highway Act, and with the state's proceeds from car-registration fees. They quoted a farmer: "Under this new and largely increased auto license we are going to be paying for paved roads whether we have them or not; I think we better have them."

On July 25, the *Bee* ran a report from a committee of the board of supervisors who'd visited other counties where concrete had been laid. "We went away with open minds on the whole question," these worthies concluded, "and came home convinced that concrete roads . . . are practicable, durable, and a good investment for the people of Greene County."

The convoy arrived the next afternoon. The temperature was in the nineties, and the men were covered with dust and grime. They made camp at the county fairground, worked on the trucks, showered at a local cement plant, and were ferried in a fleet of cars to dinner at the country club. Back in town afterward, the Goodyear band played in the main square; soldiers danced with the local girls until about ten-thirty. So many people came to town that the streets were choked with cars. McClure spoke to the crowd from the bandstand, as did Austin Bement from Detroit (the Lincoln Highway Association's secretary had joined the convoy earlier in Iowa), and Dr. Johnson made his pitch for pavement.

Unlike the railroads, he said, with highways America had built the rolling stock first, then found there was no roadbed on which to run it. That had to change, he argued, not least as a matter of economy. Any tax a farmer paid for roads, he'd earn back several times over in savings on gas, and on wear and tear to his vehicles and tires. More important yet, he lost money every time he couldn't get a crop to market on account of the mud. In other words, it wasn't that they couldn't afford pavement; the real point was that they couldn't afford bad roads. In language doubtless calculated for his western Iowa audience, he told them that voting no was like "saving at the spigot and wasting at the bung hole."

Early the next morning, the convoy left for Denison. Two days later, Greene County voted yes to a million dollars for paved roads by a majority of three to one—the biggest margin yet seen in the state.

WHEN THE FIRST settlers started moving into western Iowa around 1850, the conditions they had to contend with were harsh: "A trackless wilderness, remote neighbors, wild beasts in evidence, fifty miles to the nearest post office, no base of household supplies, no bridges across streams, oftentimes obliged to go from seventy-five to one hundred miles for provisions." The land around Jefferson was a place of sloughs and wetlands—people warned new settlers they'd be web-footed in a couple of years—and yet this place and this region, in little more than half a century, was made the larder of the world.

Sadly, the war that had pushed prices for produce and land through the roof came with another kind of price tag—and one of the first to pay it was a young man named Merle Hay. He was a farmer's son from Glidden, twenty miles west of Jefferson; he enlisted in May 1917 and sailed for France in June with Company F of the 16th Infantry. After four months' training, in hand-to-hand fighting in the small hours of November 3, Merle Hay and two others were the first American troops to be killed in action in World War I. He was twenty-one years old.

Glidden's population was 850. Of the eight boys who went to war from here in May 1917, only two returned.

Merle's parents, Harvey and Carrie Hay, lived on North Main. The convoy pulled up along the street, and the officers went in to pay their respects. The movie crew filmed the moment—but this time, they and the army men were marking something more important than the road.

TO EASE THEIR passage into Glidden, a team of local men had gone out the evening before to a bad spot in the road south of town and patched it up with shovels and several wagonloads of cinders. The convoy's officers were tactfully complimentary about Iowa's roads—they'd developed a canny habit of telling the people of whichever state they were in that the roads of the previous state were worse—but the trucks were now proof in town after town, county after county that only concrete would do.

There was a hill just east of Glidden that the locals thought had a perfectly decent piece of road. When the convoy went over it, they left ruts a foot deep or worse. The highway had soft stretches in it now that set the trucks' engines overheating as they plowed through the yielding earth. Wheels slipping in the dirt, the Mack pulling the pontoon trailer couldn't climb even a gentle hill; the Militor had to tow them both. One of the machine shops couldn't manage any grades at all, and for several days another truck had been shoving it nose-to-tail up every rise they came to.

To beat the dust, the vehicles spread out until the train covered five miles of road. At least a good breeze had picked up now, carrying the worst of the swirling clouds away from them. The men took a break for lunch in Carroll; it wasn't on the schedule, but the town's enterprising boosters had pinned down McClure in Jefferson the night before. He'd agreed to stop for them; it was, after all, another crowd for Dr. Johnson to address.

McClure was less accommodating with the eager promoters of Council Bluffs and Omaha. These two cities on opposite banks of the Missouri both hankered to have the convoy stay with them for their Sunday rest stop. Why, they thought, should that honor go to the rustics of Denison, a little town merely four thousand strong, when sophisticates like themselves awaited so near at hand?

McClure put his foot down with the delegation from Omaha. He told them, "The train is an official army affair, and is not out for entertainment and advertisement." This was something of a half-truth—but he had a schedule, and he was sticking to it. Denison got the convoy for two nights and a day, and it was the biggest thing that had ever happened there.

The announcement of its coming was front-page news in the local *Bulletin & Herald,* up there with the other really important item of the moment: GOOD BALL TEAM BEING DEVELOPED. Denison won the opening game of the baseball season the following week, beating Charter Oak 8–3. With plans in hand for a game against a team from the convoy, it sounded as if the soldiers had better watch out.

The rival *Review*, meanwhile, grew urgent in its excitement at having put one over Council Bluffs and Omaha. Given good weather, they expected huge crowds. They'd heard that two hundred people planned to drive from the village of Ida Grove alone, and they urged all these folks to do Denison proud.

The crowds that gathered over the weekend of the convoy's visit were the largest the town had ever seen; only the populist orator and presidential candidate William Jennings Bryan had come anywhere close to being such a draw. From surrounding towns and counties, thousands came to stroll through the camp in Washington Park. Soldiers and local people mingled in the warmth of the summer evenings on the teeming streets. Big crowds heard the Goodyear band play two nights' running on the courthouse lawn; on Saturday the street was cleared for a dance that went on until midnight, while the local women's clubs served ice cream, cake, and canteloupe.

So many people came to enjoy the party that the *Review* counted over six hundred cars parked around just that one part of town where the dance was held. For some, of course, this was too much temptation, and three of the cars were stolen by joyriders.

Hundreds more autos came to Denison the next morning; the soldiers couldn't even eat breakfast without a crowd gathering to stare. As the thermometer rose into the humid nineties, the local churches sent cars for any army men wishing to refresh their souls at Sunday service. By afternoon the heat was fierce, and it helped reduce the much anticipated ball game to absurdity.

The army were hopeless; Denison scored at will, until the game was abandoned in the sixth inning "due to heat and lack of interest" with the home team leading 19–1. At least Mutt and Jeff helped entertain the crowd. One stood six feet, eight inches tall, the other was four feet, seven inches short, and evidently they made about as odd a catcher-pitcher pairing as you could wish to see.

Away from the ballpark, many of the men took time out from the festivities to catch a movie at the Opera House. Blanche Sweet was playing in *The Unpardonable Sin*—"The soul stirring picturization of the most tremendous tale of love and adventure ever written"— but one soldier at least was too busy for Hollywood or baseball.

Like the amorous Private Gollick in Chicago Heights before him, Private Harry J. Paul got married, to Miss Charlotte E. Rohr of Cedar Rapids; county clerk Monaghan did the decent thing, opening his office specially to issue a license. It's not reported what McClure thought of this latest strike on his men from Cupid's arrow—but it seems another of his men had less respectable intentions.

Helen Wakefield was fifteen years old. She lived on a farm a few miles outside Mondamin, fifty miles southwest of Denison by the Missouri River, but a week before the convoy's arrival she'd run away from home. Her parents knew she'd been writing to one of the soldiers in the motor train, so they alerted Sheriff Green and his men to be on the lookout for her.

About midnight that Sunday evening, Deputy Sheriff Johnson arrested her on the grounds of the Central School. The girl "confessed to intimate relations with the soldier in question," but said she'd return home and behave if the police let her go. Her father duly collected her on Tuesday morning; what McClure did about the soldier isn't recorded.

More upset was caused by a "local celebrity" named Ike Mentor. Only recently discharged from the army himself, and already a habitué of the local courthouse, Mentor went to Washington Park on Sunday afternoon "with the evident intention of causing some trouble."

His first attempts at provocation were ignored; he met more soldiers later that evening on Broadway, and this time his insults struck home. Perhaps he wasn't impressed with their showing on the ball field, but expressing himself of the opinion that the soldiers were "a lot of bums" wasn't calculated to win him admirers. Before he made his escape it won him, instead, a punch in the face.

Holing up in a building a few blocks away, Mentor was surrounded by a picket of irate soldiers until some of the officers arrived to avert the looming fracas. Doubtless shivering with a delicious thrill of schadenfreude, one of the Omaha papers reported that Denison had been the scene of a near riot. Pride affronted, the *Bulletin & Herald* retorted that "everyone against one does not constitute a riot." If Mentor had had any local men on his side, the paper continued, "he didn't need an adding machine to count them."

AMID THESE VARIED excitements every truck had an oil change, and every vehicle was inspected and overhauled. The officers held a meeting and agreed that their biggest problem continued to be feeding the men. Lieutenant Shockey doubling as both mess and supply officer couldn't manage both roles, and an urgent request for an experienced man to run the kitchens went off to Washington.

That dealt with, the convoy pulled out early on Monday morning, heading seventy-two miles southwest for Council Bluffs and the Missouri River. Passing through Dunlap and Woodbine, Logan and Missouri Valley, the men were feted all the way. Again they choked on the Iowa dust—a still day, reported McClure, made conditions the most trying they'd yet experienced—and again the people of these little towns had lemonade ready by the gallon to help them cope.

A reception committee from Council Bluffs came to Missouri Valley to greet them. Not for the first time McClure bit his tongue and told them the roads were fine. "The dust was there," he said, "but we don't mind that if the road is good. You have to take the dust wherever it is found. Your road was the equal of any I have found in this state."

Equally poor, in other words—but that would change. The convoy, said McClure, "is doing more for good roads than anything else in the history of the country. You will see more good roads in process of construction after this trip than you ever had any idea of." He was right; 1919 was the year Iowa finally decided to get out of the mud. By the mid-twenties, the Lincoln Highway was paved clear across the state—and paving Iowa's roads was an enormous job.

Thomas MacDonald's successor as the state's chief engineer was Fred White. Rolling up his sleeves in 1920 to spend the money most counties had now voted for their roads, White issued a clear warning. He said, "By the time we get those roads paved, the first of them will be worn out and ready to start again. So let's go into it with our eyes open that we are starting something we will never finish."

Even as he said this, the price of corn was tumbling from $1.60 to 60¢ a bushel. The golden age was over; the first stirrings of the Depression were starting to be felt in rural America. Those farmers' sons who'd had such high hopes of the future found their fathers' land wasn't worth $350 an acre after all—so what were they to do?

More than a few of them went to work building cars in Detroit, and many others went to work on the roads.

CHAPTER SEVEN

★ ★ ★

Across the 100th Meridian

WHEN THE CONVOY was passing through western Iowa, the editor of the *Carroll Herald* wasn't there to see it. He was on vacation in Colorado, and he naturally wrote back to his hometown readership on this fast-growing new phenomenon, the automobile vacation. A cross-country car trip, he said, was "one of life's big experiences. It is harmless to look at, sweet to contemplate and not bad to take. It is not an easy experience, however."

He'd driven over seven hundred miles, and Nebraska had been a trial. He'd found "mud, mud, everlasting mud." He'd had flat tires, he'd been stuck on narrow trails with oncoming cars and no passing place in sight, he'd watched night fall and wondered if he'd find any place to stay. To deal with it, you had to be a "good sport"—but at least it was, he said, "a sort of democratic undertaking, where the man in the Ford is as important and is vested with the same right as the man in the Packard."

The other pleasing thing about it, from a more parochial point of view, was that the roads in Nebraska made Iowan roads look good. Nebraska's "well-advertised transcontinental highways," grumbled the Voice of Carroll, "are not worked and are in a deplorable state of neglect . . . with hills that had not been tickled with a road tool since the disappearance of sod houses."

The Lincoln Highway's 1918 guidebook was more tactful. It conceded that "many sections . . . are not yet in the best possible shape." Rather than criticize, however, it used the condition of the highway to push an argument central to its case for good roads in general, and for the Townsend Bill in particular. Nebraska—and even more so Wyoming, Utah, and Nevada—were too large and too sparsely settled to pay for improving their highways by themselves. In short, this was not a local issue: "The road problems in these states are national problems."

They wanted Americans to think about roads in a whole new way. The night before the convoy left Iowa, when Dr. Johnson spoke in Council Bluffs, he said, "Once a road led to somewhere near in the vicinity. Now it will connect the extremities of the country." For it to do that, the federal government would have to build it.

THE LINCOLN HIGHWAY through Nebraska followed the Union Pacific all the way across the state—nearly five hundred miles. The railroad had leased fifty feet of its right-of-way to a few counties on the route, so the road could run beside it and avoid endless right-angle jogs along section lines. Otherwise there were many such turns and frequent grade crossings, with all the risk attendant upon that. The imperceptible ascent from Omaha to the High Plains was thus a long, slow, kinked, sand-and-gravel haul, and it would take the convoy ten days to cross the state.

They spent a day's preparation at Fort Omaha. Leaving Bayliss Park in Council Bluffs at seven-thirty in the morning, the trucks rumbled up Pearl Street onto Broadway, crossing the Missouri on the Douglas Street bridge. The eccentric notion that they should use the pontoon trailer to cross the river had soon been abandoned. McClure said briskly, "We can't throw a pontoon across that stream in a week. The banks on both sides are bad too."

The trailer had been imposing a heavy strain on every truck that tried to tow it, so rather than drag it all the way to California, McClure now got rid of it by ceremonially presenting it to Mayor Edward P. Smith of Omaha instead. Somewhat bemused, the mayor had no clue what he might do with a pontoon trailer, but said uncertainly that he would "keep it for emergencies."

Smith's tenure in office was, in fact, a kind of perpetual emergency; the convoy would have been a welcome shot of light relief. His city was, in the resonant phrase of the day, "wide open," and his attempts to reform it very nearly cost him his life.

In 1919 Omaha was a thriving city of 200,000, with a robust sense of its own worth—it liked modestly to call itself "the biggest agricultural city in the world"—and, as any self-respecting big city should do, it boasted a colorful crime lord. Vice boss Tom Dennison had loomed large in Omaha life for two decades. He had a sweetly oiled political machine, and four-term Mayor James C. Dahlman had stayed studiously silent about his rackets.

Dahlman was loud enough in other ways. A former Texas cowpuncher, he once caused something of a stir on a visit to New York by lassoing a few of its citizens. Under Dahlman's regime, when Nebraska went dry in 1916 Tom Dennison's liquor flow in Omaha didn't slow up very much—and these were not men you crossed lightly. On one occasion, when the *Omaha Daily News* accused a city commissioner of falsifying jury lists, three murders ensued, and reporter Charles Driscoll was found badly beaten on the courthouse lawn.

Smith ousted Dahlman as mayor in 1918 and, with his radical police commissioner, J. Dean Ringer, he set about trying to clean up the city. By the summer of 1919, however, Omaha was plagued with strikes—and just prior to the arrival of the convoy, the Central Labor Union had rounded up five thousand signatures on a petition seeking the recall from office of Smith and three of his commissioners, including Ringer.

Naturally, Smith saw Dennison's hand in this. He charged that those seeking to unseat him were an unholy alliance of "the radical, I.W.W., Bolshevik element of the labor party" with "the booze element generally." If they succeeded, he warned, they'd make Omaha "a closed shop industrially, and a wide open town otherwise." An extra layer of disquiet was added to this volatile mix by the city's mounting racial tension. Omaha's black population had risen above ten thousand, having doubled in a decade, and widespread, often false reports of black men assaulting white women were helping to stoke an ugly climate.

Two months after the convoy passed through, on Friday, September 26, one Will Brown was identified by a young white woman as her rapist. He was an improbable suspect—he was crippled with rheumatism—but he was hauled off to a cell in the new courthouse all the same. On Sunday evening a mob numbering several thousand gathered there, started a fire in the building, dragged out Will Brown, shot him, hanged him, then mutilated and burned his body. While they were at it, they beat Mayor Smith unconscious and strung him up too. His life was saved by Russell Norgaard, who managed to lower him to the ground, and by three policemen who somehow got a car to him through the seething crowd.

The *Omaha World-Herald* won the Pulitzer Prize for a dramatic editorial it ran two days later, titled "Law and the Jungle." The piece concluded with a quote from Abraham Lincoln on the paramount need for reverence of the law—but the city's reformers had been too much discredited by the disorder, and Jim Dahlman became mayor again in 1921.

The riot had another consequence; it radicalized Omaha's black population. One among them who went on to promote the cause of African-American unity was Baptist minister Earl Little, whose son Malcolm would later change his surname to X.

THERE'S A GRIM irony in the fact that, for over fifty years after the creation of the Lincoln Highway, there were places all along the road named for the Great Emancipator where black people couldn't stay.

McClure, Jackson, and the many thousands who went before and after them could use the Lincoln Highway guidebook or the AAA's famous Blue Books, which had started appearing in the East back in 1901—but black Americans needed guidebooks of their own. The *Negro Motorist Green Book*, for example, was first published in 1936 "to give the Negro traveler information that will keep him from running into difficulties, embarrassments, and to make his trip more enjoyable."

After noting that the Jewish press had long published information about which places wouldn't welcome them, the preface of the 1951 edition finished thus: "There will be a day sometime in the near future when this guide will not have to be published. That is when we as a race will have equal opportunities and privileges in the United States. It will be a great day for us to suspend this publication, for then we can go wherever we please."

Other guides offered similar help. Along the five-hundred-mile course through Nebraska of what had once been the Lincoln Highway, the 1961 edition of the Bronze American National

Travel guide listed hotels and motels where black people could stay. There were nine of them. In Wyoming, there were three.

WHEN THE CONVOY came to Omaha, a summer heat wave was peaking. Forest fires raged amid a deepening drought in the West; in the city by the Big Muddy, temperatures were topping one hundred. In Krug Park and at the municipal beaches, girls were reported to be wearing excessively skimpy bathing suits. Superintendent Weirich of the public welfare board decided to investigate, and to consider whether to enforce the wearing of stockings. Upon his return, he anounced that he would be taking no action. "I had a very pleasant time," he said, "oh yes. I saw many stockingless bathing suits."

Stockingless women were strolling downtown as well. Traffic Officer J. J. Dudley was an Omaha landmark, "the human semaphore" at Sixteenth and Farnham—but when two women in their mid-twenties sauntered past nonchalant and bare-legged, even the stolid Dudley "was so overcome for a few moments that his long arms lost their cunning . . . the area of visibility between their slippers and their skirts was about eight inches."

Omaha was hot, it was at risk of infection from shocking Parisian fashions, and it was noisy. From early on a weekday morning there were squeaking auto brakes and honking horns, there were yelling newsboys and profanely raucous deliverymen, there were trucks and messenger boys and factory whistles. Into this bustle and hubbub came the rumble of the convoy.

The streetcar bridge across the Missouri onto Douglas Street is gone now; all that's left is the concrete abutment on the Iowa bank. It was just short of a mile long by twenty-eight feet, and it had a big Lincoln Highway arch across it saying WELCOME. It stood a block downstream of the bridge that carries Interstate 480 into Omaha, and the convoy came across it at eight-fifteen on the morning of Tuesday, July 29.

McClure led the way over the bridge, to be greeted at Tenth and Douglas by the beleaguered Mayor Smith. He left the searchlight on Seventeenth Street between Farnham and Douglas so it could put on a display that evening, then passed four miles north through the city to Fort Omaha. The chamber of commerce had made elaborate plans for the convoy's visit, but—expressing polite regrets—McClure turned them down.

There was work to be done. He planned to use his first chance to camp in a military facility to give the train a total overhaul before they tackled the West. Only forty years earlier, Fort Omaha had been General Crook's base for the Indian campaigns on the plains; since then it had been in and out of use, before finding a role during World War I as the army's balloon school. Goodyear made many of the crafts the army used, and during the summer of 1918, ten or twelve of them were in the air every day. More recently, early in July, when the convoy was setting off, the school had sent up a scientist who planned not merely to set an altitude record over thirty thousand feet but to communicate with Martians while he was at it.

Under the command of Lieutenant Colonel Jacob Wuest, the base also housed a meteorological school, a signals department, and—of most import to McClure—a branch of the Motor Transport Corps with three officers, 135 men, and some 150 cars, motorbikes, and trucks. It was ideal; the convoy parked around the center of the base, covering an area about four city blocks square, and the men started work on their vehicles. Not the least of the jobs was changing tire after tire that had been shredded raw on the Iowa dirt.

Colonel Wuest turned one of the barracks into a giant mess hall and made sure they got a decent feed. The soldiers' only complaint arose when they found they were expected to sleep in the barracks too. They demurred, protesting that it was far too hot to sleep indoors, and were granted permission to bed down on the ground as they'd been doing for three weeks now.

During the afternoon, Wuest also arranged balloon rides for several of the convoy's officers; Elwell Jackson was among them, though sadly he recorded no details of his flight. Wuest sent up another dirigible as night fell. Before a crowd of thousands, the searchlight downtown picked it out against the darkening sky. Four thousand feet up and several miles away, it stood out "as if pasted in the sky."

Meanwhile, McClure and nearly all his officers—having turned down the chamber of commerce, citing their work at the fort—had dinner as guests of the local Packard agent instead.

MCCLURE TOLD WASHINGTON that his vehicles were being maintained in "generally excellent condition," particularly in the light of "the long daily mileage and the hardships and obstacles which have been overcome to date." At headquarters, however, the view was not so sanguine. The day before the convoy crossed the Missouri, Lieutenant Colonel B. F. Miller in the Motor Transport Corps' Office of the Chief submitted a damning memorandum to the Corps' senior officer, General Drake.

Miller began, "I have received from various sources numerous reports regarding the lack of road discipline and the improper care of motor vehicles on the Transcontinental Convoy. . . . Some reports have been received from ex-officers of the Motor Transport Corps in personal letters, some are rumors shifting down from representatives of the motor industry." He suggested the matter be urgently looked into, going so far as to say that an inspector should be sent out to check on the convoy's conduct and to give McClure a weighty lecture. "His attention should be invited to the fact that this convoy is being sent over land as an advertisement, and as an example of how convoys should be conducted, and not as a speed outfit." Miller warned further that if the trucks weren't properly looked after, "when bad roads are reached the effect of previous over speeding will cause the motor vehicles to rapidly go to pieces."

There was certainly no question that bad roads lay ahead. To mark the visit of the convoy, the *Omaha World-Herald* produced a fourteen-page special Lincoln Highway section, which included the news that the highway was "fair to good" as far as Kearney, but after that you'd hit "rough stuff." Moreover, the weather forecast had the heat wave breaking soon. If you were growing corn the prospect of rain was fine news, but if you were trying to drive anywhere, it was quite the opposite.

Even the "fair to good" roads out of Omaha turned out to be awful. From their camp eighty-three miles west of the city in Columbus, McClure told Washington, "The roads traversed today were of graded sand and gumbo badly rotted and four to ten inches deep with dust. . . . In wet weather these roads would be impassable to large motor vehicles."

One of the kitchen trailers finally broke apart beyond repair under the beating this dismal surface dished out, and McClure shipped the wreck back to Omaha by train. It took more than ten pounding hours to get through the day; for those held up by breakdowns, it took nearly thirteen. Between those left on the wayside and those that went straight to camp in an open field just north of the city, by day's end Columbus saw less than half the convoy in good enough shape to parade through the town.

Even so, the procession drew a bigger crowd than the Fourth of July. In Frankfort Square, speaking between performances by the local band and the Goodyear fifteen-piece, McClure said simply, "The further west we go, the better treatment we get." They danced in the street by the bright beam of the searchlight until, at around midnight, it started to rain.

THE FIRST GOVERNOR of the Nebraska Territory, appointed in 1854, was Francis Burt from South Carolina. He arrived, took office, and died two days later from the exhausting effects of the journey.

The town of Columbus was founded in 1856 as a business venture by thirteen men—ten Germans, two Swiss, and one Irish—from the town of the same name in Ohio. They'd correctly foreseen that the site would be on the route of the transcontinental railroad; they walked there from Des Moines, built a log cabin with a thatched roof, put in crops, established timber claims, and started a ferry across the Loup River.

The Union Pacific came through ten years later. It was a Sunday but, as one local newspaperman fondly remembered, "We were not excessively pious hereabout in those days, so the whole city— men, women, and children, about seventy-five in all—for an hour or two, watched the passing industrial pageantry." The track was laid before their wondering eyes at a rate of ten feet per minute.

By 1900, when Columbus was forty-four years old, it was home to nearly five thousand people. It had a new high school, a library, a YMCA, a Civil War memorial, and no paved streets. The first three cars appeared in the town in 1903, one of them bought by Max Gottberg at the St. Louis world's fair. Gottberg became Columbus's first auto dealer in 1907; in keeping with the motor trade's ever lively public relations, he once had himself photographed driving a Model T up the front steps of the YMCA.

This was the time when historians decreed that the frontier was a thing of the past—but it didn't feel that way when the convoy came through. As in Iowa, land prices were soaring out of sight, and banks were falling all over themselves to lend money. One real estate ad yelled out, "If you are not a landowner, ask yourself, WHY NOT? Are you afraid to put your money into a crop that never fails?"

Seeing no clouds on the horizon, Columbus man Ed Niewohner went three hundred miles west to Alliance and reported to the *Telegraph* back home on what he'd found. He'd had a fine trip, "uneventful except for blowing out six tires, forgetting to fill up with gas four times, and getting lost every other day." All along the way people were breaking out more land, buying more farm machinery, and putting in more crops; hotels were "full to the muzzle."

Niewohner had bought land near Alliance himself, and it had doubled in value in a year. He bet his wife against a Ford that within three years it'd double again. "Why," he declared, "any man can make money in this western land."

The bubble would burst soon enough; at least until 1929, the business to be in was the motor trade. As the convoy approached Nebraska, Robert Collins, the manager of Goodrich's Omaha branch, wrote ahead to their dealers along the highway—and in Central City, the *Republican* blithely printed his letter in full. It's about as bald a revelation of what the convoy was about as any you'll find. "If we are all to cash in on this trip," said Collins, "our newspaper editors in writing up the visit of the convoy ought to point out that transportation of this sort would be possible every day if we only had better highways, and that every voter has now a chance to help this cause by writing his congressman to get behind the Townsend Bill."

A week later, the *Republican* obliged: WAR DECLARED BETWEEN CIVILIZATION AND MUD.

BACK THEN, PEOPLE bought land in quarter sections of 160 acres apiece. Today, you drive U.S. 30 alongside the Union Pacific tracks through cornfields the size of Belgium, watching faint sprays of rainbow dance from the arcs of the giant irrigation arms. Today, freight trains and road rigs loom shimmering out of the heat haze over the paving; back then, there was no paving.

On the road through Central City to Grand Island, the rain had compacted the sandy road surface enough to keep the dust down, and had softened it enough that in places the vehicles sank to the axles. The men.pushed, the Militor and the tractor pulled, and it took ten hours to go sixty-four miles.

Perhaps the roads would have been better if Grand Island had been the capital of the United States. That, in the 1850s, had been the notion of some visionary schemers in Davenport, Iowa. The country, they thought, should have its capital in the center, and they reckoned Grand Island would be just the place.

They sent out the first settlers in 1857. During their first winter it took months for supplies to reach them from Omaha, 150 miles away, and two of the pioneers were so entirely disenchanted that they took their own lives. The company backing them failed, and the Davenport banker who'd dreamed of siting Congress on the prairie died in a Philadelphia poorhouse. The settlers survived by selling corn to the troops at Fort Kearney; they were a handful of souls in wooden huts, but then the railroad came. In 1880 the Union Pacific built machine shops in the town, and Grand Island's future was assured.

By 1919 it was home to nearly fourteen thousand people; it was also home to V. E. Evans of the Glass-Evans Ford dealership. That year Evans wrote, "Ten years ago the automobile business was in its infancy and a few of us that were so engaged were classed with the village blacksmith, absolutely no credit, and for places of business we generally had to occupy some old abandoned shack, generally the worst appearing building in the town, and when you called upon one of these places . . . you expected to see as its manager a greasy man with his overalls and jumpers sufficiently saturated that they would almost stand alone."

By the time the convoy arrived, said Evans, the contrast was so marked that "it would almost seem like an impossibility for so great a transformation to take place." Car dealerships were now the fanciest new businesses in every town you went to; people from sixteen counties came to Grand Island to buy cars. The town had held its first auto show in March, and as well as cars, there were trucks on display, many of them entirely new sights in that part of the country. No one there had ever seen an REO Speed Wagon, for example—the first truck to be equipped with electric starters and lights.

Motor trucks, wrote Evans, "less than two years ago made their first appearance in our community. Today they are shown by all the leading firms of our city. . . . With our national system of highways completed, which is the crying need of our land, the tonnage transportation of trucks will exceed that of the railways." To that end, the convoy came in along the seedling mile just east of town. There was some confusion about what route they were taking; Lieutenant Doron had arrived the previous afternoon and had immediately vetoed the parade line laid out by the locals because it crossed the railroad tracks. There followed, in the words of a memorable subhead in the *Daily Independent*, "Much Balling Up of Orders," with one arrangement made after another only to be canceled again.

They got it sorted out in the end, though not without a ticking off from Henry Ostermann at the Commercial Club. Quibbles over the route had arisen because the originally designated Lincoln Highway east of town was impassable. "The people along the way," said Ostermann sternly, "have laid down on the job. After the seedling mile was finished, cement for which was furnished by us, nothing more was done. . . . This means just so much more work for us."

A welcome party sent out to greet the train saw evidence for themselves of their inadequate infrastructure. Mayor Cleary and assorted businessmen—among them Ford dealer Evans—had to watch and wait for the best part of an hour while the engineers reinforced a bridge that had started giving way beneath the trucks. Not for the first time, confusion and delay obliged the townspeople to arrange their hospitality all in a rush at the last minute; but they managed it, with dinner for the officers and a dance for the men, and McClure thanked them graciously. "You received us when we were tired and dusty," he said, "and made us feel at home and among friends. We will not forget Grand Island."

His men had another cause to be thankful; it was the last day of July, and it was payday. The War Department sent a check for $13,000 to the Grand Island National Bank. The bank cashed it, spent the whole day splitting it into envelopes marked for each man, then delivered it under armed guard through a crowd numbering thousands to the campground in Hann's Park. The pay wagon—of course—was a motor truck.

THE WEATHER COOLED, and spotty showers persisted through central and western Nebraska. For parched cattlemen and corn growers it was "a million-dollar rain," but for the convoy it was a growing threat. It took eleven hours to get eighty-two miles from Grand Island through Kearney to Lexington; the biggest holdup came when a Class B ran into a ditch four feet deep, burying itself over the axles in soft dirt.

The Militor, reported Jackson, "gave a wonderful exhibition of its power" as it retrieved the mired vehicle. The sprag dug two feet into the roadbed, the front wheels lifted clear of the ground as the winch heaved on the rope, and the road was plowed and churned as the army's steel dinosaur took two straining hours to haul the truck back from the ditch. Not finished for the day, the Militor then towed a Four Wheel Drive the last dozen miles into camp. As Colonel Miller had warned in Washington, a speeding driver had burned out bearings in the truck's engine on the road's increasingly treacherous surface.

They were nearing the halfway point of the journey, and Elwell Jackson on this Friday, August 1, marked their arrival at Lexington as such. To be pedantically precise, according to Jackson's own mileage log, they'd not actually be halfway until they got to the other side of North Platte—but, obviously enough, measuring halfway across America depends where you measure from in the first place.

A few miles west of Kearney, an enterprising farmer named H. D. Watson had put up a huge road sign saying his land was halfway between both coasts. It was, said the sign, 1,733 miles east to Boston, and the same distance west to San Francisco. Boston wasn't actually on the Lincoln Highway, but Watson put up his sign regardless so that Kearney could be called "the midway city of the nation."

He'd been a big local booster since his arrival in the town in 1886, and his holdings had grown until he was farming eight thousand acres at the 1733 Ranch. He experimented with alfalfa, he had huge orchards growing cherries, plums, apples, and peaches, and he planted many of the trees you can still see today along U.S. 30. In the twenties, he started a tourist stop along the Lincoln Highway too—but he lost all his money in the end, and the ranch changed hands. Now it's just a pricey subdivision, and all that remains of Watson's midway dream is a name: the 1733 Estates.

THE LINCOLN HIGHWAY followed the Mormon Trail and the Union Pacific along the north bank of the Platte. In 1852, Ezra Meeker would have followed at least some part of its route; he was twenty-two, heading for Oregon with his wife and baby son. When he got there, he made and lost several fortunes. Then, in 1906, when he was seventy-six years old, he headed back east in a prairie schooner. A lot of people thought he was crazy, but Meeker just wanted them to remember the trail. Teddy Roosevelt agreed, and he greeted Meeker on the front lawn of the White House nearly two years after he'd set off from the Pacific.

Meeker lived to the age of ninety-eight and went back over the trail several more times. He did it once in a car, and another time in an open-seat biplane. He's remembered at a worthwhile new attraction called the Archway Monument that spans I-80 by Kearney; the Lincoln Highway is remembered there too, as important in its own time as the trail and the railroad before it.

By featuring the Lincoln Highway, the Archway Monument has done good service to this forgotten piece of history. In August 2000—forty years after the subject had fallen from Joyce Ausberger's textbooks in Jefferson, Iowa—the Nebraska Department of Education issued a "Curriculum Guide for Upper Elementary Middle Schools" that makes use of the monument's educational potential. One of the modules covers the highway—so at least in a small way, and at least in one state along the route, the story of the road is being taught in school again.

THE CONVOY STOPPED at the Dawson County Fairground in Lexington. It was, said Jackson, the best campsite of the trip so far—a considerable tribute, given that the town had only two thousand people.

Lexington had started life as Plum Creek Station in 1866. It was a section house, a coal shed, and a depot on a siding by the Union Pacific tracks; the early settlers initially made their homes in the same freight cars that had brought them there. They endured blizzards, droughts, prairie fires, and plagues of grasshoppers; their town survived and grew; and, natural calamities aside, it seemed the only thing wrong with the place was its name.

In 1887, when the population was approaching one thousand, the *Plum Creek Gazette* solemnly declared that "people would prefer a name less indicative of a back country post office, and more appropriate for the largest town in a ninety-mile stretch of the Platte River." They settled on Lexington; and while this may seem a trivial thing, at that time the rivalry between Nebraska's budding new settlements was fierce. If there was any move that gave a community even the slightest chance of drawing business and growing faster, people took it.

Lexington was indeed growing fast. The Cornland Hotel was three stories tall, and deemed so imposing that it appeared on the letterhead of the Lexington Bank. So did an electric streetcar; there wasn't one, but why let the truth mar a good image?

The image tarnished in the panic of 1893. There was no fair in Dawson County that year, and it didn't return as an annual event until 1908. Like the Cornland, the First National Bank was three stories tall. It had no windows on the south side, the bankers having assumed that more fine three-story edifices would go up alongside it, but they never did. The blank brick looked down on a town that stalled for more than a decade.

When Lexington revived, the brick stayed blank. The new businesses in the new century were car dealers and garages, replacing blacksmiths and livery stables, and instead of building up they built out, spreading east-west along the Lincoln Highway. As the road spurred new trade, so the pressure rose to pave it—but with America still under arms, where might Lexington find the labor?

As THE CONVOY approached, the people of central Nebraska were much exercised over the dark deeds of the "pants burglar" (or burglars). North Platte had already been subject to a wave of thefts; the modus operandi of the villain was to creep into your house, sift through your pockets while you slept, and make off with whatever coins he could find. Much affronted, North Platte's citizenry took home "large amounts of artillery and ammunition," and the pants burglar wisely relocated down the road to Brady.

"This class of crime," said the *Lexington Clipper-Citizen,* "has reached a very troublesome proportion [and] the perpetrators of the pants robberies have apparently been moving en masse from place to place." BURGLARS AT LAST ARRIVE IN LEXINGTON, proclaimed its headline on July 31—as if the town had been short of excitement—but a week later, it seemed the pants burglar had finally been caught. Unfortunately for Lexington's street-paving program, however, the pants burglar turned out to be black.

He was an "itinerant negro prowler" named William Jackson. Soon after midnight one early August night he took off his shoes on Ernest Dowler's front porch and slipped into the house, but before he could lay hands on any pants, he disturbed Dowler and his brother from their sleep. The two men chased and caught him, and by the time Officer Whaley arrived on the scene, Jackson had been so badly beaten ("or at least pretended to be," said the mistrustful *Clipper-Citizen*) that he asked Whaley "to finish the job of killing him. The officer declined."

Meanwhile, the hue and cry had alerted the citizenry, and a mob of fifty or sixty gathered just east of the Lincoln Highway garage. Here stood a few shacks where a gang of some twenty black street pavers had been quartered while they worked on the town's roads. Though they had nothing whatsoever to do with William Jackson, these men were now told "to leave town without any delay at all. The orders to decamp were emphasized by a number of shots through the windows of the house and a fusillade of bricks."

In terror, the paving gang fled in their nightclothes down the Lincoln Highway, "pursued by several autos filled with men, a number of whom had guns which they fired to expedite the flight of the negroes." They hid in fields, in ditches, in a sandpit by the railroad track; they were "rescued" by some evidently rather complacent policemen the following morning. Most went back to work only to be told they'd better not stay another night in Lexington. Promptly and understandably, they left town. Apparently satisfied with this turn of events, the *Clipper-Citizen* calmly observed, "Their places have been filled with Mexicans."

It seems, then, that black people didn't just have trouble finding a place to stay on the road. The truth is, they weren't even welcome when they were building it.

William Jackson, meanwhile—now elevated to the status of "negro desperado"—managed to escape from Lexington's jail ten days later. When he was recaptured in Fremont the following week, his failed robbery attempt earned him an ominously vague sentence of "one to ten years" at the state penitentiary in Lincoln. Two white boys from Chicago whose attempt to rob a restaurant at this time had also failed were, by contrast, given "some good wholesome advice on the subject of honesty" and a suspended sentence.

THE MEN OF the convoy were worn out by hospitality, not hostility; at the Rosenberg Garage in Lexington, they were treated to another dance. Halfway to California, the soldiers confessed to the *Clipper-Citizen* that "the greatest trial of the trip was the fact that they were so liberally entertained all along the way in the evenings that they had a limited opportunity to get necessary rest."

Greater trials awaited soon enough—and it would be apposite that their first day of true struggle should be the day they crossed the IOOth meridian. No matter where you measure your halfway point by mileage, this line on the map, in both myth and reality, is the point where the West has been held to begin since white men

first started to cross it. Intersecting the Lincoln Highway fourteen
miles west of Lexington at the town of Cozad, the 100th meridian
is where you begin to sense that the land is getting higher and
drier. This is where cornfields fade out into cattle range, where
grain silos by the rail stations give way to stockyards. This is where
mountain oysters—bulls' testicles—become a routine feature on
restaurant menus.

You have here a century of industrial history laid out in three
parallel layers, the Union Pacific next to U.S. 30 next to Interstate
80. You have here the magical barrens of the Sand Hills—a sere
desert that can turn the most intense, radiant green when the vast
blue sky sheds a blessing rain. Past Lexington, the dune range
edges closer to the road from the northern horizon, starting gently
to buckle and roll the wide land.

The convoy moved into this terrain at six-fifteen on the morning of Saturday, August 2. A light rain was falling. Perhaps mindful of the critical murmurs in Washington, McClure spent the first
hour of the day running a road-discipline drill. At Cozad they
stopped to strap chains on all the rear tires, but it didn't help. By
nine-thirty it was raining steadily, and the road became as slippery
as ice.

The first truck left the road four miles west of Cozad; another
one retrieved it. Nearby, the Mack carrying the caterpillar tractor
slithered into the ditch as well and was hauled out by one of the
blacksmith shops. The Militor rescued four Class B's one after
another before skidding onto the shoulder itself and getting buried
to the frame in sodden gumbo. It took the wrecker's crew two
hours to dig it out by hand.

After that, Jackson and McClure stopped noting each individual mishap; there were too many. By day's end, twenty-five trucks
had left what passed for the highway. In some places the crown of
the road was so steep that the vehicles had to be angled across it,
then edged forward crabwise. To add to their labor, two bridges
needed strengthening by the engineers before the trucks could
safely cross them. All but two of the motorbikes gave out too, their
engines clogged with mud.

McClure, and any other man who'd seen service in Europe,
must have been uncomfortably reminded of the Western Front.

They waded and shoveled through cloying wet earth, their legs caked in sticky filth. One man went down with pneumonia and had to be rushed ahead by train to Fort Russell in Wyoming. As they struggled on, there was no place or opportunity to get a mid-day meal served. When they reached Gothenburg late in the after-noon, after nearly eleven grim hours on the road, they'd managed to travel only thirty miles. According to the schedule, they were supposed to go still another thirty miles to North Platte before quitting. Once McClure inspected the road west of Gothenburg, however, he saw there was no possibility whatsoever that they'd make it, and he called a halt.

Dr. Johnson made sure to drive the message home on the back of this fiasco. Arriving ahead of the mired and crawling train, he sent a telegram to Secretary of War Baker to let him know that "for the first time since war was declared, the army has been forced to surrender—to Dawson County Mud."

"Really, folks," muttered the *Gothenburg Times,* "it's a shame. . . . There is no good excuse for tolerating longer the rotten roads that we know we have." "Seems like we are always talking good roads," sighed the *Cozad Local,* "and traveling rocky ones."

FOR EARL THOMAS, it was all too much. A soldier just nineteen years old from Cincinnati, he clearly viewed the prospect of more days dragging trucks through this Nebraska gumbo as too forbidding to be borne.

Jacob Glenn's new Nash Six was parked by city hall, and some-time between four and five that Saturday afternoon, Earl Thomas made off with it. For an hour or more the theft wasn't reported because the trustful Mr. Glenn, finding his car missing, had first gone around Gothenburg asking his friends if any of them had bor-rowed it.

Finally apprised of the startling fact that something dishonest had happened, Sheriff Benton got on the case. He learned that Thomas had bought gas from Emil Hagberg in Willow Island a few miles to the east; he heard on Sunday morning that a young man in uniform driving a Nash had stopped at Jurgen Aden's place to ask where the Lincoln Highway was.

This might imply that young Thomas wasn't the brightest button in the box, seeing he'd been on the road in question these past 1,733 miles or so. Alternatively, and at least as likely, it might imply that the highway in Nebraska remained no more than a vague and messy line in the dirt. Either way, however, Thomas was at least bright enough to get as far back east as Council Bluffs.

He was arrested there on Monday, turned over to the military, and taken to Fort Omaha for trial. He stated that "he had had some sort of trouble with the commander of the train" and was "generally dissatisfied with the trip"—and one rather suspects he was not the only one to feel that way.

THE NEXT DAY was supposed to be a rest day, but, eager to get back on schedule, McClure canceled it. There followed another eternal haul through barely passable bog and quicksand; truck after truck sank to the hubs. In places the highway was no more than a pair of wheel paths, each one a foot wide through the prairie grass.

The engines couldn't handle it. Fan belts sprang, bearings burned out, cylinder heads blew. At one point during the morning, the tractor had all twelve of the engineers' trucks under tow in one grinding, flailing line. Another time, five trucks needed hauling through several miles of sodden slop. Under a cloudy sky, the army crawled across the heartland like lamed bugs, khaki dots lurching through a sea of grass and sand.

The men tried chaining the trucks together, hoping those unmired would keep the stuck ones pulling on. When it didn't work, the Militor weighed in and hauled the whole line. By day's end it had taken every truck in the convoy under tow, dragging them over steep rises and deep chuckholes. Once it had to save itself again as well, winching its way back out from the ditch.

Desperate for traction, the soldiers laid anything they could find under the gripless wheels—chains, canvas, weeds and prairie grass yanked from the earth. All this engine power, and in the sopping slime it was helpless; all through the day, the task came down to raw muscle. While the motors screamed and the wheels spun and the muck flew in sprayed cascades, the men put their shoulders to the frames of the trucks and shoved them onward in groaning packs by pure main force.

The first vehicles made it to North Platte at about five-fifteen in the afternoon. After one of the machine shops dropped through a wooden bridge, the last of them didn't reach camp until past two in the morning. Along the way, some of the soldiers told the *Maxwell Telepost* that they'd had more or less good roads until they'd hit Nebraska—and some of what they'd seen here "was worse than No Man's Land."

Lincoln and Dawson Counties were left sorely embarrassed. It was a shame, said the editor of the *Gothenburg Times*, that the area "should have exhibited such roads to the distinguished visitors. Certainly one thing has been demonstrated, if indeed it needed demonstrating, and that is that the transportation problem will not be solved by trucks to any great extent until the main highways are permanent hard-surfaced roads." The proof lay in the wake of the trucks. In their battle to get from Lexington to North Platte, they left large sections of the road churned to a hopeless morass. You might say, indeed, that they were destroying the road to save it.

NORTH PLATTE WAS a Union Pacific town of some seven thousand people; it had made elaborate plans to greet the convoy, all of which were now much disarranged. The Goodyear band played and Dr. Johnson spoke, but while they did so, the convoy itself was all over the road. A day behind schedule, urging his men on through bog and breakdown, McClure himself didn't reach town until ten on Sunday evening; he found Mayor Streitz waiting for him with a floral key. Though fraught and exhausted, he accepted it with good grace, then joined those of his men who'd already made it to the city park.

It didn't take long for him to realize that they needed a rest day after all. After the beating they'd taken over the past two days, so many of the trucks needed at least minor repairs that pressing on to try to make up lost time would have been counterproductive. Without another overhaul, he'd have been driving them nowhere but the scrapyard.

McClure's decision to call a halt was a relief all round; for Dwight Eisenhower, it was doubly welcome. At the Doud family home in Denver, Mamie and her father had been charting the convoy's progress across the country with pins on a map. Now she and John Doud decided to meet the convoy in North Platte, two hundred miles away. Mamie suggested going on the train, but her father shucked that notion off, as he'd been trying to stir up enthusiasm for a motor trip ever since the spring. So they loaded the Packard with food, water, blankets, cooking kit, spare gas, a tow rope, and a shovel and set off across the plains.

The journey took from dawn to early evening, about thirteen hours, most of it in second gear. They wore dusters, goggles, and pull-down hats. When they arrived at their hotel, Mamie changed into "frothy cotton with black velvet at her wrists." She started bobbing in and out of the front door to the street, anxiously waiting for sight of the husband she'd not seen in eight months. Finally the convoy started stumbling into town, broken into scattered and weary groups, caked in dust and mud. Amid the watching crowds, she heard a voice shout her name; there was Ike, leaning from one of the staff cars, "hollering like a kid on a rollercoaster."

Mamie and her father stayed with the convoy as far as Laramie, Wyoming, before turning south for Denver and home. "This was a fine interlude," Ike wrote later, "and I decided that it would be nice, being in the West already, to apply for a leave with my family at the end of the tour—if indeed we ever reached the end."

"FORCED TO SUSPEND movement for twenty-four hours," McClure curtly told Washington. He was clearly under pressure. Beside the reprimands already coming his way over the convoy's indiscipline, he was now also being upbraided for failing to file daily reports. He'd sent no cables from either Lexington or Gothenburg; from North Platte he protested that with trucks arriving late into the night and telegraph offices closing early, sometimes it just couldn't be done. He promised arrangements "to materially increase scope and detail of daily reports." Striving to look on the bright side, he was at least able to observe that "rougher going produces more news."

The going stayed rough. When they left North Platte on Tuesday, August 5, their objective for the day was Big Springs. It was now painfully clear, however, that planning to drive heavy trucks seventy-five miles in a day through western Nebraska, especially after rain, was laughably overambitious.

Tuesday proved to be another day of ruts, chuckholes, quicksand, feeble bridges, and ramshackle detours. In places the surface of the road crumpled beneath the weight of a walking man, never mind a five-ton truck. You couldn't see by looking at it where it was going to give way; it just did. Then, with a helpless lurch, you were in it up to the axles, the wheel tops, or worse.

One truck sank so deep that it took six attempts to rescue it; the sixth time, the Militor and the tractor had to pull it out in tandem. Then, ninety minutes and fourteen miles west of North Platte, they came on a two-hundred-yard stretch that McClure described as "crusted watersoaked quicksand." They tried laying down everything they could find to stabilize it, spreading timber and vegetation across the road in their wheel paths, but only the Four Wheel Drives and a few of the lighter trucks could get through unassisted.

One by one the Militor dragged sixteen trucks through the quagmire. The tractor pulled ten others, and on eight different occasions both were needed at once. In the process they snapped a three-quarter-inch stranded steel cable, and they broke a one-and-three-quarter-inch tow rope four times. Once again, they were reduced to pushing and pulling by hand; crossing these two hundred yards took the convoy *seven hours and twenty minutes* of sweat and hard labor.

The sky behind them to the east flared with lightning and cloudbursts. Ahead to the west lay steep, sandy grades that the trucks couldn't climb, and five bridges that they couldn't cross. The engineers laid extra planking to strengthen the bridges; two of them they rebuilt entirely. Sometimes, when they couldn't get up or across they'd go around, plowing into the fields at the roadside. At one bridge, held up waiting for county officials to show up with some timber, they laid sixty feet of corduroy road across the dry bed of the creek and somehow blundered in and out of the watercourse that way instead.

No surprise, then, that they didn't reach Big Springs; fifty-three miles from North Platte, they crawled into Ogallala at eleven o'clock that night. It was, however, something of a wonder that they'd gotten anywhere at all. By any normal measure this road—as McClure was quick to point out—was simply impassable to heavy traffic. Under the circumstances—no matter if inexperienced drivers had started out not knowing how to change gear, or taking governors off the engines and speeding and trashing the vehicles—he must have felt it was about time he and his men got some credit for what they were doing.

Between the tractor and the Militor and their own bare muscle power, they'd pushed and pulled their vehicles through this swamp of a road from dawn into darkness. They'd had nothing to sustain them during these travails but jam sandwiches and water at four in the afternoon. "Entire personnel," McClure reported pointedly, "quite exhausted by severity of seventeen hours continuous duty." The *Keith County News* was kinder than the convoy's superiors. "The impression left," said the paper, "was that of a sturdy, fearless, intelligent and energetic lot of men."

Perhaps the trials of the road were knocking them into shape—and, if ever they had a chance to look up from their struggles with that road, they could now see that it was leading them into an extraordinary land. McClure noted this too; doubtless mindful of Washington's request for better copy but plainly sincere in this and other messages from the West, this stickler of a man began to reach for poetry. "Territory traversed is sparsely settled," he wrote, "very rugged, and many of personnel have seen for the first time part of the wild west with its sage, sunflowers, sand, cactus and rattlesnakes."

They would soon be four thousand feet above sea level. They were in the terrain that topographical engineer Lieutenant Stephen H. Long in 1820 had called "the Great American Desert," saying simply that it was "uninhabitable." It wasn't, as things turned out, so long as you paid the land and the climate due respect—and McClure now decided to do that.

The next day he limited the run to twenty-two miles, stopping at Big Springs so the men could get some rest. Although they'd set off from Ogallala at seven-thirty, it took them six hours to go that short distance. Steep grades winding through sand dunes obliged the tractor and the Militor once again to haul virtually every truck through the worst soft stretches. By now, however, they'd started to get the hang of it. The past three days' experience, McClure reported, "enabled more expeditious handling of this work."

Big Springs was a tiny settlement with barely more people in it than there were men in the convoy; it had been incorporated as a town only two years before the trucks arrived. The men camped in an open mowed field—but maybe things were looking up now. An experienced mess officer joined the motor train here, so at least the food might get better.

LAYER BY LAYER, shade by shade, the landscape grows more vast and harsh, more empty and imposing. Kimball, the convoy's last stop in Nebraska, stands 4,709 feet above sea level; it was originally called Antelopeville, a coal and water station for the railroad. When the *Western Nebraska Observer* was first published here in 1885—on an old army press, by a nineteen-year-old boy named Charles Randall—the paper eagerly proclaimed that the town was "a marvel of growth, with a social and intelligent class of people." At the time, there was barely one of those people per square mile.

They were certainly intelligent enough to appreciate the worth of the Lincoln Highway. In 1914, fearing that the road and its traffic might yet be diverted to Denver, Kimball's businessmen went out to smooth its dirt surface with shovels, and to put up signs from Big Springs to make sure you drove their way. Then, to brighten it up where it ran through town along Third Street (as U.S. 30 still does today), they planted four hundred trees. In western Nebraska, after all, trees were a rare and cheering sight.

Five years later, these people had done a better job of maintaining their stretch of the highway than the larger towns to their east. From Big Springs the convoy made eighty-six miles in eleven hours, with few of the troubles the past few days had visited upon them; they reached Kimball by six in the evening. The soldiers washed the day's dirt off in an irrigation ditch running through the county fairgrounds; that evening the town put on a dance, with dinner for the officers in the Wheat Growers' Hotel.

The hotel is still there today, a long, rectangular, two-story brick structure on Oak Street, across the tracks from the grain elevator. It's in a sorry state of repair, with boarded windows and FOR SALE signs, but the facade is still attractive. It could be a beautiful building, if there was money to restore it.

As people stopped riding the train, as new roads were built, and as business spread out of American towns to flow alongside them, so many of these little downtown hotels have disappeared. The few still standing are mostly flophouses now. But you can stand outside the Wheat Growers' in the white heat of the Nebraska sun and you can imagine the smoke and talk and laughter at that officers' dinner on their last night in the state. They were, of course, promoting the industry that would put places like this hotel out of business—but no one knew that in 1919. Just a few years earlier, after all, there'd been only a dozen cars in the whole of Kimball County.

Amid the speeches and the interviews, as he'd done all through the state, Dr. Johnson told anyone who'd listen that if they'd help get the Townsend Bill passed, the Lincoln Highway would be paved for five hundred miles from Omaha to Wyoming inside of five years. In fact, it took a little longer than that.

On November 5, 1935—sixteen years after the passage of the convoy—a ceremony was held on U.S. 30 two and a half miles to the west of North Platte. In homage to the golden spike that had marked the completion of the transcontinental railroad, state engineer A. C. Tilley cut a golden ribbon to mark the final piece of paving on the Lincoln Highway across America. In the thirties, people still called it by that name.

The celebration was elaborate, and attended by several thousand people. A caravan representing the different types of transportation used along the Great Platte River Road since the days of the pioneers passed the speakers' stand; among the parade there was a prairie schooner, a horse-drawn buggy, a Model T, and a 1912 truck. Franklin D. Roosevelt sent a message of congratulation from the White House, commending the fact that "the perilous trail of the pioneers is at last transformed ... into a coast-to-coast highway."

That evening, Nebraska Governor R. I. Cochran spoke at a

banquet in the Pawnee Hotel. Two decades earlier, when the graveling of the highway began, he'd been the district engineer in North Platte. The Lincoln Highway was the first road finished, he said, "because it was planned that way."

It had taken a while, but the road inspired by Carl Fisher and urged on by Henry Joy was finally complete. As Fred White had warned in Iowa, however, once you start on a road, there's no end to it. Today, they like to joke in Nebraska that the state has two seasons: winter and road construction.

CHAPTER EIGHT

★ ★ ★

Human-Skin Shoes

Henry Ostermann crossed into Wyoming forty-eight hours ahead of the convoy. Accompanying him as he scouted the road were the state highway engineer and the regional manager of the Goodrich tire business. Public relations men for Willys-Overland, Firestone, and Goodyear traveled ahead of the trucks as well, while the Goodyear band serenaded the offices of every newspaper they could find.

"Just now," observed the *Wyoming State Tribune*, "Cheyenne appears to be the mecca for a great variety of cross-country transportation." They called the convoy "the Goodrich tour." Ostermann carried publicity shots for the papers—trucks outside the White House, trucks in mud, trucks breaking through bridges and culverts, the smallest man in the army inside a tire—and he carried film of the convoy shot en route to be shown in cinemas all along the road.

Ostermann's party stayed at the Plains in Cheyenne and at the Connor in Laramie. Both buildings still stand today, though pretty timeworn, but in 1919 these were high-toned establishments. Looking across the Lincoln Highway to the fanciful Italianate tower of the Union Pacific station, the Plains was at the heart of Cheyenne social life for half a century, right into the sixties. In Laramie, the Connor was "the only modern, up-to-date hostelry in town," so much so that you could make long-distance calls from every room.

In these well-connected surroundings, Ostermann rallied the local boosters. Laramie had three Lincoln Highway consuls, one of whom was Elmer Lovejoy. Lovejoy died in 1960, at the age of eighty-eight; his name lives on in Laramie today over a smart little bar by the railroad tracks. In 1919, he was one of the characters about town.

His family moved to Wyoming when he was eleven; ten years later, in 1893, he opened a general repair shop at 412 South Second Street called the Lovejoy Novelty Works. While this rather makes it sound as if he sold fireworks and whoopee cushions, the real novelty was that in 1895, the inventive Lovejoy produced a chain-driven automotive wagon with tiller steering and a one-cylinder engine—Wyoming's first car.

Local accounts differ as to whether this effort was powered by steam or gas. He's also credited with devising various other car-related gadgetry, including (in 1918) patented designs for an automatic garage-door opener. With bicycles and autos being close cousins in those early days, he also built a tandem for himself and his wife. He once cycled six hundred miles from Laramie to Woodbine, Iowa, "for no reason," said his brother-in-law. "That was just Elmer."

In time the Novelty Works became Lovejoy's Garage, and the local dealership for Franklin and Studebaker. In 1914, Lovejoy produced the *Wyoming Auto Guide*—which, like other such local efforts at the time, was hectically, deliciously optimistic. If you cared to go after the record, he wrote blithely, you could get across the state in twenty-six hours. In the Laramie Valley, "the engines of the automobile sing a sweet song and the wheels whir as they roll over the hard surface of the well-marked trail."

Small wonder, then, that the transcontinental tourist had quit the stuffy old train for the freedom of the road. "It is the coming pleasure tour," declared Lovejoy, "through one's own country, over good roads, the sweet air filling one's lungs, the steady hum of the engine making gladsome music to one's tired mind."

Wyoming at this time was promoting itself as the "Switzerland of America"—but tourists seduced by Lovejoy's lyric hymn to the state's roads must on occasion have been rendered speechless with disbelief. The contrast between the paeans of the boosters and the reality on the ground was all too vivid, all too often.

John C. Thompson was a local journalist who, for some years through the middle of the twentieth century, wrote a column called "In Old Wyoming." The truth about car travel in Lovejoy's day, he

said, was that you "generally limped along in the twin ruts worn
by the wheels of wagons. To attain a speed of forty miles an hour
was phenomenal and, if attained, it could be sustained only for brief
distances. A journey of 150 miles in a day was remarkable indeed."
As it turned out, the convoy would be hard put in any of the long
and tiring days ahead to cover even a third of that distance.

THE LINCOLN HIGHWAY ran 425 miles across the state through
Cheyenne and Laramie, Medicine Bow and Rawlins, Rock Springs
and Green River and Evanston. As in Nebraska, it followed the
line of the Union Pacific; sometimes it followed it too exactly for
comfort.

It was graveled for a part of the distance and graded dirt for
much of the rest, but in some places it used an old roadbed abandoned by the railroad in 1901. The rails and ties were gone, but the
indentations were not; between convict labor and the fact that it
rains less in Wyoming, the highway here could be a better ride
than it was in Nebraska, or it could be a juddering washboard.

You can still see phantom stretches of the original road today,
trailing through the high desert alongside Interstate 80. Wheatland and pasture fade out here into an arid vastness of sagebrush.
Thinly peopled and majestically harsh, this is country where place-
names have a resonance both poetic and functional—Lost Cabin,
Muddy Gap, Point of Rocks, Ten Sleep—and where those places
often prove to have only the most tenuous hold on the unforgiving
land. Settlements slip off the map and into history as if they'd
never been. If any brawling shanty that hoped to become a town
wasn't made a division point on the railroad, it usually died as
quickly as it had grown notorious, leaving nothing in the alkali
dust but a handful of bent nails and broken glass.

Places that did survive did so not least on the back of through
traffic—from the Pony Express to the interstate—and they survived in terrain that grows more fierce the farther west you go.
That's why, as the local joke has it, Cheyenne got the government,
Laramie got the university, Rawlins got the prison, and Evanston
got the insane asylum.

The eastern section of the route was first located in 1865 by

General Grenville M. Dodge; evading pursuit by a band of Indians around the head of Crow Creek, he realized he'd found a good approach into the Laramie Mountains. Two years later he picked the site for Cheyenne by Fort Russell, and the town's economy grew around the railroad: passenger depot, stockyard, freight house, and machine shops.

Half a century and a new world later, when McClure led the convoy into Cheyenne, stores and businesses closed so that people could watch them pass, and factory whistles blew—but not at the machine shops of the Union Pacific or the Burlington Railroads. Still central to the town's economy, in 1919 these substantial institutions employed some twenty-five hundred people, but at the time they'd been threatening to go on strike.

So perhaps they didn't join in because the atmosphere in the shops was tense; or perhaps also they had some intimation of what the convoy might mean for the future of their business. General Dodge may have surveyed the railroad, after all, but his name ended up on a car.

RUNNING TWO DAYS late, McClure and his men crossed the state line at Pine Bluffs on Friday, August 8. Cheyenne lay at the end of a sixty-six-mile run—and the people there knew how things had gone in Nebraska.

They'd had cables alerting them to trouble and delay. One said tersely, "There is plenty of mud," while another urgently requested Fort Russell to ship them a cylinder-head gasket for one of the trucks. Unfortunately, no one at the fort or in the city had ever heard of the type of gasket in question, and without specifications, no one had any idea how to make one.

They were short on wide-awake mechanics, perhaps, but they were long on welcome. The convoy was met east of town at Hillsdale by Governor Carey, Mayor Stone, and General O'Neill from the fort, with a retinue of dozens of motorists. The mounted band of the Fifteenth Cavalry waited at the city limits, ready to escort the convoy up Sixteenth Street and Capitol Avenue to Frontier Park.

The trucks had had few mishaps on the way—the gravel gave

134 : AMERICAN ROAD

better traction than the mud and sand of Nebraska—but it had
been another eleven-hour day all the same. Climbing over six thousand feet above sea level, the engines labored in the thin air. The
skies threatened rain all day, and as the convoy neared the city, it
poured down hard for an hour. Between that and the time, already
late in the afternoon, plans for a revue and reception at the capitol
were abandoned. The trucks made straight for the park, where a
rodeo awaited to entertain them.

It was cold enough for overcoats, but the rain stopped in time
for the show, and it was heralded by a spectacular double rainbow
shining over the arena. Despite the inclement weather, thousands
of people came out, nearly filling the two-deck steel stand. They
saw a lively display of bareback riding, bronco busting, trick rop-
ing, and wild-horse racing. Local sensibilities were gratified when a
group of soldiers from New York said they'd rather take their
chances going over the top than bulldog a steer.

They made camp at Fort Russell. Before the convoy moved on
in the morning, as in many towns and cities before them, Cheyenne's boosters made sure the trucks were decorated with promotional slogans. Wyoming was enjoying an oil boom, and the state's
businessmen and politicians wanted more people moving there. By
way of enticement one of their banners read proudly, WYOMING IS
SPENDING $7,000,000 ON ROADS.

COLONEL MCCLURE DIDN'T know where the Continental Divide
was. Along the route of the Lincoln Highway then and the interstate today, it splits around the Great Divide Basin, with the eastern branch by Rawlins and the western branch running through
Table Rock. As it's one of the geographic fundamentals of the continent, you'd expect an army map to show it, and you'd expect the
man leading a convoy from ocean to ocean to be able to mark the
moment when he'd gained the Pacific side of the mountains.

It seems, however, that McClure didn't have a decent map, and
that he and Lieutenant Jackson used the Lincoln Highway's 1918
guidebook instead. This erroneously sites the divide between
Cheyenne and Laramie, by the Ames Monument on Sherman
Hill—presumably the result of an editorial slip, because a few

pages later it then places it correctly west of Rawlins as well. Maybe Jackson and McClure didn't read ahead those few pages, since, obeying Detroit's guidebook, both men now reported to Washington that they crossed the divide on Sherman Hill.

It was cold, and in the afternoon the wind got up to forty miles an hour. The ground was dry as bone, the grass dead for want of water; recent rains had given sign that the drought might soon break, but so far the earth had just sucked all the moisture up. Heading out of Cheyenne into this parched high wilderness, the convoy climbed the natural ramp into the Laramie Mountains first surveyed by General Dodge—it's called the "Gangplank"—until they reached the Ames Monument.

The monument commemorates Oakes and Oliver Ames, the financiers largely responsible for the epic creation of the transcontinental railroad, as well as the epic corruption that went with it. At 8,247 feet above sea level, a squat pyramid of rough-hewn granite blocks standing sixty feet tall, it was erected by the Union Pacific in 1882.

The convoy stopped for lunch here at two o'clock that Saturday afternoon, in weather so clear they could see Pike's Peak in Colorado, 175 miles to the south. The railroad used to go right by this spot, but in 1901 it had moved to a new line a few miles south. Of course the Lincoln Highway is long gone too, and now the interstate runs a mile off to the north.

There's an exit with a sign, and a rough dirt road that looks as if few people use it. They stream past on the four-lane doing seventy; away from the modern road, away from the world the convoy helped bring into being, the monument is a piece of history bypassed and alone on the red mountain dirt.

THE ORIGINAL ROUTE dropped southwest from the monument on Hermosa Road to Tie Siding, then ran north into Laramie on what's now U.S. 287. In 1919 a new, shorter road was just being finished through Telephone Canyon, along the line the interstate takes today past the Lincoln Monument—but McClure didn't want to risk tangling with the last of the roadwork. He opted for the original road, and it was rough.

In some places it was little more than a pair of wheel tracks. The solid tires on the trucks were wider than the wagon ruts, and the abrasion as they rode half in, half out of the scoured lines rapidly shredded them. In other places the grades were so steep that the convoy had to pause, letting each truck tackle the climb alone lest one fail and crash down upon another. The Mack carrying the tractor broke through a weak wooden bridge, but they were used to that by now; getting the truck hauled out and repairing the bridge took just twenty-seven minutes.

Nonetheless, traveling these fifty-seven miles occupied the best part of twelve hours, and they didn't reach Laramie until past seven in the evening. McClure thought it worth every minute of their exertion—the day's trip, he told Washington, "was through scenery of marvelous beauty"—but he also thought rest for the men mattered more now than speed. Rather than try to make up mileage and get back on schedule, he settled for a day off the road that Sunday in Laramie.

Laramie had started life as "Tin-town," a motley of tents and shacks where the Overland Stage and the Emigrant Trail crossed Elizabeth Creek. It moved to its present spot to meet the advancing railroad in 1867, and—like so many of these Union Pacific towns—its early days were famously turbulent. The town's first mayor resigned after three weeks, on the grounds that the place was ungovernable. The second man in the job was a saloon owner who ended up getting lynched; since it seems the men wielding the rope on this occasion were the "good guys," one has to wonder what the bad guys were like.

Things had settled down somewhat by the time of the convoy, but perhaps it says something about the place that one of the local papers was called the *Boomerang*; it had been christened after the editor's mule. Certainly, the Albany County Fairground was still a dry and dusty spot, and more than a few of the visitors who came to look at the trucks traveled in horse-drawn vehicles.

Laramie was a town of just over nine thousand people. That weekend, said the *Boomerang*, the convoy "formed the center of attraction for the whole city. . . . Scarcely a minute of the time from Saturday evening until [Sunday] night passed without numerous visitors being in evidence at the camp." There was a dance that Saturday night. The next morning the men serviced their vehicles, presented themselves for a medical inspection, then had liberty for the day. The wind blew chill and hard, and a rainstorm skeltered through in the afternoon; staying out of the weather, the soldiers went to the movies.

They were on the road again at six-thirty the next morning.

WHERE THE INTERSTATE superseded U.S. 30 farther east, the earlier road has remained in place to carry local traffic. However, Wyoming is still so sparsely populated that when the four-lane was finished there in 1971, the state let U.S. 30 fall off the map; there weren't enough people or taxes to justify maintaining it.

The only exception is the loop northwest from Laramie through Medicine Bow. From before the advent of the automobile, this stretch of the route was laid out to avoid the Medicine Bow Mountains—and U.S. 30 still runs along this original, historic line of transcontinental travel because when the federal engineers put in Interstate 80, they thought they could go a quicker way. They thought they could save time and mileage by driving their new road straight around the flank of Elk Mountain—a decision over which the locals have been having a good laugh, if in some cases a rather bitter one, ever since.

Elk Mountain is 11,156 feet high, and it snows up there. In consequence, I-80 gets closed, and oftentimes all the traffic diverts back around to the north on U.S. 30. Any satisfaction to be had from muttering at the feds that "we told you so" is, however, entirely offset by the fact that the handful of little places along the old road have been devastated by the loss of the traffic.

The hamlet of Bosler took it worst. There were seventy-five people there in 1919, doubtless hoping their little place might amount to something. They had a hotel and a garage, a phone company and a newspaper and two little schools—but now there's nothing there at all. After I-80 was finished the last souls in Bosler packed up and left, leaving a ghost village of empty mobile homes and scrawny shacks.

From the old road you can see Elk Mountain all the way, a huge, elongated, snowcapped triangle of black rock looming on the southern horizon. People who stick to the interstate over there miss out on a stunning drive through mountain-fringed plains of sagebrush and orange-gray dirt, flecked with white salt pans.

Above all, they miss out on the Virginian Hotel in Medicine Bow. The Virginian was the title character of Owen Wister's influential novel, published in 1902, which did more than any other to shape the popular image of the cowboy and the West—both romantic and violent—at that moment when the frontier was beginning to pass into history. Eight years after the book appeared, August Grimm built a hotel in Medicine Bow named after this character. In effect (in the manner of tourism since the trade began) he created in real life the place where something first happened in fiction.

The hotel was built of concrete block three stories high; it had the first electric light and sewerage systems in town. Though Medicine Bow was home then (and is now) to only a couple of hundred people, the Virginian was the largest hotel between Denver and Salt Lake, and it's still in business today. You can sit at the bar and imagine the officers of the convoy eating there that Monday night in August 1919, while outside the building the men were treated to a barbecue and an open-air dance, and the trucks stood arrayed across a sandy hillside south of town.

The wind had blown strong all day, and they'd had rain and hail. In this dismal weather they'd reinforced a dozen bridges with timber left in place for them by the Wyoming Highway Department, and they'd toiled on the road nearly twelve hours to go fifty-nine miles.

EVEN THE ASSOCIATION's guidebook conceded that stretches of the Lincoln Highway here were "very rough." The next day they had nine miles of good hard dirt out of Medicine Bow; pretty much all the rest of it was a nightmare. The wind roared over the plains at forty miles an hour, whipping clouds of dust and cinders from the roadbed about their faces as they shuddered over the old railroad grade.

After one of the trucks sank into the cinders and they'd hauled it out, they laid their portable corduroy to get through the soft stuff. They had to stop fourteen other times while the engineers strengthened a dozen bridges and entirely rebuilt two more. During this endless bridging of empty creeks, one of the lieutenants had a finger crushed. The medics patched him up, and the trucks pushed on.

Where the trail left the old rail bed they crawled up steep and winding gradients, teetering dangerously on the faint and slender track, spaced apart for safety, engines racing as the wheels clawed for grip. All the while the chill, grit-laden wind howled through their unprotected cabs. It was, McClure told Washington laconically, "very tedious going [through] territory of a most desolate character. . . . Extremely dry atmosphere and intense sandy dust caused considerable hardship."

At about six in the evening they made it to Fort Steele. There were more people in the convoy than there were in the town, but they had hot coffee and doughnuts waiting all the same, and it must have been pretty welcome. The soldiers, noted the *Rawlins Republican,* "were mighty hungry."

Knowing they would be, the anglers of Rawlins over the past few days had been fishing en masse in the North Platte at Saratoga—there was trout on the menu that night—but it was apt that Rawlins should provide fine refreshment. The town was named after General John A. Rawlins, who'd joined Dodge's surveying team after the Civil War. Hot and tired on the parched high plains, he'd remarked to his men that if ever a place were named after him, he hoped it'd be a spring of cool water. They duly found Rawlins Spring on October 12, 1867, and the railroad followed them to the water.

In this tough country, as the convoy was learning, you had to work hard to get by. J. D. Woodruff was a Rawlins man who came to this spot in 1866; he later said, "I love Wyoming. . . . I like it because it is hard, rough and unyielding and because one must make a fight to gain its favors, and because one can appreciate the good of Wyoming so much better after the struggle of conquest."

HARD, ROUGH, AND unyielding—that was certainly the way it turned out in Rawlins for Big Nose Charlie Parrott. Big Nose had

$1,000 on his head, after he killed two deputies during a robbery attempt on the Union Pacific in 1878. Caught and jailed two years later, when he tried to escape he was hung from a telegraph pole at the bottom of Fourth Street.

At the time Rawlins was home to maybe fifteen hundred people. Between the railroad, mining, livestock, and an increased military presence suppressing the rebellious Utes, the town was doing nicely. This prosperity had brought along two doctors—Thomas McGee and John Osborne—and with McGee's assistant, Lillian Heath, they conducted a macabre experiment.

They wanted to know if the brain of a criminal was different from that of respectable folk, so with Big Nose Charlie's cadaver conveniently at hand, they cut the top off his skull to have a look. Whether their investigation produced any profitable theories isn't recorded, but Miss Heath—who's said subsequently to have become the first female doctor west of the Mississippi—kept the lidless skull on her desk for years thereafter.

John Osborne, meanwhile, thought he might as well make the most of the opportunity Big Nose presented. Flaying skin from the body's chest and thighs, he proceeded to tan it, and to make from it a lampshade and a pair of two-tone shoes; he made a death mask as well. Then he went into the livestock business, got himself elected governor of Wyoming, and wore these human-skin shoes at his inauguration.

You can see the shoes in the Carbon County Museum on Ninth and Walnut; the toes are white, shading to a dirty brown on the heels and uppers. The museum has the lampshade and the death mask as well. The death mask has no ears, on account of Big Nose's struggle with the rope as he died.

THE NEW U.S. Pacific Fleet was passing through the Panama Canal, headed for San Francisco—an exercise in metal modernity to match the journey of the convoy overland. In Rawlins, McClure received a telegram from San Francisco's Mayor James Roth, letting him know that the city was watching their progress with keen interest. The convoy, he hoped, would arrive in time to meet the fleet. No doubt McClure hoped the same—but whether it could be done remained to be seen.

They moved on at six-fifteen in the morning into the Red Desert, the center of the Wyoming sheep range, a place virtually empty of people. All they saw that day were a couple of watering points for the railroad at Creston and Latham Stations, and the tiny settlement of Wamsutter. Otherwise, said McClure, it was "mountain desert of most desolate and monotous [*sic*] character" in which they found "dry air wind and dust hardship continuous."

The carburetors gagged on the dust, and so did the men. A lot of the time they were on the old railroad right of way; trucks slithered off it into deep sand and chuckholes and were hauled back on again by other vehicles or the Militor. One of the water tankers rolled 270 degrees onto its side, but they got it righted and under way in twenty minutes.

Again, the bridges were a problem. It seemed their timber became brittle and fragile in the waterless air, and it was hard to tell if a bridge would hold or not until you were on it. One of the machine shops sheared through the planks of one bridge over a gully twelve feet deep and only narrowly avoided crashing to the bed of the creek below. The engineers built a dirt-and-timber crib to hold it up until the truck was rescued, and they had to strengthen half a dozen other spans as well before the convoy could safely get across them.

They made fifty-eight miles in eleven hours; they camped on a barren, sandy plain by Tipton Station. No one lived there except the Union Pacific crew, and the nearest natural water supply was sixteen miles away. Today, it's not even on the map anymore.

MCCLURE'S ADJUTANT AND statistical officer, Captain William C. Greany, later wrote a report that somewhat overdramatized the circumstances of the convoy's progress. Going further than any of the other officers involved, Greany claimed that in determining whether it was possible to move a military force across the continent by truck, they were "assuming that railroad facilities, bridges, tunnels etc. had been damaged or destroyed by agents of an Asiatic enemy. The expedition was assumed to be marching through enemy country and therefore had to be self-sustaining throughout."

In reality, should the Japanese ever occupy any western portion of the United States—a possibility much feared at the time—it's not likely that they'd thoughtfully leave piles of lumber by every rickety bridge for their advancing opponents, go fishing for trout to feed them, or put on an endless supply of dances and free cigarettes. Why Greany should have stretched the heroic image to that point is therefore hard to imagine (at least without succumbing to unworthy suspicion about his motives). After all, the convoy's progress through the West was now becoming, day by slogging day, a steadily more impressive triumph of hard work and determination over profoundly inimical conditions. There was no need to fantasize about the landscape being populated by hostile Asiatics; the landscape itself was an enemy quite formidable enough.

As Eisenhower later noted, however, at least a few of the officers who came from the East, and who had never seen terrain like this before, found the experience pretty grueling. Innocents abroad, the only idea they had of the country had been gained "from highly colored books and stories, usually printed on pulp paper." For Ike and his friend Sereno Brett, eager to enjoy themselves amid the wearing daily struggle with the road, these urban ingenues were a godsend.

Brett was with the 326th Battalion of the Tank Corps; he was a decorated veteran of the Western Front. On September 12, 1918, on the opening day of the St.-Mihiel offensive, he'd led his men on foot (America still hadn't made any tanks) into a hail of machine-gun and artillery fire. His citations state that he displayed "extraordinary heroism" and that his leadership was marked by "the greatest resolution, skill, and devotion." He was awarded the Distinguished Service Cross, the French Legion of Honor, and the Croix de Guerre.

Now this Oregon native was twenty-seven years old. Ike remembered him as a man "of swarthy complexion, short, strong, and muscular. He had piercing brown eyes, the sort that seemed to look right through the person to whom he was talking." He also, like Ike himself, had a sense of humor.

These two had been exploring "the theatrical possibilities" of the expedition for a while now. In western Nebraska, going ahead of the convoy in one of the reconnaissance cars, they'd shot a jackrabbit, then propped it up in a bush a hundred yards from the road. That evening, they took two of the easterners back along the road with them; they said they planned to do a little shooting, but they carried only .45-caliber pistols.

When they reached the spot where they'd left their now stiffened rabbit, Sereno called out for them to stop. "At that distance," wrote Ike, "and in dimming light, one could see him only in imagination"—but they described the rabbit with such precision that the easterners had to admit they could indeed make him out. Sereno then said Ike was one of the finest pistol shots he'd ever known, and invited his partner to take a crack at the target. Ike "carefully aimed the pistol in the general direction of the North Pole" and fired.

"You've got him! You've got him! He fell," proclaimed the delighted Major Brett.

The easterners—who hadn't seen the rabbit to begin with— now had to agree that this man from Kansas was a truly skillful shot. Sereno, meanwhile, scampered off to get the rabbit. He got near enough to the car that they all could see it, then he tossed it aside, saying, "Well, let's turn back."

The greenhorns protested that the rabbit would make "a nice addition to our rations" (which says something about the state of the convoy's mess). Ike and Sereno told them it'd be lousy eating and drove away; they weren't going to let them see that the animal had been dead for twelve hours.

As the convoy advanced farther into the wilds, a few of the more experienced officers now began warning the others that Major Brett had shell shock and was "a trifle touched." Playing along, Sereno took to setting up his own camp a small distance from the rest of the convoy. As they bedded down for the night in the howling emptiness of a place like Tipton Station, he would then add to the wind a volley of "weird and strident cries. . . . In the morning when he woke, he'd give one or more of these whoops, just on general principles."

The easterners began to worry. Couldn't something be done for the poor man? Ike said that he, and only he, could control Sereno in his fits. These "fits" became more frequent; Ike took Sereno aside and calmed him, while the others fretted amongst themselves over their unstable traveling companion.

The pranks grew more cruel, and the easterners grew more alarmed. One night Sereno climbed a bluff 150 feet above the camp and moaned and howled in the darkness like a coyote. Ike said it wasn't a very good imitation, but the others didn't know.

Come dawn, Sereno hurled his bedroll over the cliff top. The uneasy young officers watched it tumble into the camp, and wondered whether the mad major would follow—whereupon Sereno came racing down the path, said Ike, "kicking gravel, screaming, yelling, throwing things, and heading directly for the tent of one of the easterners. The man, who had been looking out of the flaps of his tent, took off, shouting to me, 'Stop him! Stop him!' "

"Well," said Ike laconically, "I had my chore and dutifully performed it."

He described one of their victims as "a man who was more gullible than he should have been about conditions beyond the Hudson River." Naturally, however, Ike was far too decent to identify him.

Captain Greany, meanwhile, wrote grandly that their living conditions "were comparable to those generally experienced in the advance zone of battle operations." Sereno Brett could have corrected him on that. It was sweat and labor, no doubt, it was a long and arduous trek—but it wasn't the Western Front.

PAST TIPTON AND the western branch of the Continental Divide, the desolate plains give way to land more buckled, with gullies and outcrops of shattered sandstone edging nearer to the road. Rolling through here on I-80 is to be granted a fantastic deception; take away the paved highway, and you are stripped of any vestige of civilization.

Someone had slipped up. McClure's schedule told him it was sixty miles to Green River, and it wasn't. It was seventy-six—and while sixteen extra miles today with air-conditioning and a windshield is no more than a couple of songs and an ad break on the radio, to the men of the convoy it was a large extra ration of back-breaking work. After leaving Tipton at six-thirty, they were on the road for nearly fourteen hours.

They'd had trouble sleeping; the temperature in the open desert had dropped to forty-five degrees. Now the weather gave them dust storms, with winds touching fifty miles an hour; one of these near Rock Springs was so thick, said McClure, that it "totally obscured vision." They encountered only fifteen miles of mercifully good, hard, graded dirt road at day's end; for the other sixty-one they had to battle with clogged eyes and throats through this desert gale over a trail that was barely a scratch mark on the earth.

The rutted wheel paths wound up and down through sand holes and washouts in wild passes and canyons. Some of the time, wrote McClure, they saw "magnificent palisades of stratified earth and rock rising to heights of seven hundred feet." Dust permitting, the view otherwise was of "utter desolation strewn with bones of animals/the intensely dry air absence of trees and green vegetation and parched appearances of landscape exert depressing influence on personnel." It was, he noted wearily, "altogether most tedious day of expedition."

They strengthened four bridges, rebuilt a timber culvert, and detoured around four others. Grit fouled the spark plugs, the gas lines, the carburetors. One of the kitchen trailers broke its coupling and rolled away into the ditch; a motorbike sidecar broke down and was loaded onto the Militor. The wrecker towed a lamed Dodge five miles into Rock Springs—and in that town they knew very well how bad the road was, especially on this last stretch from Point of Rocks.

Arguing before the convoy's arrival that an effort should be made to secure a talk in the town by Dr. Johnson, the *Rock Springs Rocket* said the Townsend Bill's promise of federal funds for road building "will be of interest to residents of this city." Any of them who traveled the Lincoln Highway knew, after all, that east of town it was "in a terrible condition and almost impassable." It was, indeed, so bad that the wealthier class of tourist had been known to give up on it entirely. They'd load their cars on the train back at Wamsutter and take them off it at Rock Springs.

The convoy came into town over the Elk Street bridge about five o'clock, "after many hard experiences with some of our bad roads." Watching the dust-coated trucks pull to a halt on C Street, the paper noted that the trip "must be at best a grind."

They stopped for an hour. It wasn't on the schedule, but McClure was persuaded to allow it at the last minute, even as the first trucks were entering the town. A team from Firestone's Salt Lake branch was there to meet them with ice cream and cigarettes; while the soldiers took a break, the street was thronged with people.

It was the same in Green River. They got there at eight-fifteen in the evening, and camped for the night in the baseball park. Eighteen hundred people lived in the town; the *Green River Star* said that almost every man, woman, and child of them gathered to see the convoy. It was, reported the paper, "a sight that will long be remembered by all who viewed it."

FIFTEEN MILES APART, Rock Springs and Green River are neighbors who, like neighbors everywhere, like to have a good snipe at each other. Rock Springs was and is the larger of the two places; it started out as a coal-mining town for the Union Pacific, which, running a profitable near monopoly, owned most of the mines. Sporadic booms drew people of fifty-six different nationalities—a fantastically diverse ethnic mix, which, conveniently for the railroad, made it harder for labor to get organized. This mix is now cited in the town as a point of local pride.

In Green River they look down their noses and say tartly that what they don't tell you in Rock Springs is that none of those fifty-six nations get along. Rock Springs retorts that in the homey county seat under Castle Rock down the road, they're just a bunch of inbred snobs.

It's true that Green River was never quite so much of a "hell on wheels" town as most of the other railroad stops. With its reliable supply of good water, it already had a couple of thousand people there waiting to make money when the railroad arrived. The townsite with its store and hotel was owned by Jack Field, who'd come north from the Colorado gold mines. The Union Pacific didn't want to pay Field his price for the property, so it set up a station eleven miles west at Bryan, on the Blacks Fork, instead.

The population of Green River fell from two thousand to one hundred in a month. Then, in 1872, a drought dried up the Blacks Fork, and the railroad had to pay Field his price after all. Everyone moved back and Green River revived; today, nothing remains of Bryan but a historical marker on a cinderbed turnout by Highway 374.

Green River is an oasis overlooked by magnificent buttes. It used to keep mountain lions in a pit to amuse people getting off the train, and it had stores and stalls selling fossilized fish to the tourists. Whatever inclination it might have to look down on dusty Rock Springs, however, in truth the two towns have much in common.

Both started out, in the words of one early traveler, as "a brown dot in a vast space." Both have had crazy booms and busts; in a harsh land, the goal of both was to get on the map and to stay there. Achieving that goal was made possible first by the railroad and then by the Lincoln Highway.

As far as the highway went, however, both towns had portions of notoriously wretched road. In 1909, Harriet White Fisher was in a party driving east through this area; it took them a whole day to cover the forty or so miles from Granger to Rock Springs, over "long stretches of sand with high centers." Arriving in Rock Springs, they found an Irishman and an Italian sitting on a bench outside a restaurant; penned nearby stood two mules. It transpired that these men made their living by waiting for motorists to get stuck, then charging them to have the mules pull them out from the sand. The experience of the convoy suggests that, ten years later, the road hadn't gotten much better.

At the time, Rock Springs had just one paved city block, from the Union Pacific station up C Street to city hall. The suspicion locally was that the railroad didn't favor any kind of major street-paving program; it would be funded out of property assessments, to which the railroad would have been substantially the largest contributor.

Whether that's true or not, for a period of about ten years the people of Rock Springs tackled the problem by having a "street day" once a year. Stores and businesses closed, and every able-bodied man went out with shovels, rakes, trucks, and wagons to spread and roll cinders on the downtown streets. They were volunteers, of course—though if you didn't take part, you were likely to find yourself fined by an impromptu citizens' court.

In the circumstances, it was the best they could do. To do any more—to get a hard surface laid through the endless miles of windblown mountain and plateau in western Wyoming—was entirely beyond them. In terms of either labor or taxes, there simply weren't enough of them. When the Lincoln Highway Association spoke of the road problem being a national problem, not a local one, this was exactly the kind of place they had in mind.

These, then, were people who needed the Townsend Bill as much as anyone did. When the convoy came through, it wasn't reported in either town whether Dr. Johnson spoke or not—but the night before the trucks arrived, Goodrich's man gave a talk at the Oracle Theater in Rock Springs. He told his audience that the Lincoln Highway was worth a dollar to the town for every man, woman, and child who passed through on it.

DEPARTING GREEN RIVER, McClure was impressed; he described "green buff and pink tinted stratified rock and sand of wondrous formations and beauty." The road, unfortunately, didn't give him much time to enjoy the view. For the most part, it was better than the past few days—a firm surface of compact gravel and clay—and the weather was kinder too. The wind was down to a patchy breeze, and a welcome hint of moistness infused the air.

The bridges, however, were worse than anything they'd seen yet. Even the new timber left to reinforce them wasn't up to standard; again and again they were delayed as wheels sheared through planking, trucks teetered over creeks and gullies, and the engineers toiled to strengthen each enfeebled span. There were so many holdups for these patch-and-mend operations that even the meticulous Jackson didn't bother counting them; McClure put the tally at twelve. Other sources have reckoned that, in crossing Wyoming, the men of the convoy repaired or rebuilt no less than forty-nine

On July 7, 1919, by the south lawn of the White House, the Zero Milestone was unveiled by Secretary of War Newton Baker (seated in a white suit behind the speaker). This was the starting point of the First Transcontinental Motor Train.

Carl Fisher of Indianapolis, the man who first thought of the Lincoln Highway. "A road across America," he told his friends. "Let's build it before we're too old to enjoy it."

"The Spirit of the Lincoln Highway" was widely used in promoting the road. Taken at Owensmouth, California, this photograph shows Captain W. S. Gilbreath, secretary of the Hoosier Motor Club, near the end of Carl Fisher's Hoosier Tour from Indianapolis to Los Angeles in 1913.

3

Henry Bourne Joy of Detroit. Abundantly energetic, Joy built Packard into the largest luxury carmaker in the world, and did more than any other man to make the Lincoln Highway a reality.

4

5

Henry Joy in the first Packard, built in 1899. Joy kept it in the foyer of the plant in Detroit to remind all concerned how the business had started.

6

Franklin Augustus Seiberling, founder of the Goodyear Tire & Rubber Company. Seiberling succeeded Henry Joy as president of the Lincoln Highway Association in 1917.

7

Henry Ostermann, the Lincoln Highway's raffish field secretary, in his official Packard Six in 1913. The highway logo is on the car door. Six years later, Ostermann piloted the First Transcontinental Motor Train 3,251 miles across America.

Austin Bement, secretary of the Lincoln Highway Association from 1915. Bement said later that, for several years, he placed at least one thousand words about the highway in American newspapers every single day.

8

Gael Hoag of Ely, Nevada. Hoag succeeded Ostermann as the highway's field secretary in 1920, was heavily involved in the Utah controversy, and wrote a history of the Lincoln Highway in 1935.

9

10

Packard sent its cars on arduous expeditions every year, and Henry Joy often drove them himself. Taken in 1911, with Joy on the left, this image shows him setting off for the Rocky Mountains from the factory on East Grand Boulevard.

The first Packard Twin Six en route from Detroit to San Francisco in 1915. Rain in the Midwest turned the roads into cloying gumbo. The conditions in this image, said Joy, were "only slightly worse than the average."

In Iowa, on Joy's 1915 trip to California. "A small car following in our ruts," Joy reported, "had to give up at this point east of Tama."

13

First Lieutenant Elwell Jackson, second from left, the convoy's meticulous reckoner of snapped fan belts and clogged carburetors. Ike took this picture himself.

14

Lieutenant Colonel Charles W. McClure, commander of the First Transcontinental Motor Train. After fourteen years of service, it would be his last job in the army.

15 Harvey Firestone, in the white suit at left, greets officers of the convoy before lunch at his country mansion near Columbiana, Ohio. Ike is the six-footer on the right.

16 Ike on the right, and his good friend from the Tank Corps, Major Sereno Brett of Oregon, second from left. The young man between the two officers is Harvey Firestone's son.

The Militor—$40,000 of custom-built "artillery wheeled tractor." For all involved, this bizarre vehicle was the convoy's most priceless asset.

Sometimes the Militor rescued mired vehicles, but on more than a few occasions, the men had to push them through by brute force.

19

The rickety span of the High Bridge over the Mississippi between Fulton and Lyons.

20

The Lincoln Highway Bridge in Tama, Iowa, was placed on the National Register of Historic Sites in 1976.

21

As the expedition advanced, so three hundred men became steadily more numb with exhaustion.

22

Throughout the journey, the convoy's film crew shot scenes of the men's travails. The film was shown in theaters all along their route.

23 *Pilot Car –*

Convoy pilot Henry Ostermann arrives in Salt Lake City in his gleaming white Packard Twin Six.

24

Thousands lined the streets to see the convoy parade into Salt Lake City. Ike made sure to capture the moment.

25

"Stewart seemed to work overtime here," Ike dryly noted, as the fair maids of Utah made ready to present Colonel McClure with a floral truck. Sadly, Utah was less hospitable to the Lincoln Highway than it was to the convoy.

26

There was only one way to cross the southern end of the Great Salt Lake Desert— and it wasn't an easy way.

27

"Disgusted at the desert and trip." Private Edward Mantel's terse note sums up
the convoy's experience of western Utah.

28

The convoy camps in Citizens' Park, Ely, Nevada.

29

The journey of the First Transcontinental Motor Train was repeatedly compared to that of the forty-niners before them. In the desert mountains of the West, the trucks even look like prairie schooners.

30

The mountain trails were barely wide enough for the vehicles, with precipitous drops barely inches from their wheels.

31

"Lucky to get on road like this," noted Ike laconically. In 1919, the Good Roads Movement still had much to achieve.

32

This commemorative cartoon is from the Eisenhower Library, Abilene, Kansas.

bridges in total. During nine days on the road across the state, that's an instant engineering problem every eight or nine miles.

They didn't get to Fort Bridger until eleven-thirty that night; it had taken them seventeen hours to go sixty-three miles. The men must have been flat-out exhausted; one of them was in considerable pain as well, after a load of oil barrels had jolted across his legs in the back of a truck on the bone-shaking road.

It seems that Ike and Sereno Brett, on the other hand, still had energy to spare.

FORT BRIDGER LIES on the Blacks Fork of the Green River. It had been abandoned by the army in 1890; they started selling off the buildings and the land, and by the time the convoy came through the men had to camp in a cow field. A few stone buildings remained in tumbledown condition among the trees; around them stood a hamlet of about a hundred people with a hotel, two garages, a store, a telephone, and (according to the guidebook) "a large house at which meals may be obtained."

This, almost certainly, was the scene of what Ike described as the "finest hour" for the theatrics he and Brett enjoyed at the expense of the easterners. Ike doesn't identify the location himself, beyond siting it in western Wyoming. He merely describes their camping near "a little settlement that boasted a combination restaurant and soft-drink parlor, a post office, a telegraph station, two general stores, and a half dozen houses."

Since their other camps in western Wyoming were all in towns rather larger than that—except for Tipton Station, where there was no settlement at all—only Fort Bridger fits the bill. It's also appropriate to the prank he and Sereno now played, the site having famously been the scene of several massacres involving trappers, soldiers, Mormons, and Indians—a fact duly noted in the guidebook that Elwell Jackson was using as a journal for his daily log. Fifty years later, Ike's memory may have played him false when he recalled there being a telegraph station, but if there wasn't, that would turn out to be rather convenient.

Arriving ahead of the main train, he and Sereno went to the restaurant, where they decided that one of the more gullible easterners "should be given a taste of the authentic West." They got to talking with the locals and cooked up a scheme; then they took a table and waited for the junior officers.

As soon as they came in, the locals started "to talk and argue heatedly and loudly about the possibility of Indian trouble. It appeared that an outbreak was imminent. They were terribly disappointed, we overheard, that the motor convoy had come into the region without arms . . . then they addressed us directly."

They said they'd been waiting for the convoy to get there, hoping they'd frighten the Indians away. But, they went on, those Indians were shrewd. They'd know by now that the convoy wasn't armed.

Ike and Sereno professed their concern and said they better mount a guard on the camp. They borrowed an old shotgun from one of their co-conspirators and loaded it with shells from which (to avert any danger of the joke going awry) they'd previously taken out the shot. Then they drew up a roster for sentry duty.

"Courageously," Ike wrote, "Sereno and I and a few others took the early duty. We allotted the dreary small hours of the night to the officer for whom this episode was staged."

As midnight approached, while he made his rounds, Sereno let out a few war whoops in the darkness. The easterner came out to take the watch, now somewhat nervous about his scalp; Ike and the others hid so they could watch him.

"The recruit took his duties seriously," Ike recalled, "marching at attention around the camp as if on parade. Brett and several others spread out and from a distance would let out an occasional short yelp. Finally, just as we hoped, the sentry let go with both barrels—to arouse the camp, he explained later."

They let him explain, at great length, then went back to bed masking grins and feeling thoroughly pleased with themselves. Unfortunately, the greenhorn still hadn't caught on—and it happened, said Ike, "that one of the duties of our victim was writing up daily progress reports to be telegraphed back to the War Department."

Their victim, in other words, was that diligent reckoner of snapped fan belts and fouled spark plugs, Lieutenant Elwell Jackson of Philadelphia, who now drafted a report for the day describing

Indian trouble in the vicinity, as well as dissatisfaction among the locals about the convoy's lack of arms.

"Faster than any vehicle in the convoy," Ike and Sereno shot off around the camp to find the man with the message before it was sent. Then they went to McClure and pointed out that if this news went back to Washington, the War Department "was unlikely to understand our brand of humor."

McClure was an experienced professional officer; he was a lot more likely to get on with men like Brett and Ike than he was with a reservist technician like Jackson. He went along with the gag and crossed out that part of the message about Indian trouble without bothering to tell Jackson that he'd done so. Thereby, said Ike, "a number of us were saved lengthy explanations in original and three or more carbons."

Ike said their victim never realized he'd been fooled—but one can easily see from this story how Jackson might have come to his low opinion of the convoy's commander. As for McClure, he sent no telegram from Fort Bridger; he reported on this long day's travel from their next stop at Evanston, noting that there'd been no telegraph station at Fort Bridger for him to do so from there.

Either there wasn't or, if Ike was correct to recall that there was, it was closed, or McClure had simply decided not to use it. But one way or another, McClure quietly censored the news that some of his officers had been up half the night playing an involved practical joke on one of their colleagues.

They were, Ike contentedly recalled, "a troupe of traveling clowns."

THE MUSEUM AT Fort Bridger today is in a farmer's old milk barn. The original Lincoln Highway turned right in front of the gate to the fort, running along a dirt track to a bridge over the Blacks Fork. On the left side of the old road stand some crumbling stone buildings; the second one along still has a sign saying FORT MOTEL, while the third one has the painted words TOURIST SUPPLIES just faintly visible on the faded walls.

Back at the fort's entrance, overgrown with a grove of beech trees to the left of the gate, an eight-unit cabin motel stands in tottering disrepair. There used to be a Lincoln Highway Motel franchise whose colors were yellow and black, but the owner of this place didn't want to join; he painted it orange and black instead.

Linda Byers is the superintendent of the Fort Bridger site for Wyoming State Parks and Historical Sites ("I hold down the fort"); she said they'd acquired this ruined motel a couple of years ago. Now they were looking for a way to fund its restoration, so they could add it to the site. She said, "We want to restore it, definitely. We're just tickled to death to have it. It's a part of the place. Out here, history so far has always been the pioneers and the Union Pacific—but now people are realizing that 1910, 1920, those are important times too." Gesturing toward the bare wood shacks falling apart in the shade of the trees, she said, "This is the next chapter."

When I-80 was built, this chapter through Fort Bridger was bypassed; having no need for it anymore, the state tore up most of old U.S. 30. Here and there between miles 30 and 10 on the interstate going west, you can still see pieces of it snaking away over the hillsides. To the south, the snowcapped Uinta Mountains in Utah rise beyond rolling plains of jade sagebrush.

In 1919, this section of the trip was brutal; mercifully, it was also short. They made thirty-five miles from Fort Bridger to Evanston in seven and a half hours; for eight of those miles, the trucks labored up and down grades as steep as 12 percent.

They had to stop nine times to fix bridges and culverts; one bridge was so unsafe that they didn't even bother with it. One by one the trucks dropped down the near-vertical sides of the creek, then hauled themselves (or were hauled) up and out the other side. A few miles from Evanston, one of the machine shops broke down; Jackson's beloved Militor towed it into camp in the Uinta County Fairground.

At least it was a Saturday. At least here, after the struggles of these last few long days, they could pull up for a day and have a rest—or that's what they thought. Unfortunately, it didn't turn out that way.

It was eighty miles to their next scheduled stop at Ogden, Utah. When McClure's scouts came back with reports that the first half of the run was "very rough with steep grades," he decided it was too risky to try to tackle the whole drive in one day. They would instead leave Evanston at midday, get across as much of the bad road as they could that Sunday afternoon, and bivouac out on the road.

The need to leave Evanston was given extra impetus when, that Saturday night, motorcycle dispatch rider Sergeant Wallace "Casey" Brouse was badly assaulted in town. He was left unconscious, with the convoy's surgeon unable to determine how serious his injuries might be. Brouse was sent ahead to the army hospital at Fort Douglas, which made McClure even more keen to get out of Evanston. The feeling among the men, he reported, was running high; best to get them out of Wyoming fast, before they sought revenge.

It was an unfortunate way to leave the state. Compared to the trials that lay ahead in Utah, however, and the wider controversy the Lincoln Highway would generate there, it was—for all but Sergeant Brouse—a minor affair.

CHAPTER NINE

★ ★ ★

The Utah Controversy

UTAH PRESENTED THE Lincoln Highway Association with the thorniest problem of any state on the road. The nub of it was to choose between three potential routes running west through the state—to decide which was most practical, most direct, and of most benefit to most people.

The first option was to follow the original line of the Union Pacific from Ogden around the north of the Great Salt Lake. This, however, meant the road wouldn't go to Salt Lake City; it also meant it would cross northern Nevada down the Humboldt Valley through Wells and Winnemucca. This was fine if the motorist wanted to go to San Francisco, but it closed off the choice of turning south for Los Angeles—and that was where 60 percent of Salt Lake's through traffic actually wanted to go.

The second option had the same drawback. If the road went south of the lake, then due west across the Great Salt Lake Desert to the state line at Wendover, it still funneled the traffic to Wells and San Francisco, and it still shut out Los Angeles. It had, moreover, to cross some seventy miles through one of the world's most inhospitable places. There was no water out there, except for the alkali brine that migrates in slow waves through the off-white mud flats—undermining in the process any roadbed not built to the most exacting and costly standard.

No one really knew how to build a durable road through this awful terrain in the first place. True, the Western Pacific had gotten across here in 1907, but it had huge resources, and it needed them; it had to haul in enormous tonnages of rock and gravel fill. Neither Utah nor the Lincoln Highway Association had anything approaching the kind of money that a railroad could throw at this problem—and even if they did, Henry Joy still believed they'd be spending vast sums of cash and energy to go the wrong way.

The third option—the one they chose in 1913—was the most southerly of the three. It parted company with the railroad and followed the route of the Pony Express instead. From Salt Lake City the Lincoln Highway went west through Grantsville, south into Skull Valley, and on from there to Fish Springs and the state line past Ibapah. It was more circuitous than cutting straight across to Wendover, but it had two advantages. First, by running south around the worst of the desert, the motorist would never be farther than twenty miles from water. Second, the traffic would be brought into central rather than northern Nevada. There, at the town of Ely, the tourist could continue to San Francisco on the Lincoln Highway or turn southwest to Los Angeles on the Midland Trail.

Joy and his colleagues believed the central route through Nevada was an easier, more direct line for their road than the Humboldt Valley. With the junction at Ely offering both final destinations, they also believed it was the line that would draw the most traffic.

In the widest perspective, they had a good case. If you're thinking of how best the largest number of people might cross the West—rather than how best they might cross just one state or another—then the Pony Express route had a great deal going for it. Indeed, in 1913, it was the only route that had any semblance of a road on it at all. It was long faded since the days of the mail riders and the overland stage, and it was subject to "blowouts," in which sections of the trail simply turned to dust and blew away—but at least it was there.

Despite its advantages, however, neither Salt Lake City nor San Francisco had the widest perspective. They had their own local perspectives, and neither favored central Nevada. San Francisco had no interest in tourists turning south for Los Angeles at Ely; why should that brash upstart get the business when the Bay Area could have it? Salt Lake City, meanwhile, wanted tourists staying in Utah for as long as possible; it didn't really want them going west at all. If they had to go to San Francisco, fine, get on and go there—but if southern California was the goal, it suited Utah better if tourists turned that way from Salt Lake, instead of taking the Lincoln

Highway through empty country to Ely. If they did that, they could run south on the Arrowhead Trail by way of Provo and Cedar City, and remain in Utah for three hundred more miles of garage and hotel bills.

In consequence, both Salt Lake and San Francisco had mutual cause to subvert Joy's chosen route in Utah. They wanted tourists heading different ways, to be sure—north of the Lincoln via Wendover, or south of it on the Arrowhead—but neither city had reason to back Ely. These conflicting interests would, in the end, lead to bitter controversy, but in 1919 the situation had not yet been resolved. In 1919, getting across Utah was a nightmare whichever way you went.

THE CONVOY HURRIED out of Evanston before anyone else got hurt and crossed into Utah down Echo Canyon under cloudy, drizzling skies. As McClure's scouts had reported, the road was dreadful. It's called the Eisenhower Highway today, but in 1919 it was a rough trail with sharp descents and many dangerous turns. For much of the way, it was barely wider than the trucks.

Giant, weatherworn red cliffs loomed above them; their wheels crept along the edge of precipitous drops. They took seven hours to go forty-one miles to the mining camp at Echo and, once again, Sergeant Wood and the Militor did noble work. From dawn they towed a machine shop with a broken piston; twenty miles out they had to drop it and go back sixteen miles to pull another truck from a broken culvert. By the time they'd gotten back to the lamed machine shop, then towed that another five miles, it was getting dark. Between their feeble headlights and the vertiginous rim of the canyon trail, it was too dangerous to go any farther.

Wood and his crew spent the night on the road; when they got to Echo at nine the next morning, the convoy had moved on for Ogden. The cook had, at least, remembered to leave them a meal. After forty-five minutes to rest and eat, Wood pushed on through Devil's Slide and, amid thick clouds of dust hanging over the road on a windless day, caught up with the others at Morgan.

Morgan was and is a blissfully beautiful little town tucked into fertile alpine meadows under snowcapped peaks. It had dressed in its finest to greet the army; while the Female Relief Society of the Mormon Church served refreshments, Bishop Anderson made a speech of welcome and presented McClure with two keys—one silver from the town, one gold from the state of Utah. A band played, the streets were lined with flag-waving schoolchildren, and the convoy was given half a dozen cases of locally canned peas; these, apparently, were famously good.

Welcoming though Morgan was, however, it wasn't on the Lincoln Highway, and it was odd that the convoy had come here at all.

THOUGH NOT AS important as the issue of how to cross the desert to Nevada, the route in Utah had been problematic from the beginning here too. It made more sense from the fork at Echo to go directly southwest to Salt Lake City over the Wasatch Mountains and down Parley's Canyon—but in 1913, at the behest of Governor Spry, Joy had instead drawn the line northwest through Morgan and Weber Canyon to Ogden.

Two years later, with Spry no longer in office, the road was rerouted to cut out Ogden and go the quicker way—yet still the convoy went by the first and longer line. Including Ogden was probably a mix of politics and commerce; if nothing else, the presence of the Browning armaments firm would have drawn the army. Equally, McClure may not have wanted to push his trucks up the climb into the Wasatch. Whatever the reason, the people on the Lincoln Highway in Summit County took the detour as a grave affront.

The county commissioners wrote in furious protest to Utah Senator Reed Smoot in Washington. Ogden, they said, had "endeavored to get the Lincoln Highway but failed owing to infeasibility of routes." It was a longer way around, the roads were worse, and sending the convoy there to satisfy Ogden's merchants was an "unjust and absurd proposal." They went on to say that, after all the work they'd done to bring their portion of the highway up to boulevard condition, "it would be the grossest injustice and the most humiliating slight to the people of Summit County" to deprive them of the convoy.

It did them no good; the convoy pressed on down the dizzying descent into Weber Canyon. The sky here becomes a thin and distant strip wedged between vast, craggy faces of jumbled gray rock. The convoy crept between towering walls of stone, pausing at one sharp turn while the engineers shored up the crumbling edge of the road with a timber wall. The Militor towed the machine shop all the way.

Caked in dust, at last they were met at the Ogden city limits by Mayor Browning and a coterie of local businessmen and officials. Hundreds lined the streets, among them young women (specially selected for their looks) handing out baskets of peaches and watermelon slices. "During the few short hours that you are to remain here," proclaimed the mayor, "the city is yours, and we hope that you will enjoy yourself to the fullest capacity."

The officers were feted at a banquet, the men were ferried in special streetcars to the baths at the sanatorium, and there were dances in the park and at the Elks Club. Telegrams were fired off to Washington in support of the Townsend Bill, asking that the proposed appropriation for federal road building be increased to $1 billion—and, with similar chutzpah (seeing as Ogden wasn't actually on the Lincoln Highway), a commemorative granite milestone was dedicated at city hall.

In neighborly fashion, Mayor Browning took his chance to have a swipe at the moaners in Summit County. The gist of his speech was reported in the *Standard:* "Though forces had been at work against Ogden entertaining the convoy, yet the outfit had come to this city over good roads instead of being compelled to travel an execrable road over the mountain pass by a little-traveled way to a city further south."

Which is, of course, just another way of saying that there was no such thing as a good road if it didn't lead to your town.

UTAH DIDN'T IMPROVE the Lincoln Highway west of Salt Lake City because it didn't have the money and, even if it had, there was virtually no one out there anyway. Instead, understandably, Utah spent what money it had on the north-south traffic in the fertile valley by the lake where the people were.

Spending money meant roadwork, and then as now that was

the bane of the motorist. In the summer of 1919 roadwork projects were so ubiquitous that the *Ogden Standard* devoted an editorial to them. At each construction site there was a detour. A detour, said the paper, "is a sign, a sweep of dust, deep ruts, and much anxiety. It is something more—it is an outrage on the traveling public." The paper could not recall one summer in the past six years when the journey to Salt Lake City could be made without "vexatious turn outs [with] clouds of dust and racking holes." Told that the road would soon be concrete all the way, rather than rejoice the writer could foresee only an eternity of maintenance work and "everlasting despair." "Hope crushed to earth shall rise again," the *Standard* solemnly concluded, "if Hope avoids the region of the steam roller."

Heading for Salt Lake City from Ogden, the convoy couldn't manage to do that. Still towing the machine shop, the Militor ran into a soft spot on a detour. The machine shop broke through the crusted road surface; trying to pull it out, the Militor broke through as well, and sank four and a half feet into the underlying mud.

It took three hours to get it out. Steel cables snapped and the retaining collar on a pulley sheared off, throwing the pulley thirty feet into the air so violently that it sliced clean through a large tree limb overhead. Luckily, no one was hurt. In the end the men gave up trying to tow the wrecker out and shifted it instead by shoveling all the mud away, building a ramp, laying planks, and letting it drive out of the crater by itself.

The Militor then towed the machine shop out along the planks behind it. Altogether, the operation took three hours, but it had to be worth it. After all, a lot of the men felt by now that if it hadn't been for the Militor, they'd never have gotten this far in the first place.

FROM OGDEN TO Salt Lake City today is thirty-four miles. Some idea of how meanderingly indirect these early roads were can be gathered from the fact that McClure pegged their mileage on this day at fifty-two, while Jackson put it at seventy-three. The discrepancy could be explained in several ways, but by now sheer exhaustion would surely have rendered them prone to the odd factual inaccuracy. Besides, no matter how tired they were, the last major city before California awaited them, and it was time once again to put on their party faces.

Salt Lake City was determined that the reception they laid on should be among the best of the journey. The convoy's arrival coincided with the annual Governors' Conference, and many significant politicians were in town to see the show. The local motor trade planned an enormous spectacle, urging every owner of a motor truck to join the convoy's escort, and to sport banners on their sides promoting good roads. Detailed plans were in the hands of the Utah State Automobile Association, whose intention was to mount nothing less than "the greatest demonstration of motor vehicles of this sort ever assembled in the country."

On the day, the *Salt Lake Tribune* estimated that about 150 trucks turned out to greet the army, with hundreds of cars besides. All the way into town, while bands thumped out tunes and factory whistles blew, huge crowds lined the streets. By the time the convoy reached South Temple every available inch of space on the sidewalks, in windows, and in doorways was jam-packed.

At the Pioneer Monument, half a dozen young women presented McClure with a truck made of white and purple flowers; it was six feet long. McClure had it gingerly set in his car, and promised he'd take it all the way to the Pacific. One assumes he was, in reality, about as likely to do that as he was to fly there unaided.

Nonetheless, he graciously accepted this lavish if impractical token. He was, said the *Tribune* eagerly, "a courteous, intensely earnest and wonderfully energetic officer." Utah Governor Simon Bamberger stood on the steps of the monument, looking on with at least a dozen other state governors. The convoy passed before them, and then (McClure having vetoed plans for an extended parade past the capitol) they proceeded directly to their camp in Walker's Field on Main Street.

The field looked inviting, with a thick carpet of grass. The first trucks drove onto it, and promptly sank to the hubs in the soft soil. The tractor had to tow them all out; they gave up on the field and parked in an impromptu bivouac along the street instead. The men were driven to Saltair for a swim in the lake, and a dinner dance was held for the officers at the Hotel Utah's Roof Garden. No doubt, at this event more last-ditch efforts were made to persuade McClure to stay in town the next day. As usual, the city's movers and shakers had been pleading with the War Department for the visit to be a longer one; as usual, McClure wasn't having it.

He had lost two days from his schedule in Nebraska already, and he was about to lose more. Ironically, he and Jackson had told Washington that the road out of Wyoming through Echo was "the worst road in Utah"—but compared to what lay ahead, it was a flawless boulevard.

AMONG THE HOST of politicians and businessmen in the social throng around McClure was one man with a very particular interest in the outcome of the convoy's passage over the Lincoln Highway. His name was Bill Rishel, and he was popularly known as "the desert bedouin."

He was born in 1869 in Punxsutawney, Pennsylvania; when he was four years old, his family moved west to Omaha. His father was a carpenter, a Civil War veteran who put up barracks for the army. He followed the work to different forts in Wyoming and Colorado, then settled in Cheyenne when Bill was eleven years old. They lasted there a decade, until things turned sour in the early 1890s. With the Union Pacific in receivership and the payroll withering, Rishel's parents decided to return to Pennsylvania. Bill didn't want to go with them, so he looked around the West and reckoned Salt Lake City was the place for a young man in a hurry—and Big Bill Rishel was pretty much always in a hurry.

A friend from Cheyenne met him at the train station. Bluff and hearty, Rishel said to him, "Show me a Mormon."

"Dolt," replied his friend, "they're all Mormons."

In a bicycle store, Rishel got to talking to a racing man. "I found we talked the same language," he recalled. "I liked him. Was I surprised! Mormons were just like anybody else!"

This tone of hale, exclamation-pointed bluster is pure Rishel. Weighing 225 pounds and standing six feet three and a half inches, he put himself about the town and was soon a well-known figure. A keen and able cycle racer—a victim of the time's endemic "handlebar fever"—he became the secretary of the Beck's Hot Springs Bicycle Track Association. This was partly owned by a railroad man named Simon Bamberger, who would in due course become Utah's governor. Rishel promoted races on Bamberger's circuit and then, in 1896, he got involved in the biggest race there'd ever been.

It was one of William Randolph Hearst's many inspired creations: a bicycle relay race all the way across the continent. It was sponsored by Hearst's *Examiner* in San Francisco, by the *New York Journal,* and by the Stearns Manufacturing Company, producers of the Yellow Fellow Bicycle. Rishel organized the first section of the race in the West and set to working out the route. With long sections of the Overland Trail fading back into the landscape since the advent of the railroad, he wondered if it might be possible for the race to cut through the Great Salt Lake Desert instead. To find out, he announced that he'd cycle across it himself.

Told that it would surely be suicide to try such a thing, he snorted with disdain. Why, he said, he had ridden "every kind of terrain. He was steeled against pedal fatigue. Why couldn't he ride across a salt bed?"

His mother once said that, as a child, "he was always competitive and adventuresome." Now, in company with a friend, he spent twenty-two hours to go a hundred miles through the infernal muck and heat of the mud flats. They ran out of water and spent at least as much time carrying their bikes as riding them. Having survived, Rishel said he wouldn't do it again for a million dollars— and as it turned out, he and his companion were the only men who ever did do it.

He still expected the relay racers to go through this ordeal, and he planned to lay out ten-gallon water bags under canvas shade for them all the way across the route. But, come race day, a well-timed rain made the desert an impassable bog; the fortunate riders went around the north of the lake to Ogden instead.

Rishel himself rode five sections of the race, in four different states. Spotted in Reno, he was "a giant in a yellow and black sweater who spun around the city with a speed bewildering to behold . . . the bedouin of the alkali desert."

LIKE SO MANY other wheelmen, Rishel moved early from bicycles to cars. Indeed, though some dispute the claim, he later said he'd driven the first automobile in Utah. It was a blue Locomobile, shipped in a crate as a demonstration model to a cycle dealer named Charles Wilkes in 1900. By then, Rishel was sports editor of the *Salt Lake Herald*. Cars fell under the rubric of sport, so Rishel went to help Wilkes unpack the new vehicle, read the book of instructions, and drove it six blocks downhill on West Temple. Then he found it didn't like climbing hills, and he had to push it six blocks back up again.

Wilkes became the city's Oldsmobile dealer; Rishel produced an item that he said he was "convinced was the first cross-country road map ever drawn." Guiding the motorist from Omaha to San Francisco, it was based on the route of the Hearst bicycle race. Rishel had fallen in love with the new machines; in 1909, when he lost his job at the *Herald,* he flung himself into the motor business full-time. "Boys," he announced, "this is where I declare myself. Never again will I accept a position or work on any job where somebody over my head can step in and say, 'You're through!' From now on, I work for Bill Rishel and no one else."

He organized a dealers' association, published a state auto directory, and promoted an annual car show. Within two years he forgot about working for Bill Rishel and no one else and became auto editor of the *Salt Lake Tribune*. Like many major papers, the *Tribune* had a pathfinder car (with appropriate sponsorship), and Rishel drove all over Utah mapping routes around the state. When the Lincoln Highway Association was formed, he paid his five dollars and joined up straightaway.

To begin with, he and Gael Hoag got on well. Hoag was the Lincoln Highway's state consul for Nevada; he was an Ely man who'd moved there in 1902, hoping to make his fortune in the copper boom, and he'd been instrumental in the founding of the Nevada State Automobile Association. His collaboration with Bill Rishel was such that, in 1912, when Hoag published a route guide from Salt Lake City to Reno, the starting point was Rishel's office.

Over time, however, as the association persisted in pushing the highway along the Pony Express route to Hoag's base in Ely, the friendship soured—because Rishel wanted the road to cross the salt flats to Wendover instead. Partly it was plain ornery doggedness. He'd cycled across, then he'd tried to take a car across and he couldn't, and it seems he'd simply gotten really determined to beat the desert. In the words of one local historian, "He was one stubborn man. The Lincoln Highway people were stubborn too, but Rishel must've been about the stubbornest cuss that ever lived."

There were, however, more mercenary reasons. Rishel was the secretary of the Utah State Automobile Association—and, at least in part, that organization had been helped into being by the California State Automobile Association in San Francisco. The latter was determined to ensure that traffic came their way by Wendover, instead of driving farther south through Ely to Los Angeles. To that end, San Francisco subsidized the Utah body—they even shared the same club magazine—and Rishel duly backed the Wendover route. Gael Hoag would later charge bluntly that Rishel was on the Bay City's payroll for years.

Thus began a long and heated argument—an argument that would eventually go all the way from the desert to Washington, D.C. There, it would land on the desk of Thomas MacDonald, the Iowa engineer who'd become America's chief road builder.

How to lay a road west from Salt Lake City through the parched and empty sagebrush south of the salt flats to Ely was a problem that had vexed the Lincoln Highway Association from the outset. Part of the difficulty is that the mountain ranges here, and onward all the way across Nevada, run north-south. Any road through this territory must therefore crest a succession of rugged passes between an equally imposing succession of vast and arid valleys.

The first impediment was the Stansbury Range, between Tooele and Skull Valley. This was originally deemed too formidable, and in 1913, the road went around the top of Tooele Valley to Timpie Point instead. This was a landmark where the Stansbury Range dropped down to the southern shore of the Great Salt Lake. If you went due west from here, it was also the last chance for water until you'd crossed seventy miles of white furnace to Wendover. Avoiding the perils of the route preferred by Rishel, the Lincoln Highway therefore dropped south into Skull Valley from Timpie.

There was, however, a pass through the Stansbury Range south of Tooele that, if it could be improved, would save a dozen miles off the journey. It is called Johnson's Pass, after the founder of the settlement of Clover, on its eastern side; State Highway 199 runs through it today, but back then it was far from inviting. On the western side, a spot called the Narrows was especially tricky, being barely wide enough for a wagon.

In 1915, a group of Tooele's leading citizens toured the pass and ended up snowed in at Orr's Ranch in Skull Valley. They approved the route anyhow, though Governor Spry protested that the worst of it was too narrow even for a man on horseback. That January, Henry Joy proved him wrong by driving his Packard through it, snow and all. To be fair, he didn't quite make it unassisted all the way—he needed horses to tow him the last hundred feet to the top—but characteristically, he blamed himself rather than the state of the trail. "I could have gone over without aid," he claimed, "by better knowledge and driving on my part."

Once through the pass and into Skull Valley, Joy's putative road dropped southwest around the base of the salt desert. Joining the Pony Express route, it went by Fish Springs and the tiny settlement of Callao, then on through the Deep Creek Mountains to Ibapah and the state line. It was a lonely, winding, faraway road—it was barely a road at all—but again, if only the money could be found, an opportunity existed to straighten and shorten it.

In tandem with Henry Ostermann, the proposed realignment was originally the work of Gael Hoag. In 1915, urged on by Bill Rishel, Utah had tried to build a road across to Wendover; it was expensive, the labor conditions were hideous, and it fell to bits in no time, thus apparently confirming that construction through many miles of salt flats was a lost cause. Down at the southern end of the Great Salt Lake Desert, however, the flats narrow considerably. Between Granite Rock and the mouth of Overland Canyon, only seventeen miles of the worst terrain needed bridging.

If the association could find some way to get this work done— to get the desert cutoff built and Johnson's Pass widened—their new version of the Pony Express route would be more than fifty miles shorter. This would make it (in Detroit's opinion) unanswerably the best way to cross that barren quarter of the continent. It would be "the keystone of the Lincoln Highway arch."

How then to get these new sections built? Utah couldn't afford it, so there was only one other way. Carl Fisher and Frank Seiberling said they'd pay for it themselves.

FRANKLIN AUGUSTUS SEIBERLING was born on a farm outside Akron in 1859. His father was an inventive man who ran a successful mower and reaper business, and who took out several dozen patents on farm machinery. Frank dabbled in milling, in a streetcar company, and in a twine and cordage firm—then, in 1898, when he was thirty-nine years old, a panic on Wall Street left him "a good many thousand dollars poorer than nothing."

One of his worthless holdings was a small slice of stock in a bankrupt Akron strawboard business. By chance, he met the company secretary in the lobby of a Chicago hotel. In a deal typical of his cavalier style, he offered to buy the firm's $150,000 plant for $13,500, with $3,500 cash on the barrelhead—and this when he had not a penny to his name. He raised the money among friends in Akron the next day, planning to have the factory make strawboard again. Then one of his friends said to him, "Go into the rubber business, Frank. It is alive."

Seiberling knew nothing about rubber, but he had his father's inventiveness, he was a popular man well respected by those who worked with and for him, and he was abundantly energetic; he was at the factory gates at six-thirty every morning. In November 1898, with a staff of thirteen, the Goodyear Tire & Rubber Company began production. It made tires for bicycles and carriages, as well as assorted sundries; its first sale was a batch of little tubes and hoses for pharmaceutical bottles, priced at $25.80.

Then the automobile arrived. In 1900, there were 4,192 cars registered in the United States; by 1909, that figure had climbed to 123,990. During these early years, Seiberling's new tire firm was a long way behind U.S. Rubber and Goodrich, and for a while he skated on the thinnest financial ice—but in 1908, twelve hundred

Model T's came off the line on Goodyear tires. Within a few years, Seiberling was the biggest tiremaker in America.

He lived in a spectacular mansion called Stan Hywet, on the west side of Akron. The name was Old English for "stone quarry," and when construction had started in 1912, the site was so huge that it had its own railroad spur to bring in the building materials. The house is a Tudor Revival with sixty-five rooms; it originally had two massive boilers that burned a ton of coal a day in the wintertime. It had thirty-seven telephones and a switchboard in the basement, and it had an electronic card table that shuffled the deck for you. Four presidents have stayed here; Seiberling's grandchildren used to ride horses up and down the corridor that runs either side of the main hall. The flagstones have artificial footprints sanded into them by order of Seiberling's wife, who wanted her guests to think the family had been there for generations. Stan Hywet was for many decades the largest house in Ohio; it was new money, certainly, but it was huge money too. By 1919 Seiberling was employing twenty-five thousand people, and his sales would soon pass $1 million a day.

This was the man Bill Rishel took on—this man, and much of the American automobile industry that stood beside him. This was the man who'd offered Carl Fisher $300,000 in the blink of an eye, when Fisher first thought of building a road across America. Five feet and four inches of bold vivacity and reckless bonhomie, this was the man who took over the Lincoln Highway Association from Henry Joy during the war—and, in the summer of 1917, this was the man whom Gael Hoag took out into the southern end of the Great Salt Lake Desert. He wanted to show his boss how their road might go a better way.

In November 1916, Carl Fisher pledged $25,000 of his own money for the widening and grading of Johnson's Pass; in return, it would be renamed Fisher Pass. At the same time, Frank Seiberling promised $75,000 of Goodyear's money for the stretch of road across the desert. Once built, it would be called either the Goodyear Cutoff or the Seiberling Section.

Fisher did his part from a distance—he was too busy investing his money and energy in the development of Miami Beach—but in August 1917, Seiberling went to look at the desert for himself. Ostermann and Hoag drove him out to the flats with the association's secretary, Austin Bement, and it wasn't an encouraging experience.

They got bogged down repeatedly; they were out there for hours. In the blinding, shadeless heat they had to dig themselves out from the sodden salt filth, until finally it seemed they'd never get out at all. Hoag was bitterly dejected; he had to start walking back to find help, and it felt like surrender. Seeking funds for his road to Ely, he had subjected one of America's wealthiest men—a man now fifty-eight years of age—to a dismal, potentially deadly fiasco.

Behind him, Ostermann finally freed the car—but still it got worse, because now he gave Seiberling "an awful mudbath. . . . He'd hit every little channel of water wide open to make sure the car would get across and not be stuck, and the mud and the water just flew every which way."

They caught up to Hoag and headed out of the desert; Seiberling sat silent and pensive in the back. As Hoag recalled, "We assumed he was utterly disgusted with the whole project. Bement and Ostermann and I winked at each other from time to time, expecting to hear him say at any time, 'Well, boys, it's no go.'

"After a while Mr. Seiberling straightened up and we all sort of braced ourselves. We felt the ax was about to fall.

" 'Boys', he said, 'I've decided $75,000 won't do it.'

"Of course, the next thing we expected him to say was: 'It's too big a job; let's ditch it and take up something else,' and that would have been a deathblow to our plans. But what he actually said was: 'Let's make it $100,000, and if Goodyear won't put up the other $25,000, I will.' "

A CONTRACT WAS agreed between the state of Utah and the Lincoln Highway Association on March 21, 1918. Six miles of pass and seventeen of desert cutoff would be built by the state, with $125,000 to be donated for that work by Fisher and Goodyear.

Seiberling would further personally contribute up to $5,000 a year for five years for maintenance costs, once the cutoff was built.

The contract was drawn up by Utah's attorney general, Dan B. Shields. It was approved by Governor Bamberger and signed by Shields, along with Utah's secretary of state, the state auditor, and the state engineer. Fisher, Seiberling, and the association's secretary, Austin Bement, signed for the Lincoln Highway. It was agreed that work would be completed by July 1, 1919, and an opening ceremony was envisaged. Bement imagined the scene in the association's newsletter: "One can picture the silent satisfaction of the gathered shades of Jim Bridger, Kit Carson, Brigham Young, Donner, Fremont, Lander, and the scores of other intrepid pioneers who braved the dangers of this region of desolation and hostile savages, and advanced along this same western trail the frontiers of an American Empire in the making."

Work progressed in the desert through the early summer of 1919. Convict labor dynamited the pass, and the road was graded and graveled. They moved west toward the cutoff and built a bridge of hewn logs and rock abutments over the north fork of Government Creek. Out on the flats, a grade was raised across seventeen miles, and more work teams started to gravel it. They went from west to east on this section, from Black Point at the foot of Montezuma Peak, because the mines at Gold Hill had a railroad spur; that was the nearest place to which they could ship in their heavy equipment.

Then, as the work advanced, the convoy came into play. In Detroit, it seemed natural that the road builders should arrange their opening ceremony to coincide with the army's passage over these new sections of road. The problem with that, however, was that no one could say for sure when the army might actually get there.

In mid-April 1919, Bement returned to Detroit from a meeting with officers of the Motor Transport Corps in Washington. The convoy had still not been finally authorized—the army was waiting for the association to submit "our complete plan and detailed data"—but Bement now thought it certain to happen. He therefore wrote to the secretary of the Utah State Automobile Association—one Bill Rishel—about what form the ceremony at the Goodyear

Cutoff might take. At this stage, evidently, they were not aware in Detroit of the extent of Rishel's opposition to their route.

Bement wanted the truck train to be the first to use the cutoff. He wanted every newspaper they could chivy along to be there, and the Pathé News movie cameras too. He wanted speeches by Seiberling, and by the governors of Utah and Nevada; he wanted to arrange "a good publicity stunt by breaking a bottle of champagne on the road, or something of that sort."

One of Rishel's staff members wrote back to Bement and told him, "The suggestions offered in your letter are good with perhaps one exception. I cannot vouch for the safety of a man who would attempt to dispose of a bottle of champagne in such a manner in these parts." At the end of April, Bement assured them that he wasn't insistent on the champagne. By the time the convoy set off, Prohibition was in force anyway, and the issue was moot.

Bement wrote to Rishel again on June 10, after he'd had a cable from the General Staff saying the convoy was now sure to make the journey. He and Ostermann, he said, were "called to Washington to assist in effecting detailed plans for the trip, and the publicity in connection with it." He then professed himself anxious, since apart from the matter of the champagne he'd had no word from Utah about what ceremony they proposed for the opening of the cutoff.

It looked by now as if the convoy wouldn't pass Salt Lake City before the middle of August. Since the cutoff was due to be finished six weeks earlier, "with great regret" Bement suggested they abandon their attempt to have the dedication coincide with its passage. Still, there had to be a ceremony of some sort.

Rishel had changed jobs, taking charge of Utah's touring bureau, and his successor at the automobile association in Salt Lake was T. De Witt Foster. Foster cabled Bement on July 10, "Banquet Lincoln Highway men Utah Commercial Club July 22 Governor Bamberger to speak." He planned that the next day they'd go out to Gold Hill; they'd meet a delegation from Nevada, and they'd formally open the road the day after that. Foster said, "Bring as many in your party as possible."

The dates didn't work. On the day proposed for the banquet Seiberling would be in Los Angeles, while Bement, Ostermann, and Henry Joy would be in Cheyenne. Could Foster not push his banquet back by two days?

Foster tersely put the whole thing off to September, saying without explanation that Bamberger had recommended they do this. By now, the convoy was on the road already. On the salt flats, meanwhile, though the work was supposed to be finished, only seven miles out of seventeen had been graveled along the cutoff.

Carl Fisher was in Indianapolis. He told Bement he didn't care when they held their ceremony, because he wasn't going anyway. "I have visions of a long, hot, dirty trip some place out in Utah. . . . I would willingly give my right leg up to the knee to get out of this trip." He pleaded hay fever and said he was going back to Florida as fast as he could. He needn't have worried. The ceremony never happened; the cutoff was never finished.

At the same time, while Utah was spending the money donated by Fisher and Seiberling at the south end of the salt flats, it was still spending its own on the central route to Wendover as well. L. A. Nares, president of the California State Automobile Association in San Francisco, now cabled Bill Rishel and urged him to use his influence with Utah's senators in Washington to have the convoy take that road instead.

Rishel had a better—and craftier—idea. He told Nares, "If the army tries to cross our Wendover Highway, I will stand guard with a shotgun and defy them. By all means, let those big trucks over the 'Seiberling Section,' and there won't be any Lincoln Highway anymore."

THE CONVOY LEFT Salt Lake City at six-thirty on the morning of Wednesday, August 20. The men would soon be entering some of the most hostile terrain in America, and they were already pie-eyed with fatigue. McClure said it was seventy-four miles to Orr's Ranch that day. Jackson said they traveled "sixty miles excellent roads," then in the very next sentence said they'd gone fifty-two. In the light of what happened to them that evening, the word "excellent" is an odd choice as well.

Three trucks remained behind for repairs, and the Militor

stayed with them in case they broke down again once they got under way. When they did get going, the Militor itself broke down repeatedly, finally packing it in for good just west of Tooele. Sergeant Wood and his two-man crew had been fixing it by the roadside as they went, but by then it was late at night. They had to quit and sleep out where they'd stopped.

Ahead of them the main train moved on to find Johnson's Pass (now theoretically Fisher Pass) in good shape. The roads from the city to this point had been good concrete or gravel; the pass still had steep grades and dangerous turns, but it was well surfaced with broken stone, and they got across without any problems.

The trouble began as they dropped into Skull Valley. The last six miles were on a desert trail that was two feet deep in places with alkali dust and fine sand. There had been no rain for eighteen weeks; it was like trying to drive in talcum powder. The trucks sank into the dust until their undersides grounded on the earth, their wheels spinning to no purpose in thick layers of tractionless grit.

Each foundered vehicle had to be jacked up and dug out by hand. With nothing else available, the men stripped sagebrush from the desert and laid it in the wheel ruts. Bearings, valves, brakes, and clutches sprang loose under the strain; for the men, it was sweat-laden toil in a baking, dry-mouthed heat. There was no wind. In some places the dust hung about them as they worked; in others it rose in slow clouds several hundred feet high.

They labored on into the darkening night; they didn't reach Orr's Ranch until ten-thirty, after seventeen hours on the road. Four trucks didn't make it at all, staying out in the desert where they'd ground to a halt and not crawling in to the ranch until ten the next morning. Their crews hadn't eaten since leaving Tooele. McClure noted his men's exhaustion and started worrying about whether they had enough gas and oil to get through to Nevada. He might have started wondering if their water would last as well, but he didn't mention it; he was more concerned about the Militor, which was thirty-seven miles behind them, on the other side of the pass. Elwell Jackson would subsequently (and angrily) report in detail on what happened to it.

Jackson had left Salt Lake nearly four hours behind the main train. Six miles west of the city, he found the Militor by the side of the road. Sergeant Wood told him he'd been stopped for an hour trying to fix a broken fan-belt lacing. He was annoyed, because he'd been asking again and again for a replacement for this part, and it had never arrived. Now he improvised; he laced the belt with an eight-inch strip of rawhide and prepared to press on. Jackson left ahead of him, assuming the Militor would catch up by lunchtime. In fact, he wouldn't see it again for three weeks.

Wood and his men made four more miles, then the tie rod securing the top of the radiator to the dashboard sheared off its thread. Again Wood improvised, plugging the hole in the radiator, then bracing it in position with a wire cradle. The repair took half an hour; he drove a few more miles, but now his rawhide lacing worked loose. The fan belt slipped, the engine overheated, and once more the Militor ground to a halt.

Wood waited two hours, hoping one of the service trucks might show up to help him, but none did. He tried creeping forward a mile or two at a time, stopping and starting so the engine wouldn't blow. Along the way, he used his enforced stops to replace the governor and the carburetor; they were failing on him too.

Finally he made it to Tooele. At a garage in town he fixed the fan belt and filled his main and reserve gas tanks. No rations had been sent back for him or his men. They ate in a Tooele restaurant (at their own expense, Jackson tartly noted), then pushed on again at eleven-fifteen that night. They hoped to catch up to the convoy at Orr's Ranch, but they'd made only five miles when a bearing worked loose. They couldn't fix it in the dark, so they bedded down where they were.

Early the next morning, an officer named Bissell from the service unit came back and looked over the problem with Wood. Ahead of them, the convoy was setting off from Orr's Ranch toward the unfinished cutoff through the salt flats. Bissell and Wood decided that if they got the Militor back to Tooele they could fix the broken bearing, then catch the main train if they drove all through the day and the night. Wood had already gotten gas; Bissell agreed to leave extra oil, rations, and a relief driver at the ranch up ahead of them.

They backtracked to Tooele and went to work. Later that morning, McClure showed up in his Cadillac. He told Wood to take the Militor back to Salt Lake City and to ship it by rail to Eureka, Nevada; he could rejoin the convoy there. Wood must have stared at him in disbelief. He'd fixed all the problems except the bearing, and he'd soon have that fixed as well. He had gas, oil, and rations organized; he could catch up with the convoy by tomorrow. McClure "insisted that this was impossible."

Doubtless dejected and more than a little disgruntled, Wood got back to Salt Lake about midnight. Yet again, Jackson noted, no rations had been sent back to the sergeant or his men—and Wood had also now been ordered to give the wrecker a complete overhaul before he put it on the train.

The next morning he took it to the Shaw Motor Company, Salt Lake's agency for the Four Wheel Drive, but they had no mechanics who knew how a Militor ran. Before he could leave for Eureka, Wood had to spend five days reconditioning the vehicle by himself. He'd gotten most of the way across America, he'd towed every single vehicle in the convoy, he'd often driven into the small hours, and on several occasions he'd gone all through the night—yet now, with the Pacific just a couple of states away, McClure had abandoned him in a garage in Utah.

Meanwhile, Jackson got to Orr's Ranch at about nine in the evening. On the road, he met Bissell bringing rations to those truck crews who were still stuck in the sand. Bissell told him what McClure had done with the Militor, and Jackson was appalled. Abandoning military decorum, he railed in his next cable to Washington that McClure's action was "entirely unwarranted" and that every single observer agreed. The Militor, he later reported, was "unquestionably the most valuable vehicle in the entire convoy."

The next morning, McClure ordered Jackson to ride over the cutoff ahead of the convoy from Orr's Ranch. Jackson and two other officers got across to the work camp at Black Point. They looked at one another, they looked at the state of the road and the salt flats, they thought about the Militor left behind them in Salt Lake City, and they wondered how on earth they would ever get through this.

———

ORR'S RANCH HAD been settled in 1898 by a Scot named Matthew Orr "who found it difficult to live at peace with his neighbors" and so went to a place where he wouldn't have any. The ranch was a cabin and a cluster of poplars by a spring in the magnificent, mountain-fringed emptiness of Skull Valley. The Orrs dammed the spring to irrigate a few acres of alfalfa and lived alone here, but for maybe the occasional passing Goshute.

Then the Lincoln Highway came. On the original line of the road, the Orrs were the last people for forty-two miles, until you reached John Thomas's place at Fish Springs. As the tourist traffic increased, both they and Thomas did well from it. They kept gas in barrels, served reputedly excellent meals, and built a couple more cabins so people could sleep before they tackled the desert.

The convoy set off from here for the Goodyear Cutoff at six-fifteen in the morning of Thursday, August 21. Before they left, McClure cabled Washington from Tooele to warn them, "Until desert is crossed and Ely Nevada reached no communication possible/will wire details earliest possible moment."

There'd be plenty to report; it would take them two days to cross the salt flats. Just to get to the start of the cutoff at Granite Rock took eight hours, digging their way through dust and sand. From about noon even the tenacious sagebrush started thinning out, until finally there lay before them the gray-white blankness of the alkali barrens.

Here they found that the unfinished roadwork on the east end of the cutoff had left it impassable. They had to detour onto the featureless salt; it had a thin, crystallized crust, which every truck broke through, and beneath that was a cloying silt that held the wheels like glue. The caterpillar tractor was no use; the tracks simply skidded around in the muck. In the end, there was only one thing for it: one by one they put a rope on each truck, and between fifty and a hundred men started pulling each vehicle across the flats by hand.

They went at it from two in the afternoon until long into the small hours. On this day, in theory, they were supposed to reach Ibapah; even if the cutoff had been finished it's unlikely they could have done so, but without it there was no chance. In the dust-blown white glare of the pitiless sun, the convoy broke into fragments. The men strained with every muscle to haul the trucks inch by inch, foot by foot toward any faint hope of firm ground; they added the salt of their sweat to the salt of the desert. They may have been a rabble to begin with, but their efforts now, said Jackson, were "almost superhuman."

Those officers who got across in their cars to the Black Point construction camp established an emergency control point there. By midnight, none of the trucks had made it that far. Strewn across the desert and separated from their baggage, here and there the men snatched an hour's rest on the pallid ground, then dragged themselves up to push and pull their way forward again. At three-thirty in the morning a kitchen unit of seven trucks got through, but their fuel tanker was stalled far behind them, and they couldn't cook a meal. Those who got fed—and not all of them did—had cold baked beans and hard bread.

Another batch of trucks made it past the cutoff at eight in the morning; McClure now sent a messenger to Gold Hill to tell Washington how bad it was. He said he didn't expect the last of his vehicles to make it off the flats before noon that second day. They were running out of gas; he sent a tanker to Gold Hill to remedy that. Worse, they were running out of water. The water truck was placed under guard, and each man rationed to one cup to see them through the night. "Mere existence," McClure said grimly, "was chief concern."

They were saved by a man named Walter Paul, the superintendent of the road-construction crew. He hauled two water tanks twelve miles by horse team from Gold Hill to Black Point and "exerted every effort at his command to assist in relief."

Part of the convoy now lay parched and bedraggled at the foot of the Deep Creek Mountains; other trucks still toiled behind them on the flats. "Personnel utterly exhausted by tremendous efforts," said McClure. "The novice sees in the Salt Lake Desert utter desolation and isolation/the excessive heat and glare/absence of live vegetation and water/silence/deceptive mirages and apparent lack of means of exit," he concluded laconically, "tends to reduce the morale."

The last vehicles made it across at about two in the afternoon. McClure knew that to try to press on any farther for the sake of his schedule would have been futile to the point of cruelty. The men were filthy, bruised, and worn; he ordered them to examine and repair their vehicles as best they could, and then to rest. They would aim for Nevada the next day.

WOULD THE MILITOR have made any difference? Probably not; it would likely have been just one more truck on the end of a rope. Jackson thought McClure had been wrong to abandon it, but maybe the studious engineer was finally letting loose his exasperation at the commanding officer who'd connived in his humiliation at Fort Bridger, and maybe in fact McClure had done the right thing. If the Militor had mired on its own, trying to come across the salt flats many miles behind the others, what would Sergeant Wood and his men have done then? Walked out?

In the wake of the convoy, meanwhile, the Goodyear Cutoff was in wretched shape. Those scouts whose motorbikes were still working reported twenty-five separate tourist parties stranded on impassable stretches of truck-churned trail. They would, like the soldiers, be forced to spend the night out there. When darkness fell, McClure ordered the searchlight projected along the road, so they could at least see where they had to aim for in the morning.

A few days later, Bill Rishel drove out to Frank Seiberling's road; he said it looked like a plowed field. Even allowing for his tendency to exaggeration, it's not hard to imagine the condition in which the army had left the unfinished keystone of the Lincoln Highway arch.

Rishel said later, "There were ruts hub deep and holes large enough to bury an ordinary touring car. The new grade looked like a terrain shelled by modern bombers. There were almost enough new planks buried in the mud to build a bridge across the mud flats." He exulted. Just as he'd foreseen, the route of the Lincoln Highway in Utah had been destroyed by the very expedition that was supposed to promote it.

CHAPTER TEN

Ghost Road

THE CONVOY PUSHED into the Deep Creek Mountains from Black Point. One truck had been damaged beyond repair in the desert; it was towed to Gold Hill, then put on the train to Fort Russell to be scrapped. Two others stayed behind until the service unit had fixed their snapped and buckled parts. Between mending those two, then repairing other vehicles that broke down or rolled off the road, the mechanics couldn't catch the main train. They reached Tippett's Ranch, in the vast emptiness of Spring Valley, at midnight and pulled up there.

The bulk of the convoy camped twenty miles farther ahead; they'd spent thirteen and a half hours going fifty-one miles. At one point they passed a pond by one of the far-flung ranches scattered in the sagebrush, and McClure called a halt and made the men bathe. They hadn't washed since Salt Lake City.

The next day was a Sunday, but he kept them moving. They were five days behind where they were meant to be; he pressed them on over the hair-raising bends and grades of Schellbourne Pass through Nevada's Schell Creek Range. Vertical, unprotected drops fell hundreds of feet beneath their wheels; Jackson thought it remarkable that they made the crossing without accidents. He said they went seventy-seven miles to Ely in eight hours and, given the conditions, that seems remarkable too. More plausibly, McClure put the day's mileage at fifty-one.

These daily numbers, however, and the convoy's schedule more generally were becoming irrelevant. The road in Nevada was so bad that all they could do now was go as far as possible each day, then stop wherever darkness found them.

WHEN THE LINCOLN Highway was first drawn across the map, Nevada's population was about eighty thousand—rather less than one person per square mile in the fourth-largest state of the forty-eight. Half of them weren't naturalized Americans; they were Mexicans or Japanese on the railroad crews, or prospectors come from all over the world dreaming of silver and gold. The only highway they cared about led to a mining claim. Even if they did want good roads, there weren't remotely enough of them to pay the kind of taxes that would build them.

The state's Department of Highways wasn't organized until 1917; it came into being only because the 1916 Federal Aid Road Act required it. The department's first report candidly admitted that before 1911, "the State of Nevada did not participate in any manner in road improvements." That year, $20,000 was allocated for convict labor; when it ran out, nothing else happened for six years.

The first construction program was planned in 1918. It envisaged three gravel roads running east-west (one of them the Lincoln Highway) and one running north-south. In a state covering 110,000 square miles, the total length of the system they hoped to provide was just 1,450 miles, and even attempting that much was problematic. This desert state was "more devoid of roadbuilding materials than any other," and large stretches of construction ran through waterless terrain—in one case, for sixty miles. This challenge was taken on by a new highway department with a staff of precisely thirteen people.

In 1919, the cost of labor and materials soared, and the department found itself "forced to seriously consider the advisability of ceasing the attempt to do construction work at all." At least half the proposed road system hadn't even been surveyed, let alone built, and unless or until the Townsend Bill passed, it seemed the only chance to get anything done was to find money from private sources.

The northern route, following the railroad down the Humboldt Valley, had lively boosters. Backed by San Francisco, towns like Reno and Lovelock had created the Victory Highway. This was the road that would come from Salt Lake City through Wendover, and they improved about a hundred miles of it by their own efforts. The Bay City and other interests in northern California ("being desirous of providing an inducement to eastern tourists to visit that region") promised $450,000 toward the work, if Nevada would issue a bond to match that amount.

By 1922, only $5,000 had actually materialized—but the Lincoln Highway Association wasn't asleep in the face of this challenge, and while San Francisco promised money, Detroit produced it. In July 1919 General Motors offered Nevada $100,000, and Willys-Overland another $20,000. It was meant to patch up the worst sections of the central route, and—unlike Utah—Nevada was grateful.

The Department of Highways recorded the donation in their second biennial report. "Too much cannot be said," they enthused, "of the energy and unselfish spirit displayed by the founders of this organization. . . . In no small degree, they take the function we believe should belong to the Federal Government."

In Eureka today, where U.S. 50 passes the courthouse, a stone plaque records the contribution made by General Motors toward getting the road built; but when the convoy came through, that work was all in the future. Along one stretch marked for improvement with the money from Detroit—along eighty miles of theoretical road between Eastgate and Austin—the highway department didn't even know what was out there. It said simply that it "had not had an opportunity to investigate this territory with any thoroughness." The Lincoln Highway, in other words, was a rutted dirt trail through an empty map.

AT GAEL HOAG'S urging, the dusty little copper town of Ely had worked hard to make ready for the army. Eighty thousand square feet of mill tailings dumped in an old ballpark were flattened, covered in soil, and seeded with grass to make a camping spot. Ely's workers laid in a water supply and built showers; with twenty cars now passing through Ely on the Lincoln Highway every day, it meant they'd have a place for the tourists as well.

They called it Citizens' Park, and local businesses raised

$2,000 to pay for it. Of course the grass hadn't grown by the time the convoy came to town; McClure grumbled that it was "bare and extremely dusty." He set the men to replacing wrecked tires and giving the trucks an oil change. A band of Shoshone wandered among them all afternoon, staring fascinated at the dirt-streaked soldiers and their work. No doubt many of the soldiers stared back; for the easterners, this was another world entirely.

After what they'd just been through, at least the new showers were a hit. When they were told there was plenty of water the men, said the *White Pine News,* "gave a cheer for Nevada and a groan for Utah." But Ely had, in fact, done well to manage any food or entertainment at all. Four weeks of industrial action on the Northern Nevada had brought the railroad to a standstill, and the town was running out of supplies.

A meeting of local businessmen reported that "many articles of foodstuff were already exhausted." Here and elsewhere, however, the railroad men were sealing their own doom. In the absence of trains, garage men had started running taxi services from Ely to Cobre, 140 miles to the north, leaving at five every morning. Another winner was C. D. "Frenchy" Vautrin; he got a contract to bring the mail to town in his car.

Now the army came, with their commercial backers. Crowds gathered to stare at the huge pneumatic tires on Firestone's truck outside the Northern Hotel, and on the Packard that brought the Goodyear band to play at the courthouse. As the convoy's recruiting officer, Captain Murphy, told all who would listen, "The future means good roads and motor transportation."

THE LINCOLN HIGHWAY through Nevada today is U.S. 50, also known as "the Loneliest Road in America." In the 250 miles between Ely and Fallon, there are only two settlements. These two, Eureka and Austin, have barely a thousand people between them— and even that may be an optimistic count.

In their heyday in the 1870s and 1880s, there were many more; at its peak, nine thousand lived in Eureka alone. Dubbed "the Pittsburgh of the West," the town had sixteen smelters, with toxic air to match, and mined so much lead that it could control the world price. As each lode ran out, however, Nevada was left dotted all over with towns either shriveled or abandoned entirely.

More might have come of Austin and Eureka if Utah had stood by its contract to take the Lincoln Highway through the Goodyear Cutoff to Ely. Instead, in a state famous for ghost towns, U.S. 50 today is a ghost road. It won the title of "Loneliest Road" in a *Life* magazine article in July 1986, whose anonymous writer muttered with ill temper that the road provided "neither services nor anything to do along the way."

Understandably piqued, and possessed of a dry western humor, the locals responded by producing a Highway 50 Survival Kit. This includes a scorecard; have it stamped as directed along the road, send it to Carson City, and Nevada will reward you with a certificate, a decal, and congratulations on having made it. Even the state legislature went along; it officially designated U.S. 50 as the Loneliest Road and put up signs to say so.

This jest has, however, obscured the highway's more significant past. At the otherwise excellent Sentinel Museum in Eureka, there's nothing about Henry Joy's road. The lady at the desk said, "I had a book about the Lincoln Highway once"—and then, like the road itself, her voice trailed off into silence.

On pavement today, it's a breathtaking drive through an enormous, spectacular space. In 1919, the guidebook said correctly that the journey "is one of great interest and diversified beauty." It went on to say, laughably, that "no difficulties should be encountered at any point."

"COULD NOT MAKE objective," McClure told Washington, "due to danger in going through canyon in dark."

The convoy left Ely at six-thirty in the morning. Hearing the trumpet call reveille before dawn, the *White Pine News* dryly inquired, "Who wakes up the bugler?" From Ely they crossed Robinson Summit, then Little Antelope Summit in the White Pine Mountains. The latter pass is so consistently sinuous that even today, speed restrictions are posted all the way. The mountains are green with scrubby pine, cedar, and white mahogany. Far below, giant dust devils whip across the sand flats in Long Valley, three or more at a time, each with a pale tan central column as distinctly formed as a tornado.

The trucks crossed the valley floors in dust-filled ruts that were twelve, sometimes eighteen inches deep. A relentless dry wind blew at twenty miles an hour, scouring grit across their faces. In the mountains the trail ran up steep, twisting passes climbing over seven thousand feet above sea level. The convoy meant to make it to Eureka—but after fifteen hours on the road, the snaking rise and fall of Pinto Pass through the Diamond Range was too perilous to tackle after nightfall.

Seven miles short of Eureka, McClure called a halt at ten o'clock that night. They stopped at Pinto House, the remnant of a mining camp in the mouth of the canyon, and slept as best they could on the ground around the trucks. During the night they were disturbed by rain, by cattle roaming among them where they lay, and by the repair unit finally catching up to them at four in the morning, after another day spent nursing the breakdowns.

The men were so tired by now that their telegrams seem only barely to cling to intelligibility. Cabling headquarters from Eureka, McClure said he was in Austin, Texas. He thought they'd gone seventy-six miles, while Jackson said it was forty-six. McClure was more accurate on this one; he was less so when he said they'd been driving over thirty hours that day, though it surely must have felt like it.

They moved on at seven-fifteen, then stopped for half an hour in Eureka. Jackson noted wearily that the Militor hadn't gotten there, and that it was now aiming to rejoin them farther along, in Carson City. Even as he wrote this, however, the unfortunate Sergeant Wood was still stuck in the garage at Salt Lake.

Eureka had planned a dance for them the night before—and had gone ahead and danced without them anyhow—so McClure made sure to thank them with the same courtesy he showed in every town. They were, he said grimly, "on the last end of a decidedly hard journey."

But perhaps, here, they had their first hint of blue ocean at the end of the highway. Though still battling through desolation, it was in Eureka that they met their first Californians—a news crew and a party of journalists sent to greet them by the *Oakland Tribune*.

The crew shot film of the Red Cross handing out iced tea and smokes, then followed the convoy down the lonely road to get footage of the trucks creeping through Devil's Gate. Now, the soldiers must have thought, one last push and we're there.

THE SCHEDULE HAD them running seventy miles from Eureka to Austin; it was impossible. By four in the afternoon, they'd gone half that distance. At a place called Willow Spring, a place of so little account that it didn't appear in the guidebook, McClure called a halt. Gas lines were clogging, springs were breaking, magnetos and carburetors were choked; the trucks needed work, and the men needed rest. "Remarkable that equipment remains serviceable," McClure said numbly, "with abuse given by these deplorable roads."

They stared about them at the blank emptiness of a sagebrush plain forty-five miles across. There was one house and two people, and no other sign of humanity as far as you looked to any point of the compass.

Austin was thirty-three miles and two climbs away. Hickison Summit tops the first ridge, and it's an easy ride today through a deep cut carved into the crest, then down a swooping descent banked around the flank of the mountainside; but here and there along the road, scraps of original trail still show in the sagebrush. Two wheel paths of red dirt snake haphazardly over the rough contours of the desert, with the sparse scrub grown back between them. You watch the land jolt and stagger about you, ragged and worn, and you have to wonder how anyone ever drove a vehicle through this.

The Toiyabe Range was more demanding yet. Two passes rise seventy-five hundred feet above sea level, and the drop down Pony Canyon into Austin is rapid and vertiginous. The convoy tackled it at four miles an hour; they lost another vehicle here, when one of the kitchen trailers rolled on a steep grade and was wrecked beyond repair.

There lay waiting for them "the town that died laughing." Austin had erupted into hectic life in the 1860s, when silver was found—purportedly by a Pony Express rider's horse—and it claimed at one time to have ten thousand people. It probably wasn't that many, but it was plenty enough, and Austin was the node around which a whole mesh of camps grew up. Among the likes of Clifton, Kingston, and Amador, it was the one place that grew from tents into township because, in return for their help building a road down Pony Canyon to the flats, it offered traders and businessmen free ground for their stores and saloons.

The International Hotel was brought from Virginia City in 1863, complete with fixtures and fittings; the bar had come from Bristol, England, via San Francisco in 1849. You can still lean on it today, and two of the three mirrors before you are original. The man who broke the other one was hung. He shot a man at the bar, the bullet went through his victim's head and broke the glass, and that was the end for both of them.

In 1919, the International hosted the convoy's dance. The men had arrived early in the afternoon, leaving time for the district attorney to take McClure and his officers on a sage-hen hunt. Meanwhile, the welcome committee had set up showers in the four cells of the county jail. Eager to wash off the dust of the road, one of the soldiers observed that he'd "never seen so many men trying to break into a jail."

Despite the liveliness of its welcome, Austin was already much declined, though the wonderfully vivid *Reese River Reveille* was trying hard to promote another silver bonanza. Across the masthead on July 5 the paper had shouted, "It's dollars to doughnuts a boom will hit Austin within thirty days." Editorials enthused on the subject, urging the town to "STAY WITH IT AND BOOST IT . . . when you win, you will not feel like a quitter. A quitter and a knocker never started anything, and never got anywhere except to a graveyard."

The boom never happened, and, albeit with good humor, Austin faded away. A couple of hundred people remain; high on the mountainside overlooking the sere expanse of the Reese River Valley, they have a fitting monument to past dreams of fortune in the Stokes Tower.

Ansom Phelps Stokes was an easterner, a railroad magnate, and a mine investor; the tower, a three-story folly built of native granite, was raised up the mountain by hand winch. Modeled on a medieval tower Stokes had seen near Rome, it was built in 1897 as a summer home for his sons. It had plate-glass viewing windows and a fireplace on each floor. They spent one season here, then let the place go. Now the windows are empty, the structure is dangerous, and it's surrounded by a chain-link fence. It gazes with hollow eyes over the wide majesty of the desert, with the dry beams of the wrecked winch still pinned to the rocks at its feet.

Austin had been made the seat of Lander County in 1862, two years before Nevada was given statehood; it lost that prize to Battle Mountain in 1980. Up there, of course, they have the interstate— but if you're not in a hurry, what fun is that?

As for the *Reese River Reveille*, it was a four-page weekly founded in 1863. When the convoy came through in 1919 it urged that McClure and his men be given "a royal reception, as . . . Austin just now needs all the publicity she can get."

Way out there on the Loneliest Road, Austin still has that need, but sadly the *Reveille* can no longer meet it. It was the longest continuously published newspaper in Nevada until in 1993, after 130 years, it joined the state's many other ghosts.

WEST OF AUSTIN the original route of the highway diverted southwest from the line taken by U.S. 50, running through the Desatoya Mountains on an even lonelier road that's now State Highway 722. It crosses Railroad Pass, so called because it was surveyed for the Central Pacific before they decided to follow the Humboldt instead; it drops through a plain of shimmering salt flats, then climbs to an altitude of 7,452 feet over Carroll Summit.

Even today, signs warn that this is a rough road. You drop from Carroll at twenty miles an hour through an eternity of S-bends; then the descent eases into a long, magnificent glissade that funnels into the narrow mouth of the canyon. A solitary house with a tin roof stands there, with a trailer home and a couple of barns; the road has an old concrete bridge over the tree-lined bed of Den's Creek.

This place was called Eastgate, and had originally been a station on the Overland Trail. It was either seventy or eighty miles from Austin, depending on whether you believe McClure or Jackson. The continuing discrepancy in their numbers begins to suggest that the two men, since they'd fallen out over the Militor, were now barely speaking to each other. Earlier, Jackson had written his telegrams to the Ordnance Department, and McClure had largely copied them verbatim (with embellishments for the benefit of the press) to his own superiors in the Motor Transport Corps.

Now each man wrote his own account. Jackson continued dutifully to record loose flanges and worn bearings; McClure was more inclined to note the scale and challenge of the landscape. The spare shorthand of the cables from both men, however, contains a tone of unmistakable fatigue: "Usual mountain and desert trails," sighed Jackson. "Usual deep dust sand chuck holes and ruts," groaned McClure.

Others among the convoy were in better humor, and Ike and Sereno Brett were still determined to enjoy themselves. They played bridge in the desert; in an old wooden structure covered with screening they set up boxes and boards for tables, hung lanterns, and set about dealing cards. "My young eastern friend," Ike remembered, "was on hand as a kibitzer." Growing weary of Jackson's unwanted advice, Ike went off to plan another prank with Sereno. The mad major "was, as usual, quite imaginative."

Ike returned and settled back to his game—whereupon Sereno came tearing through the screen door screaming, "Help, he's killing me! He's killing me!" He was covered in blood. Another officer rushed fiercely after him, clutching a knife that shone red. Sereno crashed through the game, sending makeshift tables and hands of cards flying, running around and back out again with his attacker in his wake, the pair of them dripping ketchup. Jackson "nearly fainted. He was white, and his hands were shaking."

Ike rushed out after his co-conspirators "to devise a finish." They bound Sereno's wounds, put one arm in a sling, and left him bandaged for the next few days. Finally one of the doctors pronounced him safe from danger, the dressings were removed—and still the luckless Jackson didn't catch on. No wonder the poor man was writing his telegrams on his own.

Perhaps this prank took place at Eastgate; it would be appropriate if it did. In the years to come, as the tourist traffic picked up through here before U.S. 50 was built, this tiny oasis would gain notoriety as "the most-talked-of stopping-place for tenderfoot travelers" because the cowboys at Williams' Ranch got in the habit of laying on a show.

In full sight of the tourists, one of them would be peremptorily shot. As the motoring parties looked on in horror, it would be explained to them that the dead man had been a cattle rustler; they were left to understand that killing a man out here was the merest bagatelle compared to the awful crime of thieving cattle. Meanwhile the "body" was strung up, apparently plugged full of bullets; it seems many easterners left convinced they'd seen a murder and a lynching. Elwell Jackson, after all, was not the first or last man to be fooled in the West.

THE NEXT AFTERNOON the convoy crossed the Fallon Sink, a place as desolate and dreadful as the Great Salt Lake Desert itself. In the doomy phrase of Nevada's highway department, it's "the lake of final disappearance" of the Carson River, an immense saline bed of gray-white muck quavering with a haze of silver mirage, and ringed about with lifeless dun mountains. The high ground seems burned to a pile of broken rock and cinder, exhausted with heat; that afternoon, it was 110 degrees in the shade.

The scene is dominated by Sand Mountain, a titanic white dune three miles long, rising 380 feet above the flats. Sand travels in treacherous drifts here, burying history as fast as it arrives; the Sand Springs Pony Express station quickly vanished beneath the dunes once it fell into disuse, and was only rediscovered in 1976.

This would in time be one of the stretches of the Lincoln Highway to be improved with money from Detroit. Thanks to local efforts, however, a rough fill had already been laid across the worst of it by 1919, and it wasn't as bad as the Goodyear Cutoff. The soldiers had to push and pull to get through, but only with some of the vehicles, and only for some of the way.

They reached Fallon at four in the afternoon; the town was all of twenty-three years old. It had started as a post office in Michael Fallon's shack in 1896 and was brought to life a few years later by the Newlands irrigation project. Water here was more important than the highway, just as silver remained the great hope of

Austin—but keeping your place on the road still mattered a good deal, certainly enough that Fallon was fierce in its dismissal of the rival Victory Highway to the north. With blind optimism the *Churchill County Eagle* declared of their transcontinental route, "There is absolutely no question that it will ever be changed."

The convoy seemed to confirm for Fallon that assured and rosy future on America's Main Street. The town made a great effort to welcome the army men, putting seventeen hundred pounds of watermelon and cantaloupe on ice for them. The officers responded with courteous if somewhat tongue-in-cheek assurances that the roads in Nevada "were not by any means the worst encountered." Perhaps relief fostered an inclination to be uncritical; now that they'd crossed the Fallon Sink, after all, they must have thought the worst was over.

Of course it wasn't—not quite, not yet. The next day, it took them twenty hours to go sixty-six miles to Carson City.

THOUGH NOT AS fearfully void a place as the salt flats, the desert southwest of Fallon is still ferociously harsh. It seems a landscape of scorched ash and wreckage, a litter of brown and gray rubble where even the sagebrush struggles for purchase. Dust devils totter and twirl under the empty glare of a silver sky; even today the road here feels like an illusion, a fanciful scratch on the bare bones of the world.

Amid these bleak barrens lies the gleaming sheet of the Lahontan Reservoir, a splash of incongruous azure painted onto blank rock and dune. It speaks with a glossy boldness of American energy, of that contrary determination to settle even the most inimical place and make it work. Started in 1911, the dam was America's largest earth structure, and it added greatly to the irrigation potential of the canal system already built from the Carson River. To come to Fallon and create an oasis there took a mix of grit and toil and chutzpah that takes the breath away quite as much as the fierce nature of the place itself.

The convoy may have been impressed at the sight of it; more likely, they were wishing someone had thought to build a decent road while they were building the dam. They had to chain the trucks together, five or more at a time, then push them by hand through unstable sand holes each time the towline floundered.

The holes were dry in some places, a foot and a half deep, and one portion of the road had vanished entirely under drifting sand even deeper than that. Other stretches were cloying wet quicksand—created, ironically, by seepage from the irrigation system—and these were so bad that even the officers' Cadillacs had to be forced through by hand. McClure noted in a tone of some astonishment (surely this didn't happen to a Packard), "Necessary even to rescue Mr. Ostermann's car."

The men laid sagebrush wheel paths where they could, or made impromptu ramps out of railroad ties. The two gas tankers buried themselves five feet deep in the mire; they broke through the hard crust of the trail's surface and sank without warning. The shifting sand on the roadside made detouring around these bad spots impossible—and that's assuming you could tell a spot was bad before you bogged down in it in the first place.

They had no choice but to drive on, sink, dig out, push, pull, strain, curse, drive on, and sink again; it took eleven hours just to get twelve miles west of Fallon. Without the tractor and a large measure of raw muscle, they'd not have gotten anywhere at all.

When they weren't in quicksand, they were on grades as steep as 25 percent. The kitchen unit got stranded far ahead of them; food couldn't be brought back to the men until five-thirty that afternoon, and some of them didn't get any at all. With the gas tankers marooned five feet deep, some of the trucks started running out of fuel. They had to ration it from one vehicle's reserve to another until (the humiliation of it!) the army was obliged to buy gas at the pump from a garage in Dayton.

The first section of the convoy finally stumbled into Carson City at eleven o'clock that night; most of the others didn't make it until two-thirty in the morning. One of the Macks and the tractor stayed back on the road, deeming it too dangerous to go any farther in the dark. At last they crawled up to the state capital at eleven-thirty the next day. Apart from the salt flats in Utah, McClure said this was the "most unfavorable combination of road conditions yet experienced . . . the most trying day of trip."

"The Lincoln Highway people," said the *Churchill County Eagle* back in Fallon, "are delighted with the successful trip made through this section; the local road boosters are rejoiced in the anticipation of this route now being chosen as a government highway, and so—everybody is happy."

CARSON CITY IS one of America's smallest and most appealing state capitals. It began life in 1851 as a trading post called Eagle Station; seven years later, Abram van Santvoord Curry bought the land and laid out a town site, unperturbed that "if all the people in Carson, Washoe, and Eagle Valley got together, there would be just enough for three sets for a square dance."

With some foresight, Curry planned lots for a state capital when Nevada didn't even exist. At that time it was still part of the Utah Territory, but Curry was rewarded a year later when the Comstock Lode was found. In the lee of the Sierra, fifteen miles from the frenzy of the dig at Virginia City, Carson was an ideally located service center. Logs were shot down giant flumes from the mountains, and the town became an enormous lumberyard.

As the wealth of the mines became apparent, Nevada was made a separate territory in 1861. With indecent haste, it became the thirty-sixth state three years later. Theoretically, a territory needed forty thousand people to gain statehood; Nevada didn't have half that many, but Lincoln needed the votes to get the Thirteenth Amendment through, and he needed the silver to pay for the Civil War. Besides, it wasn't the first time a state had fiddled the census to win seats in Washington.

The freight lines hauling supplies to the mines and taking ore from them to California employed some two thousand men and upwards of twelve thousand horses and mules. Then the "Queen of the Shortlines" was built—the Virginia and Truckee Railroad— reaching Carson from Virginia City in 1869, and Reno three years later. Carson got the engine house and the machine shop and, for a while, the railroad made the town.

Even so, ten other Nevada towns had already grown bigger than the capital. They wouldn't all last—Hamilton had fifteen thousand, and it's not even on the map anymore—but the Comstock Lode wouldn't last either. With the mines gone, it was only the business of state government that kept Carson City going, and government, in Nevada, wasn't a large kind of business. Carson's population peaked at 4,229 in 1880; by the time the convoy came through forty years later, it had fallen to less than half that many.

All the action was in Reno—and Reno was appalled that the convoy wasn't going there. Never mind that it was a city seven times larger than Carson; according to the guidebook, the route through Reno and around the north shore of Lake Tahoe was the "official" Lincoln Highway anyway. The so-called Pioneer Trail through Carson and south of the lake was just an adjunct, a branch, an afterthought. Even if you did take it, you were still advised to travel via Reno before you joined it.

Everybody knew that the Fallon Cutoff—the direct route to Carson that the convoy used—went on wretched remnants of road left over from the construction of the Lahontan Dam. It was thirty-six miles shorter, but it certainly wasn't easier.

In the weeks before the convoy's arrival, Reno's leaders therefore made strident appeals to the War Department to have the convoy rerouted their way. If that couldn't be done, they argued, the convoy should be split in two at Salt Lake City, so at least they'd get to see some of it. This, of course, would have suited the Humboldt Valley–San Francisco axis beautifully. They'd have gotten half the convoy taking the northern route through Wendover, opening up the possibility that the Victory Highway might prove a better route than the Lincoln.

Bickering between Reno and Carson grew acrimonious. RENO THROUGH SELFISHNESS MAKING ITSELF UNPOPULAR, crowed the *Carson City Daily Appeal,* claiming that Reno thought itself the only place of any consequence in the state—a high and mighty attitude that naturally irked all right-thinking Nevadans in every other place. Ely took particular umbrage, being particularly under threat of losing traffic to the Victory Highway. Reno charged that White Pine County was rife with bootlegging; Ely retorted furiously that such a slander was rich coming from Reno, known as it was for horse races, prize fights, and divorces.

The *Tribune* in Reno's neighboring town of Sparks was no less enraged, only it directed its fury not at those who'd succeeded but at those who'd failed. "Through the blundering of some pinhead," the paper spluttered, "the only way the 10,000 or 15,000 people of Washoe County can witness the caravan is to hike or ride to Carson. But Carson is all right. Their Merchants' Club is a hummer." The paper went on to congratulate the capital on its coup in being awarded the convoy, saying that it had "effectually put it over Reno and Sparks when it comes to real, live, energetic action."

Reno's problem, continued the *Tribune,* "is that the boosters in this section take all their time telling what they ought to do and patting each other in the back. A sort of close corporation, mutual admiration society. The boosters in Carson saw what they wanted and went after it—and got it. We admire them for their enterprise."

So what was the real reason the convoy went to Carson? Perhaps Ostermann and his colleagues in Detroit, alive to the threat posed by the Victory Highway as they planned the convoy's route, were determined to keep Reno out of the game. Or perhaps it was simple politics. Carson was where the politicians were, and the politicians were the people who most needed flattering—because if there was one state more than any other that had to back the Townsend Bill if it wanted good roads, that state was Nevada.

FRETFULLY THE PEOPLE of Carson waited for the army's verdict on their roads. They sent a delegation to Fallon to coordinate their preparations; they launched the Pioneer Trail Association and held a conference promoting the southern route under the banner SEE TAHOE FIRST. All the while they nagged at the highway commission to get the road in fair shape before the trucks arrived.

As the day drew nigh, word came that the lighter vehicles could be expected into the city from Fallon by noon, with the heavier trucks following two or three hours behind. Come Saturday, August 30, the citizens of Carson organized a chicken dinner to be ready for the soldiers at six-thirty that evening on the state capitol lawn. As the afternoon drew on with no sign of the convoy, they started preparing the meal, and they waited.

The first scout cars started trickling in, and still they waited. Darkness fell, and still they waited. Governor Boyle waited, and Senator Harrington, and Mayor Gilson, and the committee of the Greater Carson Club, and the Carson City band, and the ladies of the Red Cross—and the convoy members were glad beyond belief that they did.

As they stumbled into town in the small hours, they fell on the food until it disappeared "like mist on a May morning." The tables were spread with linen and ornamented with silver. The band played, and forgetting their exhaustion, the men danced on the pavement under flags and banners and thousands of electric lights strung along the streets in the balmy summer night. Then they threw their cots and blankets on the capitol lawn, and in the middle of the city they slept the sleep of men who had achieved much—who were, indeed, near to finishing a task that many had thought impossible.

The *Daily Appeal* captured perfectly the feelings of so many who saw them on their journey—an estimated 3,250,000 people in 350 different communities across the continent. "Carson extends the hand of welcome to the visiting members of the government caravan and trusts that in their two days' stay they will get a partial rest at least from their labors. They have made one of the greatest trips on record and it has been a test of their nerve, their endurance, and their patience. But it has proved the American spirit and what it is capable of."

THE NEXT DAY, mercifully, was a rest day. While church services were held on the capitol grounds, and the men were taken to Carson's hot springs for a swim, McClure went west to reconnoiter the King's Grade into the Sierra. Long stretches of the road were barely wide enough for a truck; for fourteen miles it ascended at gradients between 8 and 14 percent, with the summit of the first pass 7,630 feet above sea level. They'd been through some hard climbs already, but nothing like this.

The road was a twisting ribbon of sand and broken stone precariously cut into the mountains over sheer drops, in some places, of two thousand feet. The papers in Reno naturally said the ascent was impossible, and warned of dire calamities. If nothing else, the bridge at Cave Rock would surely fail, pitching men and machines into the bright, deep waters of Lake Tahoe below.

McClure had the soldiers go over their trucks as if their lives depended on it—because they did. He clearly thought losing people here was a real possibility. While they changed wrecked tires and checked worn parts, he called his officers to a meeting. There might be some among them who thought him a martinet, but this was going to be done right. It was their last test, and their biggest one.

They left Carson at six-thirty in the morning. Beyond them in the mountains, past the lake at the top of the ascent, the Nevada State Highway Department halted all eastbound traffic until the convoy got through. The Militor hadn't rejoined them; it was still stuck in the coils of the strike-addled railroad system, so McClure sent the tractor up first. It climbed halfway to a bad sandy turn and stood ready there to help any truck that looked as if it might start skidding.

Behind the tractor, he established a checkpoint at the foot of the incline. Every vehicle was gone over another time—testing gears and brakes, counting towropes and wheel blocks, checking oil, gas, and water—and then the heaviest were sent up first. The machine shops led the way, then the spare-parts trucks. The regular cargo trucks followed, then the ambulances, with the staff cars bringing up the rear. They were spaced one hundred yards apart; they went so slowly that a man could walk alongside them, carrying wheel blocks to anchor any vehicle that started to slide.

Motorbike riders darted up and down the line as they climbed, keeping the trucks spaced apart. For six long, nervous hours they crept into the mountains, their wheels grinding over the rough trail just a couple of feet from the edge of vertiginous slopes—until finally they came into Glenbrook on the lakeside at about two o'clock in the afternoon. They'd lost another of the kitchen trailers, overturned and wrecked, and one of the big Macks had broken down, but that was it. With evident relief McClure told Washington, "Crossing without damage or casualty may be considered noteworthy achievement for heavy equipment involved."

Still fighting their corner back in Carson, the *Daily Appeal* duly noted that the convoy had made it. "It was a nasty knock that Reno gave the road," the paper haughtily observed, "and it was absolutely uncalled for."

High in the mountains, the convoy pushed on around the

lakeshore to the California line. Hundreds of people from towns along the route ahead had driven up to greet them with a barbecue. Finally, at eight in the evening, they arrived at Meyer's Ranch. The owner had built a huge campfire and had hung lights all about the campsite; a Firestone crew set up an outdoor movie show and laid in a copious supply of cigarettes.

"Scenery throughout the route," wrote McClure, "was of unparalleled beauty and compensated for the many hardships of past several weeks."

It was Monday, September 1. Fifty-seven days after leaving the White House, they'd finally reached California. Behind them in Utah and Nevada, meanwhile, they'd left a dispute over the best course of the transcontinental highway that would fester for years.

CHAPTER ELEVEN

★ ★ ★

The Promised Land

CARLO GIUSEPPI CELIO came from Switzerland and moved to Lake Valley, south of Tahoe, in 1863. Only the Washoe Indians lived there then, but the snowy peaks and the stunning colors of the lake reminded Carlo of home. He had a store down the mountain between Placerville and Plymouth on the Cosumnes River; he kept his cattle there from October through the winter, then drove them up to pasture on the high ground in June. The journey took five or six days each way.

In 1859 Carlo had married Maria Giambini Sartori, and she bore him four sons and two daughters. Over time, as people settled the western slopes of the Sierra, the Celios did well; they bought Meyer's Ranch in 1903 and started a lumber firm and sawmill.

A long time later, Carlo's grandson Norman recalled the first cars coming over Echo Summit on Meyer's Grade. "I remember one morning," he said, "as a boy, I was out in the field and I heard some unusual noises . . . sounds I had never heard before. Well, I started running to the bottom of the grade at Echo Creek, about a mile from home. I could see these things coming down the grade, pouring out huge amounts of smoke. I don't mind saying I was really frightened." Before he got used to them, he'd hide among the trees. He said, "We had quail, bear, deer, and coyotes by the thousands. The lake changed when they started coming through in automobiles . . . that's when it all changed."

The Celios opened a hotel and store; it was, said the 1919 guidebook, a "splendid place to stop." As for the Washoes, while the tourists moved into the mountains, many of their young men moved out. Ironically, they often went to work on highway-maintenance crews. Today Meyers is just one of many resorts, with some three thousand people living there—but as this transformation began, the Celios played host to the convoy.

THE TEMPERATURE THAT night dropped to thirty degrees. In the small hours, those men who couldn't sleep because of the cold would have heard the tractor and the damaged Mack crawl into camp. A few hours later they were up again, and pushing on; it was fifty miles to Placerville, and it took twelve hours to get there.

South of Meyers they crossed Echo Summit, 7,630 feet above sea level. From here they dropped 5,800 feet down the American River Canyon on a road of dirt, sand, and broken stone; even today, it's more like free fall than driving. "Generally dangerous," McClure laconically observed, imposing the same road drill that had gotten them up the King's Grade the day before. He still took time to marvel at the dense forests of redwood and pine, and the spectacular rock formations in canyon walls towering a thousand feet above them.

They were greeted in Placerville that evening by an effigy of a hanged man dangling from a telegraph pole. Partly on general principles, and partly because they were alive to the public relations potential, the locals preferred to call their home Hangtown. They were close to Coloma, where the Gold Rush began in 1848; the story goes that in February 1849, "Irish Dick" Crone, "a desperado and a gambler," was strung up from an oak tree on the corner of Main and Coloma. It was a sensitive lynching; the mob had kindly relocated to this site, respecting the wishes of a sick man near the spot originally selected who'd been troubled by the uproar.

They'd called the town Dry Diggings at first, before the rough justice of the time made Hangtown more appropriate. Two Frenchmen, a Spaniard, and an unspecified number of Chinese are said to have gone the same way as Irish Dick. To the dismay of its livelier citizens, the town was officially renamed Placerville in 1853.

Waves of population washed in and out with the fortunes of the mines. The town peaked at 5,000 and was nearly empty at other times, before subsiding by 1919 to a modest 1,650. Mining continued, but a greater diversity of labor had arisen in timber, livestock, and fruitful orchards. Now tourism was starting too; people drove up to fish and hunt in the High Sierra, and Placerville was a handy base.

At eighteen hundred feet, they were "above the fog and below the snow"; they were "the Gem of the Mountains." Yet still people were moving out—many went to Fallon to take advantage of the irrigation—and the population of El Dorado County had fallen by 25 percent in the first two decades of the century.

To counter this trend, the people of Placerville were busy with Carson City in the Pioneer Trail Association, promoting the southern route around the lake. The road was so smooth, the *Mountain Democrat* blithely affirmed, that people had taken to calling it the "airplane route." Faced with competition from Reno, Truckee, and Auburn, the convoy's blessing of the road meant a lot, and the fact that the other towns had failed in their efforts to have the trucks go their way was much relished.

The airplane route being as smooth as it was, the *Democrat* naturally described the army's crossing of it as "enjoyable." That may have been pushing it, but they were surely right to say that after fifteen hundred miles of high desert and mountain, of dust-clogged ruts and scorching salt flats, descending the canyon now "was like coming home to God's country."

California was the promised land, the land of sunshine, fruit, and flowers. It was the land of the future; McClure's invitation to dinner in Sacramento was delivered to Placerville by airplane. Even better than that, once you got out of the mountains, it was the land of good roads.

CALIFORNIA HAD CREATED a bureau of highways in 1895. It was more a research body than a construction agency, but that changed soon enough. In 1910, an $18 million bond issue was proposed for a statewide highway system. The vote was tight (ironically, Los Angeles was against the measure) but it passed, and the California Highway Commission came into being to build the new roads. The commission asserted that when the people of the state voted for this project, "they expressed emphatic declaration that

California should be in the vanguard of the march of twentieth century progress."

California's vision was both farseeing and explicitly commercial. Highway improvement doubled adjacent land values, and it increased them more generally "within a large radius of influence." In consequence, it was thought the state would earn its $18 million back many times over before the road system was even built.

The money was spent by 1916. The commission shrugged that off, saying simply that "it was well understood that the sum would be insufficient to provide all of the roads specified." The people agreed; by a massively increased majority of nearly four to one, they voted another $15 million to keep the program going.

The great majority of the roads were concrete; nothing else could cope with the new phenomenon of the motor truck. Heavier cargo in heavier vehicles tore up all but the sturdiest roads, not least because many operators routinely broke the law and overloaded their trucks. The cement manufacturers saw their chance; in June 1918, they sold California 1.78 million barrels at below-market cost, "under an unwritten agreement . . . to encourage the use of cement in highway construction."

Meanwhile, the war sparked labor shortages and soaring prices, and the second bond issue evaporated even faster than the first one. Undaunted, shortly before the arrival of the convoy, the people of California approved a further $40 million for their roads. The commission said from the start that even this massive new infusion of money would never be enough—but in the space of a decade, California had embraced road building with a fervor that went far beyond the merely practical benefit of a decent highway.

The commission's report for 1920 concluded, "The value of the highways of California cannot be measured in dollars alone. They have a human worth far beyond their commercial value. . . . Not only is California's investment in good roads paying an immense dividend in money, but it is paying an even greater dividend in the added happiness and the added well being of the state's great human family."

Under the circumstances, the convoy effectively became redundant as soon as it reached the Central Valley. California needed no persuasion to build good roads; it had been building them for ten

years already. Along the course of its last two hundred miles, therefore, the convoy was no longer promoting the transportation of the
future. It was celebrating its arrival.

ELWELL JACKSON'S DESCRIPTION of the drive from Placerville rings
out with joy and relief. "Entire route down grade over bitumen
surfaced concrete roads lined with palm trees, through peach,
almond, orange, and olive ranches and vineyards. Populace showered convoy with fruits . . . fair and warm. Perfect roads."

Their destination was the sixty-fifth California State Fair in
Sacramento, and they were going to be a part of it. It was a huge
event; for weeks carpenters, artists, decorators, and mechanics had
been swarming over the buildings and grounds, the stables and
livestock pens making ready for "a show worth millions in a state
worth billions." The fair had moved to an eighty-acre site on
Stockton Boulevard in 1905, and new grounds and buildings had
been added since. Now, with the war ended, 1919's fair was meant
to mark in high style California's hungry ambition to become the
most productive, innovative place on earth.

By 1919, the Central Valley was one of the richest farming dis-
tricts in the world. Huge canneries and rice mills thrived, and in
the eager quest for modernity, the rice fields would soon be seeded
by airplane. In peak season, between sixty and eighty carloads of
refrigerated fruit left the city every day. With 160 passenger trains
running daily as well, Sacramento was the busiest railroad center
west of Omaha.

From the valley the food flowed out, and "a veritable sluice of
gold" flowed back to pay for it. Some 130 miles of the city's streets
were paved with asphalt; they were lined with stately buildings
and shaded by tall elms. In the business district along J and K
Streets between Fourth and Twelfth, banks and offices rose five,
seven, ten stories high, with larger buildings already in sight on
the capital's drawing boards.

Seventy-five thousand people lived here; it was the political
heart of a state whose population had more than doubled in the
past twenty years, to nearly 3.5 million, and whose potential for
growth and prosperity seemed boundless. The new Goodyear plant

in southern California was only one confirmation among many of this heady expansion, and thousands were moving to the state every day.

A picture comparing a redwood to the Eiffel Tower appeared, captioned "In California We Duplicate the Best." The *Sacramento Bee* ran an editorial pointing out that it was, of course, the Eiffel Tower that had duplicated the best, not California. The cartoonist had put "the cart before the horse; or, more modernly, the tonneau before the engine."

Over by the bay, the *Richmond News* blithely declared, "We don't know what the political outlook is, and don't care two shucks. We do know that the outlook for the biggest crop ever could not possibly be any better; also that the outlook for future prosperity in Richmond is just everlastingly scrumptuous [*sic*]. And that's enough for anybody to know."

The fair would encapsulate that mood. For a while, a railroad strike had threatened to force its postponement, but the strike was called off in good time everywhere except in southern California, and many people by then had taken to the road and ignored the stoppage anyway. Baseball teams traveled to their games by auto convoy; for the first time, the fast-expanding state motor vehicle department used trucks to carry car license plates from the manufacturer in Los Angeles to Sacramento. Army trucks carried the mail between Los Angeles and San Diego; the highway between those two cities was crowded with traffic, including a large hearse converted by one enterprising soul into a sixteen-seat bus.

Fruit growers moved en masse to shipping by truck. Los Angeles sent its entire exhibit to the fair—including displays of ostrich farming and of "crystallized vegetables"—on a caravan of motor trucks. The railroads nationwide, meanwhile, were losing $2 million a day; a cartoon in the *Oakland Tribune* portrayed them as a dying elephant. The truck dealers of Sacramento, who were by contrast gaining business left and right, contentedly planned to have seventy-five vehicles meet McClure and his men at Folsom. They aimed to make plain, with a grand parade from there, where the future of transportation now lay.

The fair opened on Saturday, August 30. So many car dealers had wanted to mount exhibits that they'd had to draw lots for the available space; their stands were arranged around the pièce de résistance, a brand-new airplane. Hotels in the city were full to the rafters; the chamber of commerce produced a folder for tourists outlining nine different motor trips round the region, and stressing how desirable a place it was to live.

On Monday, September 1, despite the rival attraction of the new Pacific Fleet sailing into San Francisco Bay, twenty thousand people came through the gates. Besides tractors, farm machinery, produce, livestock, and lectures on child rearing, diet, hygiene, and home economics, there were gaudy concession stands, fireworks, bands, boxing bouts, horse races, an art gallery, an aquarium, and spotlit nighttime stunts by a silver airplane.

Up in the mountains, meanwhile, McClure gasped to the notables who greeted him at the state line, "Please show us a good road." They were happy to oblige. With relief brimming over at the prospect, McClure admitted, "We have been fortunately blessed with good weather, otherwise we would not have made it." Some of the roads they'd traveled, he said, "belong to the Stone Age. It is impossible for worse roads to exist."

On Wednesday they left Placerville for Sacramento, leaving all their trials behind them. The highway, they gladly agreed, was "a revelation in good roads"—so much so that the newly invigorated drivers chafed at the speed limit McClure had imposed. They had a guest pilot, however, who was used to going more slowly. William Brown of Berkeley, ninety-four years old, had crossed the Sierra in a prairie schooner in 1849. He was the grandfather of the convoy's original commander, Captain Bernard McMahon, and now he guided his grandson from Hangtown to the fair.

They reached the city at about two o'clock and paraded through the business district and past the state capitol with their welcoming escort—including an artillery piece from the Western Front briskly nicknamed "Dutch Cleanser"—before heading for camp at the fairgrounds. Cheering thousands watched them pass; they were hailed as the "conqueror of every obstacle presented . . . an unprecedented argument for national highways."

Ostermann, McMahon, and Dr. Johnson waxed lyrical about their achievement and the lessons it taught. Riding alongside them was Austin Bement from the Lincoln Highway Association, busy plugging the Townsend Bill. McClure was more impassive, saying simply, "I was sent to bring the train through, and we are nearly done. . . . We have shown that it is possible to get through. I believe good roads will follow us."

A spectacular four-hundred-plate dinner was arranged for them at the local branch of the Willys-Overland Company on Thirteenth and K Streets. The menu was printed in a ten-page souvenir pamphlet; they ate razor-clam chowder, Sacramento River salmon, country-fried chicken, and "Overland ice cream." The pamphlet also contained an "Appreciation," which Ike in his memoirs erroneously attributed to California Governor William D. Stephens. It was in fact contributed by John N. Willys, president of Willys-Overland and, of course, a director of the Lincoln Highway Association. Amid justifiable high sentiment, after all, this had been Detroit's show all along.

"One cannot follow the trail of this Army Truck Convoy," wrote Willys, "without looking back seventy years to the days of the immortal 'Forty-Niners.' . . . They stand in revered tradition, makers of California and American history. So in this journey across plain, desert and mountain trail, you, too, have blazed new trails— the trails of Commerce, Highways, Mechanical Achievement, and the Protection of the Flag." For all that, the dinner's organizers knew not to let the rhetoric drag too long on weary men. Over the list of honored guests they put this reassurance: "Don't be alarmed, Boys, all Speakers have agreed not to exceed the speed limit— which is five minutes."

There was music and cabaret with a lively and varied roster of artistes. Back on the fairground, the War Camp Community Service had organized a dance for the men on a big platform in front of the General Exhibits Building, but few of them attended. The motor industry had first call on their time.

AS USUAL, SACRAMENTO tried hard to have the convoy stay another day; as usual, McClure turned the offer down. "Every morning when the men get up," he said, "they count off the number of days it will take to reach the end of this fight. They have worked from twelve to sixteen hours a day, and deserve a rest when they reach the coast."

They drove an easy forty-eight miles south through orchards and vineyards to Stockton. Jackson and McClure seem to have started talking again; presumably the increasing comfort of the journey's final days had eased any tension between them, and their telegrams from California no longer failed to match. "Personnel tired out by strenuous and continuous efforts of past several weeks," they reported, "but morale high at immediate prospect of reaching final objective."

In Stockton, film of the convoy on the road was shown that afternoon at the Lyric ("Stockton's Coolest Theater") alongside Elsie Ferguson in Paramount Artcraft's *The Avalanche.* The seat of San Joaquin County was a thriving town of forty-one thousand; like Sacramento, it was an inland port that had erupted into life when steamers decanted thousands of gold seekers after the find at Coloma. Although the gold fever had faded, cultivated fields had spread to the horizons. By 1888 California led the Union in grain production, and Stockton had ambitions to become "the Chicago of the West."

It didn't quite get that big, but by the early twentieth century Stockton was turning out all manner of farm machinery. In 1904, spurred to invention by the local problem of wheeled vehicles sinking in the soft, peaty soil of the Sacramento–San Joaquin delta, Benjamin Holt produced the world's first caterpillar tractor. This is considered locally "the most significant event in Stockton history," spawning as it did a substantial business that sold to farmers, loggers, road builders, and the military—and, incidentally, inspired the British to invent the tank. Certainly, the convoy wouldn't have made it across America without the aid of Holt's innovation.

The town boomed; in 1910 the *Stockton Record* spoke of "lightning-like growth." That year the Hotel Stockton went up, a striking building in the Mission Revival style. Unlike so many downtown hotels, this one has survived, and is presently being restored for retail and office space. In 1919, it was the site of Stockton's banquet and dance for the men of the convoy. They'd been met on Cherokee Lane outside town by Mayor Oullahan, other city and county officials, and a large contingent from Holt

Manufacturing bearing soda pop and cigarettes. They'd camped at Oak Park, swum at the Olympia Baths, and then made their way to another evening's celebration.

The mayor was considerate. In his welcome address he said he knew "that the terrors of their wearisome journey . . . were as nothing compared to facing the inevitable speakers along the route," and so he spoke only briefly. McClure replied with similarly brief thanks, before the more popular McMahon "made the hit of the evening" when he introduced his grandfather.

Asked how it had been, one of the soldiers told the *Record*, "Pretty strenuous. Up every night until eleven and twelve o'clock at banquets and dances and out in the morning at five and five-thirty to be on our way. . . . It's a great life if you don't weaken."

OAKLAND WAS SEVENTY-SIX miles away through the Livermore Valley and the stark, burnt-orange folds of the coastal range. The road had been graveled only in 1915, but California's concrete progress had pushed on so fast since then that Jackson now reported it the best section of the Lincoln Highway they'd driven on. The road, he said blissfully, was "unexcelled."

So was their reception. Oakland had been waiting two months for the convoy, following its progress across the continent with pride and fascination. Weeks of planning went into greeting the men, with Alameda County's Automobile Trade Association gleefully at the fore. Maps were printed showing the route across the state well ahead of time, when the trucks themselves were just entering Nevada. Every car owner in the East Bay was urged to join in forming a giant avenue of vehicles past the Chevrolet plant along Foothill Boulevard, through which the army would drive into the city.

The organizers were spurred on by Austin Bement; since joining the convoy in Iowa, he'd regularly updated them on its advance. They were led by Joseph Caine, the managing director of Oakland's chamber of commerce, who also happened to be California's state consul for the Lincoln Highway. Caine's ambition was a "continuous ovation" all the way down the road.

His plans didn't go entirely unopposed. When he and his

associates asked the board of supervisors to vote $750 toward enter-
taining the convoy, they met vociferous protest from board member R. C. Staats. Staats said it was the business community who
made money from "such things as wars and visits of motor transport trains," so business, and not the regular taxpayer, should pay
to entertain the army—a valid point, perhaps, but a rare voice of
dissent. Caine retorted that if the board didn't pass the money, he'd
wire the convoy that "Alameda County is not at home to visitors."
This threatened embarrassment worked, at least to the extent that
the board voted Caine two-thirds of what he'd asked for—and
preparations continued apace.

The original schedule had the convoy arriving on Saturday,
August 30, two days ahead of the Pacific Fleet. A few days before
that date, Bement cabled that they were "lost in the Nevada
desert" and would be six days late. The *Tribune* dispatched a five-
man party in a Studebaker to find them; racing to be the first Californians to greet the army, they made the five hundred miles to
Eureka inside twenty-four hours. It was, they boldly affirmed, "one
of the most daring and perilous exploits of moviemen" in recent
times. Their film of the convoy was on show at the Kinema Theater
five days later, when the soldiers were in Carson City; there were
now daily reports marking the expedition's approach.

The next morning, Monday, September 1, the Pacific Fleet
sailed into San Francisco Bay. With an airplane escort overhead,
fifty-two vessels bore fifteen thousand men through the Golden
Gate under the command of Admiral Hugh Rodman in the U.S.S.
New Mexico. One million people turned out to watch them pass in
review before Governor Stephens and Secretary of the Navy Jose-
phus Daniels; six hundred cars had followed them up the coast
from Santa Cruz in a cheering cavalcade, and now joined the masses
already thronged on beaches and hillsides around the bay.

Oakland and San Francisco gave themselves over to a week-
long party for the "jackies" or "gobs," as U.S. seamen were known.
There were dances and parades every day, and there was much concern over what might be the proper attire for young women faced
with this flood of testosterone now spilling ashore. Low-cut dresses
were banned, as was the shimmy. This "wiggly terpsichorean
movement," declared the highly alarmed Mrs. Florence Richmond

of San Francisco, was "the most obnoxious form of entertainment ever presented to the public. I, for one, will do all in my power to banish this unspeakable dance."

A tiff erupted at the university in Berkeley, where a group of young women preparing a dance show for the sailors were outraged to find their costumes criticized for being too revealing. Dancer Gladys Gervish waspishly noted that "if any of these jackies coming with the fleet have been in France, then they've seen more than bare legs and flowing draperies."

Matrons shuddered in horror at the news of stockingless women being sighted on the streets of San Francisco. In another disturbing display of female independence, Oakland's police chief was reported to be shocked at the skimpiness of the bathing suits now in fashion—but what could he do? "Pretty mermaids tell him to go chase himself," reported the *Tribune,* "and then they dive right into the Bay."

A tiff erupted between Oakland and San Francisco as well. Wednesday, September 3, was supposed to be Oakland's Fleet Day—but when it came, poor Oakland had a "dearth of sailors." Despite promises to the contrary, those wicked, treacherous San Franciscans had lured the gobs to the west shore of the bay with "counter-attractions." It was charged, naturally, that they were running their saloons wide open.

Amid this hothouse atmosphere, preparations for greeting the motor train became part of the larger celebration. The fleet and the convoy (now dubbed the "land fleet" and the "land armada") were to be feted together, representative as they were of an America newly visible in its role as world power, the master of ocean and continent alike.

To greet the convoy, Oakland's truck dealers called for nothing less than the biggest motor parade ever seen. As one of them put it, "The people of the United States look to California to do big things in a big way, and this is an opportunity we cannot afford to miss."

NEW UNIFORMS WERE sent to Stockton from the Presidio in San Francisco. Setting off at six-thirty, spick-and-span, the motor train rolled smoothly over Altamont Pass. By midafternoon they were heading through cheering crowds in Hayward and San Leandro toward Foothill Boulevard. Banners hung across the highway, fluttering on a light breeze in the blue and gold warmth of a gentle summer's day. As the first vehicles drew near, a rocket leaped into the sky, exploded, and sent a shower of Allied flags cascading on the wind.

Thousands of motorists had obeyed the call; the avenue was lined with cars as far as the eye could see, all blowing their horns in welcome. A flood of spectators poured from stores and houses as a Victory Chorus of two hundred girls sang to welcome the convoy into Oakland. Their reception, said McClure, was "tumultuous."

With the fire department taking the lead, the trucks rumbled into the city center on packed streets bright with the Stars and Stripes, raucous with applause. They passed down Twelfth onto Webster, along Seventh to Broadway, then back by city hall and the enormous Hotel Oakland to the auditorium by Lake Merritt. They parked in three long rows before the building; on the steps beneath the imposing facade, with its apt dedication "to the intellectual and industrial progress of the people," McClure addressed his men. "When we started," he said, "our motto was, 'We'll get there.' We did. I thank you."

Spread before him on the lawn in bright sunshine, the soldiers smiled and cheered, and from the crowds gathered around them rose "a barrage of congratulation." There was even greater acclamation from his men when he announced that tomorrow, their last day, they could start an hour later than usual.

They went boating on the lake and were given dinner in the Hotel Oakland's ballroom. They ate "Turkey à la Differential," with "Potatoes au Magneto." McClure planted a milepost in front of the hotel; when McMahon spoke after the meal, his popularity was such that the cheers of his men "nearly tore off the chandeliers."

Even Dr. Johnson got a cheer—in his case an ironical one for his public admission that, to avoid the worst of the Nevada desert, he'd taken the train from Eureka to Carson City. Then he said once again that every city in the West should back the Townsend Bill; once again, he urged that its projected appropriation for road building be raised to $1 billion.

Finally—speaking both for Oakland and for the Lincoln

Highway—Joseph Caine told them simply, "This convoy has made history."

The men made their way back to the auditorium. Fireworks burst over the lake, as well as a dazzling salvo of star shells and night flares. The army had used these in the trenches of France; now they lit the night to a happier purpose altogether. The band struck up, and the soldiers took to the dance floor. They had but one day left to go.

IN BRIGHT SUNSHINE on the morning of Saturday, September 6, two ferries waited in Oakland Harbor to take the convoy to San Francisco. Six of the Pacific Fleet's new destroyers were moored nearby; two of these weighed anchor to escort them through the battle-gray armada arrayed across the sparkling waves.

They unloaded at the Ferry Building; it took an hour to get them lined up in formation on the Embarcadero. Civilian and military motor escorts waited to join them on Main Street; at eleven o'clock sharp, the convoy set off toward Market Street. A platoon of policemen and a troop of the 11th Cavalry led them through the crowds, while bands played beneath vast floral arches from another parade held earlier in the week for the fleet. Above them, the windows of all the buildings downtown were packed with waving, cheering people.

Their line of march to the end of the trail was eight miles. They passed in review before the Civic Center, then drove on up Van Ness, Post, and Presidio Avenue to Geary. All through Japantown and Fillmore, families sat out to watch them on the high steps of their Victorian homes. It took an hour and a half for the full line to pass any given spot.

At Thirty-fourth Avenue, they turned toward the entrance to Lincoln Park. Here stood the Palace of the Legion of Honor, looking out over the shining Pacific; here stood a podium for the final speeches of their sixty-two-day adventure. A milestone was dedicated to match the one placed beside the White House, 3,251 miles behind them, and a pair of army airplanes circled overhead, showering the scene with flowers. Out on the ocean, the battleship *Arkansas* sailed for the blue horizon. "Another bright page in our country's history," said Mayor Rolph, "another joy for the people of the State of California."

McClure presented the laurel wreaths he'd brought across the continent for the mayor and Governor Stephens. Special medals had been cast by the Lincoln Highway Association—gold for McClure, McMahon, Ostermann, and Johnson, bronze for the rest—and every man was given his memento. Dr. Johnson completed the speaking with "a ringing oration," urging federal funds to complete the Lincoln Highway and to build a national system of roads. That, after all, was what it had been about from the beginning—and now it was ended.

"We venture the statement," said the auto section of the *Oakland Tribune,* "that if within two years the tour were to be duplicated over the same route, the Lincoln Highway, it could be made in one-half the time. Our feeling is that boulevards will exist in stretches now noted for their horrible condition. A concluding impression is that the land fleet tour has illustrated, very forcibly, the necessity for passing the Townsend Bill."

The Red Cross served a luncheon of coffee and hot dogs, cookies and pies, and then the convoy disbanded. The trucks were sent into service with the Western Division of the army; the men were detailed to posts around San Francisco.

"Theirs was a man's job," said the *Examiner,* "and they did it well. . . . They have proved once again that what Americans decide to do, they do, despite all odds of nature and mankind."

1919 SEP 6 PM 1 58
A 152 DA 25 GOVT
SAN FRANCISCO CALIF 10 25 A 6
DRAKE MOTORS RITCHIE
WASHINGTON DC

CONVOY ARRIVED FINAL OBJECTIVE SAN FRANCISCO TEN MORNING ALL EQUIPMENT ROLLING NO MECHANICAL DIFFICULTIES OR CASUALTIES DETAILS REPORT LATER

MCCLURE COMMANDING

★   ★   ★

The End of the Road

THE MILITOR ARRIVED in San Francisco five days behind the rest of the convoy. After Sergeant Wood had finished overhauling it, the railroad had taken over two weeks to ship it to the coast from Salt Lake City. It's not recorded whether Wood and his crew received their medals or not; perhaps Elwell Jackson kept these souvenirs for them.

Jackson stayed on in the city for a couple of weeks, living at the Hotel Victoria on Stockton and Bush. He watched as the trucks were gone over part by part to see how they'd fared, he wrote his report, and he fired off telegrams to Washington inquiring nervously when his paycheck might arrive. Finally he returned to Philadelphia, and received his honorary discharge at the end of October.

The following May, he presented his account of the convoy to a meeting of the American Society of Mechanical Engineers in St. Louis, Missouri. It was largely the same document he'd submitted to the Ordnance Department, though he'd tactfully excised from it any mention of his disagreement with McClure over the Militor.

After fourteen years, McClure also left military service that October. He went to work for Packard, as did his adjutant William Greany. Ironically, Packard's managers decided four years later to stop making trucks; they felt it didn't chime with the image of their luxury cars.

Greany appears to have proposed McClure for a Distinguished Service Medal; the army refused this recommendation.

McClure published his own account of the convoy in the *Quartermaster Review* in 1926. "Only those who accompanied the expedition," he wearily recalled, "can realize the obstacles to progress that were encountered." He justified his abandonment of the Militor on the grounds of "its frame having become sprung through attempting to pull itself out of quicksand." Either his memory betrayed him or this convenient untruth suggests he felt that he'd made a mistake.

Of the original eighty-one vehicles, six hadn't finished the journey. Apart from the Militor, they'd lost one truck on the mountainside in Pennsylvania, another had broken down beyond repair on the Goodyear Cutoff, and three of the four kitchen trailers had been "practically demolished" by the awful roads.

In the circumstances, however, it was remarkable that they got to California at all, and with so many of their vehicles still working. In the end, even Jackson gave McClure some credit for the "tireless energy" that helped to see them through. On short notice he'd taken charge of a disorganized rabble, and he'd gotten the job done. As for his men, many of them might not have known how to drive a truck when they left Washington, but they surely did two months later.

WILLIAM GREANY STAYED in the motor industry until his retirement in 1953. To mark that occasion, colleagues wrote to the White House to ask if President Eisenhower might like to send Greany his good wishes. Ike readily consented. "News such as this," he wrote Greany, "reminds me that it is thirty-four years since you and I—with a lot of others—went off on a jaunt across the United States. The time we took to complete that trip would make today's motorist believe that we must have done the whole thing by marching."

Greany was for many years a scoutmaster at the Church of St. Cecilia in Detroit. Every Christmas he wrote seasonal messages for the members of his troop, printed as wall hangings with festive borders. They urged decency and patriotism, and extolled the great wonders of the American landscape. Greany had, after all, seen a good deal of it. In December 1960, he put a poem called "Memories" in his scrapbook. He fixed beside it a picture of himself as a young officer with the convoy, and another of President Eisenhower. The poem read,

Happy days gone by,
Cheerful moments sped,
Ne'er to come again,
Nought but memory in their stead.

Joyful words and thoughts
Numbered with the sleeping,
Only come again in dreams,
And with the morning sun are fled.

A WIDE-ANGLE PHOTOGRAPH was taken of the convoy's personnel in San Francisco, but Ike isn't in it. When he'd seen Mamie and his father-in-law in North Platte, Nebraska, he'd decided to apply for a month's leave with his wife at the end of the trip. The request was granted, and he left California immediately for Denver.

Mamie's family spent their winters in San Antonio, Texas; this was where Ike had first met them, on his first posting at Fort Sam Houston after leaving West Point. So now, after two months' driving across America, he faced another long journey south by road from Colorado.

They had barely left Denver when it started to rain. It went on raining until, by the time they reached Oklahoma, the roads were a quagmire. They got as far as Lawton, southwest of Oklahoma City; then they had to stop for a week until the roads dried out. "There were moments," Ike recalled, "when I thought neither the automobile, the bus, nor the truck had any future whatever."

THIRTY-SEVEN YEARS LATER, President Eisenhower signed into law the biggest civil-engineering project in the history of the world: the building of the interstate system. By the end of the sixties, enough concrete had been poured into the forty-one thousand miles of that system to build eighty Hoover Dams. It's often thought that Ike's presidency was an indolent one—the joke has it that when you wind up an Eisenhower doll, it does nothing for eight years. But though the project soon went off in directions he didn't approve (he never meant for large sections of America's cities

to be ripped out and buried under freeways) Ike thought the interstates were his greatest legacy.

In 1963 he wrote, "More than any single action by the government since the end of the war, this one would change the face
of America. . . . Its impact on the American economy—the jobs
it would produce in manufacturing and construction, the rural
areas it would open up—was beyond calculation." To say that Ike
did this because he crossed the country with the convoy in 1919
would, of course, be too simplistic. He said himself that the convoy got him thinking about the need for good two-lane highways, but it was seeing German autobahns during World War II
that convinced him of the case for the interstates. Beside the economic advantages, however, by 1955 there was another, more
desperate imperative behind the call for better highways. On the
roads of America that year, the death toll was over thirty-eight
thousand.

THE ORIGINAL CONCEPT of an interstate system came from Thomas
MacDonald at the Bureau of Public Roads. In 1953, at the age of
seventy-two and after thirty-four years in Washington, MacDonald
was fired by Eisenhower. He'd been a widower for eighteen years;
now he went back to his office and told his secretary, Miss Fuller
(the only person who'd been allowed to ride in an elevator with
him), "I've just been fired, so we might as well get married."

MacDonald and his new wife went to the Lone Star State, where
he took up an appointment at Texas A & M University as the head
of a highway research center. The newlyweds traveled by train.

IN 1919, WHILE Ike was mired in the Oklahoma mud, the directors
of the Lincoln Highway Association were convinced that the convoy had been a hugely effective endorsement of their transcontinental road. More generally, they believed that it gave a massive
boost to the Townsend Bill, and to their longed-for system of
national highways.

In November 1919 Henry Joy wrote, "It is given to very few
mortals to see their dreams come true. Especially is this true when

for realization those dreams require the awakening of a whole people to a new order of things. . . . [Yet] the Lincoln Highway, in reality nothing but a dream in 1913, and by many thought to be a very wild and impossible one, is coming true."

At about the same time, Brigadier General Charles Drake wrote Joy to tell him, "If there is anything the Motor Transport Corps can do for you in the future . . . it will be only too glad to do so."

The War Department was now foursquare behind Detroit and Senator Townsend. In its annual report for 1920, General Drake enumerated the lessons that the convoy had taught. First and foremost, he said, "The necessity for a comprehensive system of national highways . . . is real and urgent."

To drive home the message, on June 14 that year the army dispatched a second motor train from the Zero Milestone. This one was to travel over the Bankhead Highway to Los Angeles, but road conditions in the South were "notably bad," and it took the new convoy sixteen days just to reach Atlanta. By the time Drake's report went to press, he had no idea when they might get to California, but he expected it to take about three months.

This was yet more confirmation of the need for good roads— but Detroit was now intimate with the highest echelons of government. On March 4, 1921, Warren G. Harding became the first president to drive to his inauguration in a car instead of a carriage. It was, naturally, a Packard Twin Six.

Eight months later, on November 9, Harding signed Senator Townsend's Federal Highway Act into law. It promised $75 million of federal funding for American roads for each of the next five years, and Detroit exulted. The new measure, said the Lincoln Highway Association, "embodies most of the essentials our organization has stood for from the start."

It envisioned "an adequate and connected system of highways, interstate in character." To that end, it required that each state should designate a maximum of 7 percent of its roads as "primary," these main roads being the only ones on which federal money could be spent. Since the Lincoln Highway was part of the primary system in every state through which it passed, it seemed that completion of a paved road across the continent along the line drawn by Henry Joy in 1913 was now assured.

WHEN THE CONVOY disbanded in San Francisco, Henry Ostermann returned to Detroit. He drove back there with Captain McMahon, the man with whom he'd devised the whole project in the first place. Ostermann's wife, Babe Bell, had died less than four months beforehand—so he now surprised all who knew him by heading straight off again down the Lincoln Highway and getting married a second time.

His bride was Sarah Simms of East Liverpool, Ohio—the same town that he'd placated with a Good Roads meeting when the convoy diverted to East Palestine. Their honeymoon was delayed; when it came, it took the form of Ostermann's first crossing of the highway of 1920. In the twelve years since 1908, it would be the twenty-first time that he'd done it.

On June 7, they stayed with friends in Tama, Iowa. The next day, Ostermann had business with the highway's district consul in Marshalltown, thirty miles to the west, so he left early in the morning to see to that, planning to return and fetch Sarah afterward. At first light, shortly after four in the morning, six miles east of Tama by the town of Montour, he pulled out to overtake a slower car. He was traveling at forty, maybe fifty miles an hour.

There had lately been roadwork at this spot. In soft earth along the edge of the grade Ostermann lost control, skidded two hundred feet, rolled twice, and was killed instantly as his head was crushed between the ground and the steering wheel. His face was so badly mutilated that it was barely recognizable.

Sarah took his body back to East Liverpool for burial in Riverview Cemetery. They had been married seven months. Distraught at her loss, she never remarried.

"He's gone on ahead," wrote Henry Joy. "No matter how great the hardships of heat or cold or storm, he was always pure sunshine."

OSTERMANN WAS REPLACED as field secretary of the Lincoln Highway Association by Gael Hoag of Ely, Nevada. He was a logical choice; he'd been an efficient booster for good roads in the West for many years. More important, he was also closely involved in the association's worst single problem.

A couple of weeks after the convoy's arrival at the end of the trail, Hoag drove through central Utah over Fisher Pass and along the Goodyear Cutoff. On his way, he met a road gang pulling out of the pass with all their equipment; they told him the road commission had ordered all work stopped on that section of the highway. At the cutoff, he found work still going on. But a few days later, a local motorist came to Hoag in Ely and told him construction on the salt flats had stopped as well. The work camp was being broken up, and the machinery shipped out.

Hoag wrote to Governor Bamberger of Utah; surely, he said, there was some misunderstanding. He quoted the contract between Utah and the association—"that work once having been begun it shall be continued with reasonable diligence until the same shall have been completed." He pointedly noted that "to this the good faith of the State of Utah is pledged," and expressed himself confident that the contract would be fulfilled "in accord with the generosity which provided a part of the cost."

He copied his letter to Frank Seiberling in Akron, who immediately wrote to Bamberger as well. Seiberling's letter was courteous, but nonetheless the president of Goodyear Tire & Rubber and the Lincoln Highway Association professed himself "startled." If the work had indeed been abandoned, he said, "I feel that I ought to know the reason and the intention of the State with reference to completion of the work as provided in our agreement."

Bamberger replied to Seiberling in mid-October. He said work had stopped because "practically all of the equipment was in very bad condition" and had to be taken in for repair. He added that winter would soon be upon them and it was "deemed advisable to stop all the work for the time being." Moreover, he was leaving for extended business in the East and would be unable to say when work might resume until his return.

In late January 1920, Seiberling wrote once more to Governor Bamberger. The tone continued to be cordial; Seiberling regretted that Bamberger and his wife had been unable to visit Stan Hywet during their time in the East, as they had done a year before. Nonetheless, he said, he was eager to see the work completed, and he asked when it was hoped that the Goodyear Cutoff might be finished.

Bamberger replied on February 3. He assured Seiberling of "a willingness to continue the work" but added that Utah was out of cash; the value of its road bonds had drastically depreciated, to the point where they couldn't be sold, and the state found itself "in a decidedly difficult situation." He then asked Seiberling for another $25,000—the money that the latter had originally promised for maintenance.

Seiberling proposed that he might purchase some of Utah's road bonds instead, to an amount sufficient to finish the work. It wasn't what Bamberger wanted to hear. Seiberling's letter was referred to Utah's state road engineer Ira Browning—who told Seiberling that he could give no definite assurance as to Utah ever finishing this section of the Lincoln Highway.

Now the tone frosted over. In early March Seiberling told Browning, "We have invested our money in accordance with a contract entered into with the State of Utah, have in good faith carried through our obligation, and I feel that we are entitled to have the state carry out its part of the agreement if it is possible for it to do so." Browning said it wasn't. Utah faced a deficit in its road fund of over $1.3 million, and the state's taxpayers weren't interested in spending money they didn't have on a road they didn't use.

Utah had reneged. The association called its behavior "rank repudiation of contract which can fairly be stigmatized as dishonorable." It seemed that "the keystone of the Lincoln Highway arch" would not be built after all.

IN 1920, AS this fruitless correspondence petered out, the apparently penniless Utah State Road Commission spent $4 million on road construction and maintenance. Naturally, the bulk of it went where the people lived, in and around Salt Lake City—but the state's choice as to where a link to Nevada should be built had also been made, and it didn't follow the line of the Pony Express.

Between Grantsville and Wendover—on the route desired by San Francisco and promoted by "the desert bedouin" Bill Rishel—Utah spent $32,000 in 1920. On the Lincoln Highway, by contrast, it spent $1,200 on maintenance that year, and precisely $8.20 on construction.

By 1922, when the Townsend Act had required that each state designate a primary system of state highways, Utah's intentions became clear. Urged on by Rishel, Utah made the Wendover route the primary federal-aid road west of Salt Lake City; the Lincoln Highway from Orr's Ranch to Ibapah wasn't even in the secondary system. Utah's leaders had abandoned it, and in 1921 and 1922 they spent no money on it at all. Meanwhile, the work begun on the Wendover road in 1920 continued in those years with a budget of over $70,000.

By the end of 1921, therefore, the Lincoln Highway Association was confronted with an unpalatable paradox. On the one hand, the passage of the Townsend Bill seemed at last to promise a national system of federally funded highways. On the other hand, in Utah, the association's own national highway was being erased from the map.

As field secretary of the association, Gael Hoag reported that from New York City to Salt Lake, the Lincoln Highway was now almost entirely accepted "as the national 'Main Street,' as a fortunate possession to those who have it, a pattern road to emulate, and a main trunk line to tie to."

Unfortunately, he went on, in Utah, Nevada, and California, "this spirit does not prevail." The fault lay in the jealousy between Los Angeles and San Francisco; the latter "has not been willing to accept the broad view" and had persistently promoted the Wendover route so as to bypass Ely. He charged that San Francisco had funded Bill Rishel ("an implacable foe") and that Rishel's people now routinely told tourists in Salt Lake that the Lincoln Highway west of the city was impassable.

Utah pressed on with the Wendover route. For two more years, lobbying, bickering, and legal argument clouded the air, while state and federal engineers studied the alternatives in detail. In 1923 the argument went to Washington, D.C., and Henry Joy spent $4,000 producing a handsome 172-page book on the subject, titled *A Brief for the Lincoln Highway in Utah and Nevada*. It was addressed to the secretary of agriculture, Henry C. Wallace;

the Bureau of Public Roads was part of Wallace's department, and the chief of the bureau was Thomas MacDonald of Iowa.

MacDonald was no great fan of the Lincoln Highway, or of pestersome private highway associations in general. He'd been enraged when Joy had criticized Iowa roads in 1916—he'd thought it "inexcusable"—and he berated the association for its "continued agitation."

His engineers recommended that the Wendover route be retained as the primary road west from Salt Lake City to Nevada. The case for the central route by way of Ely was argued persuasively in Joy's brief—though it was somewhat spoiled by the petulant demand toward the end that if the association's road wasn't chosen, Utah should give the group its money back—but in truth, the case for Wendover and the Humboldt Valley was a good one too.

Secretary Wallace backed MacDonald, and the Wendover route was finished in June 1925. Whether it was the right way to go or not, it was an extraordinary feat of construction; it included a straight gravel line over forty miles long through the very worst of the salt flats. Some $50,000 had been contributed to the work by "individuals and civic organizations of central and northern California"—so in the end San Francisco won, while the money put up by Seiberling and Fisher vanished in the sand.

In Salt Lake City, Bill Rishel congratulated himself. The desert bedouin had helped see off some of the most powerful businessmen in America—and that's why Interstate 80 goes to Wendover today. That's why, even today, the original Lincoln Highway in west-central Utah has never been paved.

THE ASSOCIATION PUBLISHED a fourth edition of the Lincoln Highway guidebook in 1921; it was dedicated to Henry Ostermann. A fifth edition appeared in 1924, dedicated to Carl Fisher as the father of the highway.

Two years later, Fisher lost much of his fortune when a major hurricane hit Miami Beach. Apart from the physical damage, real estate prices collapsed and business at his hotels dried up. Hard on the heels of the storm, the Depression killed off any hope of recovery, and in 1939 Fisher died in much reduced circumstances. He'd said he wasn't much for monuments, and (apart from the Indianapolis Speedway) he didn't get one. His name never stuck to the pass through the Stansbury Range in Utah; it's still called Johnson's Pass, on a road that leads to nowhere.

The Lincoln Highway went the same way as the fortunes of its founder. The completion of the Wendover route in 1925 was a defeat, but it was a local difficulty to which the road could be adapted. A more serious threat came the same year from MacDonald's Bureau of Public Roads, when that agency decided it would be easier for everybody if highways had numbers instead of names. In short, the highway was killed by the very success of the people who'd invented it. They'd gotten government into the road-building business—and, in the way of governments, Washington then opted for efficiency before imagination, bureaucracy before romance.

After a couple of years watching the new system evolve, in 1927 Gael Hoag wrote to Henry Joy that "the Lincoln Highway is pretty well scrambled." As far as he could tell at the time (assorted disputes continued from one coast to the other), their road was U.S. Highway 1 from New York to Philadelphia, and U.S. 30 from there to Granger, Wyoming. It became Route 305 to Echo, Utah, and 530 then 40 to Grantsville, before falling off the federal highway system altogether where Utah had abandoned it. It was a state road to Clover, and a county road (a barely improved fragment of a road) to the Nevada line. There it became State Highway 2 to Ely, rejoined the federal system as U.S. 50 to Sacramento, was briefly U.S. 99 to French Camp, and ended as U.S. 48 in Oakland.

Joy wrote back in tones of lament. He said, "We tried to put on the map of the United States a wonderful main arterial route from New York to San Francisco as a memorial to Abraham Lincoln. . . . The effort has resulted in total failure. The government, so far as has been within its power, has obliterated the Lincoln Highway from the memory of man."

Many agreed; as Hoag put it, numbers were for engineers, but names were for the people. The *New York Times* said sadly, "The traveler may shed tears as he drives the Lincoln Highway or dream dreams as he speeds over the Jefferson Highway, but how can he get a 'kick' out of 46 or 55 or 33 or 21?"

Route 66, of course, had no particular cachet at this time—and the Lincoln Highway didn't actually die in the minds of the people for at least a couple more decades. There was a radio show named after it in the 1940s; in 1939, Austin Bement drove from Detroit to the Golden Gate Exposition in San Francisco in a brand-new Hupp Skylark, and he still bore the red, white, and blue logo of the highway on either side of the car.

It had been, in its day, the most famous road in the world. Inquiries came to Detroit from Canada and Brazil, from Australia and Cuba to ask how they'd created it. So, for a long time afterward, if you lived along the road, it didn't matter what number Washington had slapped on it; you still knew its real name.

CHARACTERISTICALLY, HENRY JOY didn't long succumb to despair over the fate of his road. Never mind what he'd built at Packard; the highway, he said, "has been my greatest contribution to America's development. . . . We advanced the accomplishment of good roads beyond the question of a doubt, by many years." On another occasion he noted, with deliciously typical bumptiousness, "I was the Lincoln Highway Association."

In truth, however, after the success of the convoy and the passage of the Townsend Bill, neither he nor Frank Seiberling saw it at the top of their priorities. Joy was in poor health; despite that (or because of it), he had plans for an extended trip to Europe, and he had many other concerns and interests besides. Seiberling, meanwhile, was in increasingly grave difficulty at Goodyear.

Inevitably, by the summer of 1920, the postwar inflation had driven an overcooked American economy into the buffers, and Goodyear turned out to be hopelessly overextended. As car production halved, and demand and prices slumped, the company was left sitting on a vast excess stock of raw materials, with bills to match. Early in 1921 Goodyear was massively restructured, and in May that year the bankers forced Seiberling out. They charged that he left behind him an "utter absence of an intelligent system of finances, lack of coordination between disbursements and income, heavy contractual obligations entered into without knowing where the money was coming from. . . . There was no budget system."

That would be Frank Seiberling—and, typically, he refused to be bought out. He could have walked away a rich man; he was sixty-two years old, and he had an offer of $15 million on the table—but he turned it down. Instead, he stood by his stockholders, and took his share of the losses. He said, "I should have seen what was coming. All my fault. I take the responsibility."

He was left over $5 million in debt; he lost Stan Hywet. He wriggled and fought, his friends stood by him, and six months later he created the Seiberling Rubber Company of Barberton, Ohio. It never grew as big as Goodyear, but it did become the eighth-largest tire firm in America. He got his mansion back and, with his customary panache, in 1927 he paid off his debts by walking into the bank with the entire sum in a suitcase in cash.

Under the circumstances, neither he nor Henry Joy wanted to be president of the Lincoln Highway Association anymore. In 1920 they swapped the job reluctantly back and forth between them, before J. Newton Gunn of the U.S. Rubber Company took up the reins and gave them rest. They continued, naturally, to take great interest in the association's activities—but once the Townsend Bill was passed, the question arose as to what purpose the association now served, and what more it could actually do.

IN 1922, THE association built an "ideal section" between Dyer and Schererville in Indiana. It was forty feet wide, it had a concrete surface ten inches thick and packed with reinforcing steel, and it featured wide shoulders, a median divide, good drainage, and lighting. A memorial bench dedicated to Henry Ostermann was set beside it in 1926, in a tree-banked nook looking out over the road, and it's still there today. Unfortunately, it's hard to see it because, in one of the many ironies hanging over this story, U.S. 30 along here is now a teeming four-lane, and there's nowhere to stop.

The ideal section was the last object lesson in good roads that the association produced; too much of the rest of its time was absorbed in the Utah controversy. Joy disagreed with Hoag over

THE END OF THE ROAD : 225

their retention of legal counsel in Salt Lake City on this matter. He felt it demeaned their original ideals, and that people locally should either do their part voluntarily or not do it at all.

The dispute dragged on until 1927; the association began to waver. Seiberling suggested that since the Wendover route had been built, maybe they should just give in and call that the Lincoln Highway. Then Nevada could build a link from Wendover to Ely, and tourists could rejoin the original road from there. At first Joy said, "I cannot agree very enthusiastically." On the other hand, since a road was indeed now built "where no crossing ever was dreamt of until Uncle Sam's pocketbook was opened," perhaps Seiberling was right. Joy wrote to concur with him that they should designate the northern route and be done with it.

Gael Hoag couldn't agree, and nor could Sidney Waldon. They thought accepting the Wendover route would be a serious breach of faith with the people of central Nevada who had stood by them all this time. Joy urged them to accept the reality on the ground. The road to Wendover had been finished, and neither Utah nor Washington, D.C., would build a second road across the desert. Construction of the original Ibapah route was now "so dim a future possibility as to be out of consideration." The best road, he said, was the one that was built. "I am disappointed at this outcome, but it is not our own fault."

He told Seiberling they should "close up while the closing is good." Those wanting to stand by the original route were "a little too sentimental about the cents-dollars that, due to the perfidy of the state of Utah, has been wasted. But that is a petty matter . . . because the great work has been accomplished on a far bigger and a far better basis than our wildest dreams ever warranted us in looking forward to."

Nonetheless, in October 1927, the executive committee of the Lincoln Highway Association still decided to adhere to the original route. Joy wasn't present at that meeting, and he was annoyed at what they'd done. He told Seiberling that Hoag was only pressing on like this because he came from Ely, and because he didn't want to lose his job. He said they had $60,000 in trust funds, so they should give it all back to their donors and call it a day.

The full board of the association met on December 2 at the

Detroit Athletic Club. Its members now proposed to accept the Wendover route as part of the Lincoln Highway; the highway would then follow the link from Wendover down to Ely (though this wasn't yet built) and return to its original course.

Again Joy disagreed. If they went by Wendover, he said, they should stay with the northern route all the way down the Humboldt Valley, *because it was there*. Going back down to Ely was "pure sentimentalism." Against all their principles, it would be the first time they'd ever proposed to make the route longer.

The argument batted back and forth. Joy told Austin Bement that he and Hoag "seem to have a latent idea in your systems that the Lincoln Highway via Fisher Pass and the Seiberling Section to Ely will be built in the comparatively near future, Mr. Hoag says possibly within ten years. My best judgment would place it a century or two or three away in the future, if ever."

As it turned out, he was right. For some of the others, however, it was just desperately hard to accept. Bement told Seiberling that, after all their efforts, he could not tolerate shifting the route north to the Victory Highway "so that we can wash our hands of the situation and say that *the* road is finished—when *our* road is not." He grieved that it was the first time he'd ever disagreed with Henry Joy. Meanwhile, Joy told Waldon that if they went with the Wendover-Ely link, if they "put on the map of the United States a Lincoln Highway with such a 'broken back' in the middle of it, then I will regret all my life that I ever started the work, or ever had anything to do with it. . . . I am sorry to have to be such a cantankerous objector, and differ with my good friends; but you know the evil of my disposition, and when I feel that I am right, I have got to scrap until I am perfectly certain that I am licked!"

For once, he was licked. Roy Chapin moved that they accept the Wendover-Ely detour until the original route was finished through Utah. Bement seconded the motion, and all voted in favor except Joy. Joy said he'd expressed his views and was satisfied to leave it at that—but in the end, it didn't matter either way.

They were arguing about a road that existed only in their minds. It had existed only in their minds when they'd invented it in 1913, and it had existed only on the map for a dozen years. Then, in 1925, the Bureau of Public Roads stepped in and did everything by numbers—so now the road existed only in their minds again. The Wendover-Ely link would be finished in 1930—Ely would have a three-day celebration—and they could call it part of the Lincoln Highway if they wanted. In reality, it would be U.S. 93.

At the Detroit Athletic Club, they voted that the "active and aggressive operations" of the association should cease. Gael Hoag would lose his job; Chapin, Bement, and Joy voted him a parting bonus of $1,500.

"So far as I know," Joy wrote Bement in the last days of 1927, "everything is all over. . . . The Association seems to be in a moribund state; it wants to die and can't. No one wants to give it even any cold victuals. Our closing up with a 'blaze of glory' seems to be rather a sneaking retirement to a cold and icy morgue."

Hoag closed their offices in the General Motors building downtown, but he had one last piece of business to oversee. In 1928, with materials contributed by their friends in the cement industry, he arranged for the manufacture of three thousand concrete Lincoln Highway marker posts—just less than one marker for every mile of the road. Each had the red, white, and blue logo with the big blue L in the middle; each had a small directional arrow and a bronze medallion with a bust of Lincoln. Each bore the words "This highway dedicated to Abraham Lincoln."

Hoag organized the distribution of the markers to towns and cities on the road from one ocean to the other. On September 1, 1928, all along the length of this imaginary line across the continent, troops and Boy Scouts lowered the markers into prepared holes. They leveled them, tamped the soil in tight, and went home.

If you know where to look, you can still find a few of them today.

IN NEVADA, THE last link on the Victory Highway was finished in 1927, when the fifty-eight-mile stretch between Fernley and Lovelock was improved. The Victory Highway became U.S. 40; bitter battles continued between this road and the Lincoln route along U.S. 50 for years.

The towns on U.S. 40 said theirs was the "Main Line," and they put up signs to say so. U.S. 50's backers subsidized the

Western service station at Wendover, seeking to have it divert tourists south through Ely. The *Fallon Standard* called the Victory camp "incensed paranoiacs" and said their road was plagued with clouds of huge mosquitoes.

Despite these efforts, four-fifths of the traffic ended up on U.S. 40. That's why Interstate 80 runs along the Humboldt Valley today, and that's why U.S. 50 is the Loneliest Road.

HENRY JOY SPENT his retirement noisily riding his considerable collection of hobby horses. He ordered a new boat, *Spray III,* and gave its builders hell in detail as he pursued them with inventions and suggestions and minute specifications for every last thing on board, right down to the hooks and hangers in his wife's cupboards.

He built himself a radio station at Joy Ranch, his farm by the Selfridge Field air base at Mount Clemens. Its call sign was JOY SXAE, and he wrote with typically effusive enthusiasm about the potential of the new medium. With equally typical vigor, he also wrote to everybody he could think of—up to and including Edwin Denby, the secretary of the navy—about the vexing interference caused by Detroit's poorly tuned naval radio station. "Everybody within a range of hundreds of miles in America and Canada knew the Station NRQ was wrong," he fulminated, "except the Navy!" It was, he said, "objectionable, out of tune, and with defective and obsolete equipment"—so he went around and fixed it himself.

This, however, was only one minor example of the irksome incompetence of government. Washington provoked him in all manner of ways, and he lobbied ferociously over every issue that stirred him. He was appalled that Washington was riding its allies in Britain and France so hard for the repayment of their war debts; by the mid-twenties he was warning already of the dangers of a resurgent Germany, and once again he began preaching national preparedness. Nobody listened; by the late thirties, the United States Army ranked sixteenth in the world, behind even Romania.

He became increasingly eccentric in his tirades against pacifism, treason, sedition, and slackerism—but no one thing seems to have bothered him more than Prohibition. The Volstead Act, he said, was "insane, unwise, and impracticable," and the conditions resulting from it "a disgrace, wicked, and utterly futile." When his brother-in-law Senator Truman Newberry declared himself in favor of Prohibition, Joy snorted in derision to a mutual friend that Truman must have been drunk when he said that.

Joy became so irate over the issue that he stopped his contributions to the Republican Party; in 1927, for the first time in his life, he voted for a Democrat. "We have a condition of civil war existing in the United States today," he wrote, "where approximately one half of the people are seeking to put the other half of the people in the penitentiary." At the mansion at Grosse Pointe Farms, he had bootleggers bringing liquor from Canada into his own harbor on Lake St. Clair. Who the customer for these particular deliveries might be he didn't say, but the consequence was shoot-outs on his lawn, a search of his boathouse, and the seizure from his poor old watchman of eleven bottles of beer.

On March 11, 1927, he wrote to the deputy prohibition commissioner in Detroit, "May I ask if you think my premises are going to be a frequent battleground during the coming season of navigation, or is the situation under control? Such shooting affrays as occurred on my premises last summer are most unpleasant." A. J. Hanlon wrote back to Joy on behalf of the Treasury Department. He told him that he'd met him at Espia in Mexico in 1917, when he was on the Punitive Expedition hunting Pancho Villa. Joy had given Hanlon a carton of cigarettes, and "this I have never forgotten." It's not clear whether Joy was appeased.

He died in 1936, just short of his seventy-second birthday, after a life more full than most of us can imagine. He had been, in Austin Bement's words, "a powerful personality, an executive genius, a man among men, a [Theodore] Roosevelt type, a lover of the open road and trail." Carl Fisher had told Bement in 1923, "Any damn fool can have a notion . . . but it takes a lot of work to produce the results, and I think Mr. Joy particularly deserves more credit than anybody else."

Three years after Joy's death, his wife arranged for a monument to be erected in his memory, and she put it in the most touchingly appropriate of places. Drive west from Rawlins on Interstate 80 into the empty majesty of Wyoming, and take exit 184 onto Continental Divide Road. Turn south under the interstate, go right on a strip of deteriorated asphalt by the sign that says END STATE MAINTENANCE, then swing left after a short distance onto a narrow gravel track to the flat top of a low rise.

Here, for sixty-two years, a dark grey obelisk stood on the windswept earth. An inscription read, "That there should be a Lincoln Highway across the country is the important thing."

Helen Joy's monument to her husband was surrounded by a square iron railing, anchored at each corner by a 1928 concrete marker post. Over the years, vandals shot or prized the bronze medallions off each one. There was no sign on the interstate to tell you that the memorial stood there, and no guidebook that I came across ever mentioned it. A couple of miles to the south, freight trains thundered down the rails through the sagebrush; a few hundred yards to the north, traffic whisked salong the four-lane highway.

Then, in the fall of 2001, the Henry Joy Monument was moved from this lonely and forgotten site by the Continental Divide interchange. Thanks to efforts of local members of the present-day Lincoln Highway Association, in collaboration with the Wyoming Department of Transportation, it now stands beside the massive bust of Lincoln at Interstate 80's Summit rest area at the head of Telephone Canyon. Here, the many thousands who pass through each day can easily see it—and thus, perhaps, one of the most important men in the story of the American road finally receives his appropriate recognition.

PACKARD WAS THE only independent luxury carmaker to survive the Depression. A 1938 advertisement titled "Social Mirror" said smoothly, "The woman of social prominence cannot and should not choose her motor car as others do. For she requires more than mere transportation. . . . A large, fine Packard, more than any other car, so exactly mirrors your position."

The company spent World War II making airplane engines; after the war it lost its way. At the Classic Car Museum in Canton, manager Gary Pelger said, "They got too much like an old man's car. When I was a young guy, I'd have been embarrassed to sit in one."

Packard merged with Studebaker in 1956, and production was

moved to South Bend, Indiana. Nearly half a century later, the Packard plant on East Grand Boulevard in Detroit still stands—a vast, echoing brick wreckage of a place with a million broken windows.

The last Packard came off the line in South Bend in 1958. At Fair Acres on Lake Shore Road in Grosse Pointe Farms, Helen Hall Joy died the same year, at the age of eighty-eight. Born with money older by an industrial age than the motor people, she had outranked all in Detroit society; she had been the city's grandest grande dame.

The *Detroit Free Press* wrote, "Her death ended an era. It was an era that began in the warm glow of gaslight and terminated in the awful glare of nuclear explosion. . . . She was the city's friend, benefactor, conscience."

For forty-four years, until her death, "as proof positive that her family was pre-automobile," Helen Joy had driven an electric-powered navy blue brougham. She had bought it (or her husband had bought it for her) in 1914.

In her last years, she'd seen the mansions tumble down around her. Her brother Senator Newberry had had a stroke; his house was called Drybrook, and had been large enough that it had had "half the Detroit Symphony Orchestra in there, or more." By the end he lived with a trained nurse in one small part of it, and the rest of it was shut down.

He died in 1945. Drybrook went up for sale but nobody wanted it, so in 1950 the auctioneers moved in. The buyers made off with the paneling—the butternut, the Italian walnut, the mahogany; the crystal chandeliers went, and a church bought the senator's den for a sacristy. The house was torn down, and the lot subdivided. Before her death Helen Joy had said of Fair Acres, "This one will go when I go."

And so it did. Today, where once Henry Joy looked down across the wide spread of his lawn to the lakeshore, there's a four-lane road.

Notes

CHAPTER ONE: ZERO MILESTONE

General newspaper sources: *Washington Evening Star, Washington Post.*

3 *one of his biographers:* Stephen E. Ambrose, *Eisenhower* (New York: Simon & Schuster, 1983).

4 *"He was greatly upset":* quoted in Merle Miller, *Ike the Soldier* (New York: Perigree, 1988).

5 *"adopted with unqualified success":* Packard ad, *Washington Evening Star,* July 6, 1919.

8 *"The great feat of the motor transport":* quoted in the *Washington Evening Star,* July 7, 1919, and reprinted nationwide.

Unveiled from its white wrapping: The Zero Milestone that stands by the White House today was set there in 1923; it was paid for by the motor industry. The milestone unveiled by Secretary of War Baker in 1919 was a replica. It was hoped that President Wilson would dedicate the original marker, and one of Eisenhower's biographers actually has him strolling down the White House lawn to do so. When the convoy set off, however, Wilson was still one day's sailing out of New York, returning from the Versailles Peace Conference.

CHAPTER TWO: A ROAD ACROSS AMERICA

11 *when the car appeared:* The world's first gas-fueled automobile was a three-wheeler called the Patent Motorwagon, driven by Otto Benz in Germany in 1885. Claimants to the title of inventor of America's first car include Henry Nadig of Allentown, Pennsylvania, in 1889, Gottfried Schloemer of Milwaukee in 1890, and Charles Black of Indianapolis in 1891. However, credit usually goes to Frank and Charles Duryea of Chicopee Falls, Massachusetts. They got a car on

the road in 1893, were the first to sell it as a commercial proposition, and won America's first car race in Chicago in 1895.

the Good Roads Movement: The movement was born during the bicycle craze of the 1890s. With the invention of the pneumatic tire,
millions of Americans took to the saddle; when they got into the
countryside, they were appalled at the rutted dirt tracks they had to
ride on. The League of American Wheelmen (there were more than
a few wheelwomen too) was organized by Colonel Albert Augustus
Pope of Toledo, a bicycle manufacturer who went on to produce
automobiles; the league was the spearhead of the movement until
the car appeared. Pope said bluntly, "American roads are the worst
in the civilized world, and always have been."

12 *"more nerve than a government mule":* Mark S. Foster, *Castles in the Sand:
The Life and Times of Carl Graham Fisher* (Gainesville: University
Press of Florida, 2000).

21 *"the connecting link between the romance":* Morris Jo White, "Automobile Pioneers," *Pearson's Magazine,* July 1911.

22 *"well put up": Detroit News,* November 1, 1905.

25 *Their destination was Wyoming:* See Hoag's *The Lincoln Highway.*
Other trips undertaken by Joy—to New Mexico in 1912 and to San
Francisco in 1915—were vividly recounted in Packard's in-house
magazine.

28 *"Under no circumstances can I endorse":* I am indebted to Jesse Petersen
of Tooele, Utah, for showing me this telegram.

29 *As for Governor Ammons of Colorado:* A few weeks earlier, Carl Fisher
had led seventy people in seventeen cars on the Hoosier Tour from
Indianapolis to Los Angeles. They were lavishly feted by Ammons
as they passed through his state, which spent $500,000 improving
the road for them over the Berthoud Pass and elsewhere.

Ammons naturally assumed the Lincoln Highway would follow
the Hoosiers across Colorado—but since the Berthoud Pass was
some twenty-five hundred feet higher above sea level than Joy's
route through Wyoming, there was never any chance of that.

As one historian dryly observes: Drake Hokansen.

the association's first secretary, A. R. Pardington: Pardington was a
booster for the Indiana motor industry and an organizer of car races.
He died in July 1915, "following a breakdown from overwork."
Henry Joy wrote solemnly, "Thousands gave dollars to the cause.
Pardington gave himself."

Pardington was replaced by a Detroit advertising man named
Austin Bement. Bement was Joy's man, and an inspired appoint-

ment who became a prolific promoter of the Lincoln Highway. He estimated that, during the peak years of their activity, he placed over one thousand words about the road in American newspapers every single day.

33 *"He considered that the condition of the average roads":* Erna Risch, *Quartermaster Support of the Army: A History of the Corps 1775–1939* (n.p.: Quartermaster Historian's Office, 1962).

One line of approach was to push legislation: Pressure on legislators came from highway associations, automobile clubs, and businesses all over the country. The first result was the Federal Aid Road Act, signed into law on July 11, 1916. It appropriated $75 million over a five-year period to improve rural post roads, but it wasn't a great piece of lawmaking. There was no systematic national plan built into it, the opportunities for pork-barrel boondoggles were legion, and money went into unconnected bits and pieces of road all over the place. Nonetheless, it was a first step. It established the principle that the federal government should get involved; crucially, it mandated that those states that still didn't have a highway department had to create one or they wouldn't see any of Washington's money.

35 *Lieutenant Colonel J. M. Walker:* Adjutant General's Office, Files 1917–1925, Mexican Expedition Box 2020, National Archives, Modern Military Records Branch, College Park, Maryland.

37 *The* Chicago Tribune *called Ford an anarchist; Ford sued:* The case came to court at Mount Clemens, Michigan, in 1919, concluding while the convoy was in Wyoming. It lasted three months and had many surreal moments. A lawyer questioned at one point whether Henry Ford could actually read; Ford himself conceded that he was "an ignorant idealist."

After ten hours' deliberation, the jury decided that the *Tribune* had indeed slandered Ford when it called him an anarchist. Instead of awarding the $1 million in damages he sought, however, they gave him six cents.

A group of newspapermen in Oregon promptly got together and wrote checks totaling six cents in favor of the *Tribune*. It was, they admitted, a sacrifice, but precious freedoms were at stake— freedom of speech, freedom of the press—and they said they'd have come to the aid of the *Tribune* if the damages had been twice, nay, even three times as onerous.

One in five of them was a Packard: Or so Packard claimed. Perhaps it was one in five of those on active service abroad. When the United States joined the war in April 1917, the army had 8,039 trucks and

437 cars. Eighteen months later it had 85,000 trucks, 38,642 cars, and 23,053 ambulances.

Packard's publicity material said that "10,000 of their breed carried men & munitions on every front from Flanders to Mesopotamia. . . . It is their boast that they were first with Pershing when America entered the battle line, and that they were present on the American front in greatest numbers of any one kind of truck when the Armistice was signed."

38 *The first convoy left Detroit:* Edward Mott Woolley, "Fighting Snow on the Lincoln Highway," *Collier's Weekly,* 1918, date unknown.
the First Transcontinental Motor Train was arranged: When the convoy was finally authorized, Austin Bement wrote to every Lincoln Highway consul on June 23, 1919, to tell them to make ready. He described it as "this highly important trip, which has only been brought about by the long, persistent and continuous effort of the Association."

On December 30, 1919, the association's board held its annual meeting at the Detroit Athletic Club. Bement reported, "This run was planned in the offices of the Association; was as you know piloted by Mr. Ostermann in the Association's official Packard; the publicity was handled by the Association."

39 *"The sending of the convoy":* Joy's message was printed in the *Wyoming Press,* August 2, 1919, and in other newspapers around the country.

CHAPTER THREE:
"WE'RE GOING TO GET THERE; THAT'S ALL"

General newspaper sources: *Frederick Daily News, Gettysburg Star & Sentinel, Gettysburg Times, Chambersburg Public Opinion, Greensburg Daily Tribune, Pittsburgh Chronicle-Telegraph, Pittsburgh Daily Dispatch, Pittsburgh Gazette, Sewickley Herald.*

41 *"the government's contribution to the Good Roads movement":* Press release, source unknown. It would have been written either by Bement in Detroit, or in the Motor Transport Corps' headquarters in Washington. Either way, it appeared in newspapers from coast to coast.
"To demonstrate the practicability of long distance": Same press release as above.

42 *"was in a large measure counteracted":* Report on First Transcontinental Motor Convoy to Colonel L. B. Moody, Ordnance Department, Tank, Tractor & Trailer Division, by First Lieutenant E. R. Jackson, October 31, 1919. Eisenhower Library, Abilene, Kansas.

"the flower of the Motor Transport Corps": Doron's claim was printed in many newspapers along the convoy's route.

"Discipline among the enlisted personnel of the M.T.C.": Report on Trans-Continental Trip to Chief Motor Transport Corps by Lt. Col. D. D. Eisenhower, November 3, 1919. Eisenhower Library.

46 *The highway department's report for the years 1917 to 1920:* Pennsylvania State Archives, Harrisburg.

   a "Farmers' Anti-Automobile Association": Brian A. Butko, *Pennsylvania Traveler's Guide: The Lincoln Highway* (Mechanicsburg, Pa: Stackpole Books, 1996).

47 *"We are crossing the continent to impress upon all leaders":* Johnson's speech, which he gave virtually every night of the trip, was quoted in newspapers all along the route, and several times reprinted in full.

52 *A city of nearly 600,000 people:* Stefan Lorant, *Pittsburgh: The Story of an American City* (Lenox, Mass.: Authors' Editions Inc., 1964).

53 *"a great storm of angry remarks":* Frances C. Hardie, *Sewickley: A History of a Valley Community* (n.p.: 1998).

54 *hence the word* chauffeur: Bellamy Partridge, *Fill 'Er Up!* (New York: McGraw-Hill, 1952).

CHAPTER FOUR: A REVOLUTION IN MOVEMENT

General newspaper sources: *East Palestine Daily Leader, Columbiana Ledger, Alliance Review & Leader, Canton Daily News, Wooster Daily News, Wooster Daily Republican, Mansfield News, Bucyrus Journal, Bucyrus News-Forum, Upper Sandusky Daily Chief, Upper Sandusky Daily Union, Delphos Daily Herald, Van Wert Times.*

56 *The army film crew:* A copy of the film is in the Dwight D. Eisenhower Library, Abilene, Kansas.

57 *two men nicknamed Mutt and Jeff:* Private Tommy Stevens stood four feet, seven inches; Corporal George C. Casky was six foot eight. Stevens, weighing ninety-seven pounds, was apparently a bantamweight of some standing, while Casky had been runner-up for the Texas tennis championship in 1913.

58 *Colonel William Henry Morgan:* From an unpublished manuscript in the Alliance public library.

62 *He's a hard man to pin down, this Johnson:* According to the *Rawlins Republican* in Wyoming, Dr. Johnson was not only "a probable member of the next Federal Highway Commission" but also "instrumental in securing a highway from New York City to Bogota, Colombia."

The *Ogden Standard* in Utah described him as the "author of the legislation dealing with the disposition of motor vehicles used by the American army during the war, executive officer of the American Automobile Association, and honor guest of the Lincoln Highway Association."

63 *McClure said later that his "most perplexing problem":* Charles W. McClure, "Long Distance Motor Convoy Operation," *Quartermaster Review,* July–August 1926, pp. 26–32; September–October 1926, pp. 29–30; November–December 1926, pp. 29–32.

68 *a $45 million road-improvement program:* The figure in McClure's telegram is $450 million. Given the scale of comparable programs started or planned by other states at this time, I've assumed McClure printed one zero too many by mistake.

CHAPTER FIVE: SOLDIER WEDS IN HURRY

General newspaper sources: *Fort Wayne Journal Gazette, Fort Wayne News & Sentinel, Columbia City Post, South Bend News-Times, South Bend Tribune, La Porte Daily Argus, La Porte Daily Herald, Valparaiso Evening Messenger, Chicago Heights Star, Chicago Daily News, Chicago Evening Post, Chicago Herald-Examiner, Chicago Tribune, Joliet Evening Herald News, Aurora Beacon-News, De Kalb Daily Chronicle, Dixon Telegraph, Sterling Gazette.*

70 *the high cost of living:* Known for short as HCL. In the summer of 1919, America's political class was fiercely exercised over whether the country should join the League of Nations. For ordinary people, however, inflation was the number one topic. It was said that the price of shoe leather was rising so fast that soon everyone would be wearing wooden shoes, and there was a little ditty on the subject:

> *We are living, we are living*
> *In a grand and awful time*
> *And a quarter we are giving*
> *For things not worth a dime.*

For the promoters of truck transportation to latch on to this aspect of their case was therefore canny indeed.

71 *Clem and Henry Studebaker:* Logan Esarey, *History of Indiana* (Dayton, Ind.: Dayton Historical Publishing Co., 1923), and Donald T. Critchlow, *Studebaker: The Life and Death of an American Corporation* (Bloomington: Indiana University Press, 1996).

72 *equipment to the Allied armies worth $37 million:* The Studebaker Museum in South Bend offers this quote from the company's annual

report for 1919: "From the standpoint of profits, our war business was unattractive, netting us only 4.8% on sales and being nowhere near as profitable as our regular commercial work, but we were not in a position to choose and were devoting ourselves to a great cause."

75 *the Dixie Highway to Florida:* The Dixie Highway was another of Carl Fisher's grand promotions. In 1913, the same year the Lincoln Highway Association was formed, Fisher and his partner James Allison sold Prest-O-Lite to Union Carbide for $9 million. Fisher went to Florida and sank his money into turning a slim sand spit covered in mangroves and alligators into a holiday resort. Today it's Miami Beach; the Dixie Highway was intended to bring tourists there from Detroit and Chicago.

Growth had started with the railroad: From an unpublished manuscript in the Chicago Heights public library.

79 *a Good Roads paycheck:* I am indebted to Ruth Frantz of the present-day Lincoln Highway Association's Illinois chapter for showing me a copy of this certificate.

"the most strenuous compaign ever carried on in the state": S. E. Bradt, Superintendent of Highways, "Building the Hard Roads," *Illinois Blue Book* (n.p.: 1919–1920).

CHAPTER SIX: THE MUD COLUMN

General newspaper sources: *Clinton Advertiser, Clinton Herald, Mount Vernon Record, Cedar Rapids Evening Gazette, Belle Plaine Union, Marshalltown Times Republican, Nevada Representative, Ames Daily Tribune, Boone News Republican, Ogden Reporter, Jefferson Bee, Jefferson Herald, Glidden Graphic, Carroll Herald, Denison Bulletin & Herald, Denison Review, Dunlap Reporter, Harrison County Democrat, Missouri Valley Times, Council Bluffs Nonpareil.*

83 *The following year he stirred fierce controversy:* Though many Iowans reacted with outrage to Joy's attack on their roads, he was unrepentant. On November 23, 1916, he wrote to *Collier's* editor, Mark Sullivan, "God bless you! Bully for you! You have done a real maximum service thing. . . . Iowa can really no longer sit down in her own little mud-puddle and say that inasmuch as she is satisfied with her own mud, that no one else has any right to criticize."

84 *One historian has said that if the system's name:* Rebecca Conard, "The Lincoln Highway in Greene County," *Annals of Iowa,* vol. 52, fall 1993.

Joe Lang wrote in the Iowa Magazine: Quoted in the *Harrison County Democrat,* Logan, Iowa, July 31, 1919.

85 *It had started life as a ferry crossing:* "History of Clinton County, Iowa," Clinton County Historical Society, 1976. Joy's quote from *Collier's* in 1916 also comes from this source.

93 *"the father of the nation's highway system":* Tom Lewis, *Divided Highways* (New York: Viking, 1997).

98 *"A trackless wilderness":* E.B. Stillman, *Past and Present of Greene County, Iowa* (Chicago: S.J. Clarke Publishing Co., 1907).
a young man named Merle Hay: Joan Muyskens, "Merle Hay and His Town," *Annals of Iowa,* vol. 39, no. 1, summer 1967, pp. 22–32.

100 *with the home team leading 19–1:* The score was 19–1 in the local papers; McClure and Jackson said it was 15–1. Perhaps they were trying to cover their blushes—but with one report saying runs were batted in faster than the scorer could keep up with them, and describing the game bluntly as a farce, maybe no one knew the final tally for sure.

CHAPTER SEVEN: ACROSS THE 100TH MERIDIAN

General newspaper sources: *Omaha Bee, Omaha Daily News, Omaha World-Herald, Lincoln Evening State Journal, Fremont Evening Tribune, Columbus Telegraph, Central City Republican, Grand Island Daily Independent, Kearney Daily Hub, Lexington Clipper-Citizen, Dawson County Pioneer, Cozad Local, Gothenburg Times, Brady Vindicator, Maxwell Telepost, North Platte Semi-Weekly Tribune, North Platte Telegraph, Keith County News, Chappell Register, Sidney Telegraph, Western Nebraska Observer.*

105 *In 1919 Omaha:* Dorothy Deveraux Dustin, *Omaha and Douglas County: A Panoramic History* (Woodland Hills, Calif.: Windsor Publications, 1980). The Douglas County Historical Society at Fort Omaha (now the Metropolitan Community College on North Thirtieth Street) has a slim contemporary volume titled *Pictorial History of Fort Omaha.* Other details are from Omaha newspapers.

107 *The riot had another consequence:* Race riots were all too common in 1919; the fact that lynchings occurred at a rate just over one a week was not unrelated. During the convoy's journey, particularly awful disorders in Washington, D.C., and Chicago cost several dozen lives. In both cities, black and white gangs were reported driving around the streets, randomly firing at people of different race. At the dawn of the motor age, the United States—so inventive in so many ways—had invented the drive-by shooting as well.

The Negro Motorist Green Book: I am indebted to Carol Ahlgren of the National Parks Service in Omaha for showing me this and other such guidebooks.

110 *Lieutenant Colonel B. F. Miller:* "Road Discipline and care of vehicles for Transcontinental Convoy," July 28, 1919. Miller's memo is in the files of the Motor Transport Corps at the National Archives, Modern Military Records Branch, College Park, Maryland.

113 *They sent out the first settlers:* R. J. Barr and A. F. Buechler, eds., *History of Hall County* (Lincoln, Nebr.: Western Publishing & Engraving Co., 1920).

117 *Lexington had started life:* Russ Czaplewski, ed., *Plum Creek to Lexington, 1866–1939* (n.p.: Dawson County Historical Society/Morris Publishing, 1989).

124 *At the Doud family home in Denver:* Dorothy Brandon, *Mamie Doud Eisenhower: A Portrait of a First Lady* (New York: Scribners, 1954).

CHAPTER EIGHT: HUMAN-SKIN SHOES

General newspaper sources: *Pine Bluffs Post, Burns Herald, Cheyenne State Leader, Wyoming State Tribune, Laramie Boomerang, Laramie Republican, Rawlins Republican, Rock Springs Miner, Rock Springs Rocket, Green River Star, Wyoming Times.*

130 *one of whom was Elmer Lovejoy:* Papers in the American Heritage Center, University of Wyoming, Laramie. Lovejoy's 1914 *Wyoming Auto Guide* is in the Laramie public library.

131 *the "Switzerland of America":* In 1913, before Europe descended into war, it was estimated that American tourists on vacation on the good roads of that continent took $200 million out of the United States. Henry Joy knew all about it; his branch in Paris hired Packards for his well-heeled clientele, saving them the bother of shipping their own cars across the ocean. One motive behind the Good Roads Movement was to keep that money in the States by making it easier for Americans to go on vacation in their own country—hence the slogan "See America First."

John C. Thompson was a local journalist: A scrapbook with some of Thompson's columns is in the Rawlins public library.

139 *Big Nose Charlie Parrott:* Mary Ann Trevathan, *More Than Meets the Eye: Wyoming Along Interstate 80* (Glendo, Wyo.: High Plains Press, 1993), and exhibits at the Carbon County Museum in Rawlins.

141 *Today, it's not even on the map anymore:* At least, it's not on the Rand McNally road map of Wyoming. It's at Exit 158 off Interstate 80.

146 *It's true that Green River:* A. Dudley Gardner, Val Brinkerhoff, and Jolane Culhane, eds., *Historical Images of Sweetwater County* (Virginia Beach: Donning Company, 1993).

147 *In 1909, Harriet White Fisher:* Exhibits at the Sweetwater County Historical Museum.

   Rock Springs had just one paved city block: Robert B. Rhode, *Booms and Busts on Bitter Creek: A History of Rock Springs, Wyoming* (Boulder, Colo.: Fred Pruett Books, 1999).

CHAPTER NINE: THE UTAH CONTROVERSY

General newspaper sources: *Summit County Bee, Park Record, Ogden Standard, Deseret News, Salt Lake Herald, Salt Lake Telegraph, Salt Lake Tribune, Tooele Transcript.*

156 *the Arrowhead Trail by way of Provo and Cedar City:* From Detroit's point of view, another disadvantage to this route was that the tourist who went this way had then to cross the Mojave Desert—but that was no concern of Utah's.

157 *the route in Utah had been problematic from the beginning:* Jesse G. Petersen, "The Lincoln Highway and Its Changing Routes in Utah," *Utah Historical Quarterly*, vol. 69, no. 3, summer 2001, pp. 192–214.

159 *sank four and a half feet into the underlying mud:* It could have been worse. Shortly before the arrival of the convoy, George Romney of Smithfield was driving home from Salt Lake. With him were his wife, a family friend, and their five-year-old grandson. On a detour through Clearfield the temporary road gave way, and the car "fell into a cave." The fall was twenty-five feet, and the three adults were severely injured.

   Utah's state road engineer faced a string of lawsuits. The state agreed to reimburse one family for their wrecked car, their hotel bills, and their medical and travel expenses after they drove into a hole seventeen feet deep on the Midland Trail near Green River.

160 *the annual Governors' Conference:* The conference was initiated by Teddy Roosevelt in 1909, when he called state governors to the White House to address issues of conservation and national resources. The eleventh conference in Salt Lake City was attended by the governors of all the western states except four, with a number of

midwestern and eastern governors also present; it was intended to tackle postwar issues like inflation and labor unrest. In the wake of the convoy's passage and more oratory from Dr. Johnson, the governors also made sure to call for large federal appropriations for building roads.

161 *Bill Rishel:* Virginia Rishel, *Wheels to Adventure: Bill Rishel's Western Routes* (Salt Lake City: Howe Brothers, 1983).

164 *In the words of one local historian:* Jesse Petersen, retired police chief of Tooele, Utah. Petersen has recently served as president of the modern-day Lincoln Highway Association.

Gael Hoag would later charge bluntly that Rishel was on the Bay City's payroll: Minutes, annual meeting of the board of the Lincoln Highway Association, December 28, 1921. Hoag also said that San Francisco had "founded and subsidized" the state auto associations of Nevada, Utah, and Idaho.

166 *Franklin Augustus Seiberling:* James Carlisle, "Seiberling: A Story of Friendship," *Nation's Business,* May 1928, and Jeffrey L. Rodengen, *The Legend of Goodyear: The First 100 Years* (Fort Lauderdale: Write Stuff Syndicate Inc., 1997).

the Goodyear Tire & Rubber Company: The name Goodyear was Seiberling's tip of the hat to Charles Goodyear, the chaotic inventor from Connecticut who stumbled on vulcanization, the process of fixing rubber so it didn't melt in hot weather or crack in cold. Goodyear was a maniac for rubber; he made rubber toys, rubber umbrellas, rubber shoes and clothes. In 1851, at the first world's fair, at the Crystal Palace in London, he displayed the Vulcanite Court—a $30,000 exhibit featuring rubber furniture, rubber globes and art objects, rubber spectacles and walking sticks.

An enlarged version shown in Paris won him the French Cross of the Legion of Honor. His second wife brought him the medal in debtors' jail, his first wife having left him after deciding that a man who sold her linens and their children's schoolbooks to fund his crackpot experiments was no longer to be borne. Goodyear died a pauper in 1860, a man whose invention was ahead of its time; there would not be big money in rubber until the car came along.

167 *the biggest tiremaker in America:* Goodyear first designed a pneumatic tire for trucks in 1912. No one bought the idea (heavy loads, they thought, surely had to run on solids), and a production model didn't appear until 1916. To test it and promote it, Goodyear launched the Wingfoot Express, and the ship-by-truck movement was born. On

April 9, 1917, a five-ton Packard drove on Goodyear pneumatics from Akron to Boston. On bad roads in worse weather, the trip took nineteen days.

In better weather, with lighter loads, trucks were soon covering the Akron-Boston round-trip in five days—faster than the railroad could carry freight there and back by some margin.

On September 1, 1918, Goodyear went further; it launched America's first transcontinental trucking line. Two trucks—one of them the same Packard that would carry the company band with the convoy—set off with a pilot car and a load of fabric from Boston to Akron. They delivered the fabric, took on a consignment of airplane tires, and drove to San Francisco; they did the whole trip in three weeks.

Fisher did his part from a distance: By 1916, the development of Miami Beach was absorbing much of Fisher's energy. He continued as a director of the Lincoln Highway Association and made a substantial contribution for the road in Utah, but after 1916 he attended no more meetings in Detroit.

172 *Elwell Jackson would subsequently (and angrily) report:* Jackson's appendix to his main report concerning these events with the Militor, along with Sergeant Wood's own equally dumbfounded account, are in the files of the Motor Transport Corps at the National Archives, Modern Military Records Branch, College Park, Maryland.

173 *the tie rod securing the top of the radiator to the dashboard:* Unlike modern engines, the radiators in these trucks were mounted at the back, between the engine and the cab. So on top of their other discomforts, the drivers and anyone sitting beside them had their legs cooked all day as well.

175 *a Scot named Matthew Orr:* Charles Kelly, " 'Death' on the Desert," *True West*, November–December 1971, p. 15.

CHAPTER TEN: GHOST ROAD

General newspaper sources: *White Pine News, Eureka Sentinel, Reese River Reveille, Churchill County Eagle, Fallon Standard, Carson City Daily Appeal, Sparks Tribune.*

179 *The state's Department of Highways:* Nevada Department of Highways, Board of Directors' Reports, 1917–1930, Nevada State Archives, Carson City.

184 *"the town that died laughing":* This was the title of a 1954 book about Austin by Oscar Lewis. Mary Ellen and Al Glass, *Touring Nevada* (Reno: University of Nevada Press, 1983).

187 *this tiny oasis would gain notoriety: Nevada: A Guide to the Silver State* (n.p.: Writers' Program of the Work Projects Administration/ Nevada State Historical Society, 1940).

191 *Carson City is one of America's smallest:* Willa Oldham, *Carson City: Nevada's Capital City* (Genoa, Nev.: Desk Top Publishers, 1991).

CHAPTER ELEVEN: THE PROMISED LAND

General newspaper sources: *Mountain Democrat, Sacramento Bee, Sacramento Star, Sacramento Sunday Leader, Sacramento Union, Stockton Record, Oakland Enquirer, Oakland Tribune, San Francisco Chronicle, San Francisco Examiner, Richmond News.*

197 *Carlo Giuseppi Celio:* Betty Yohalem, *I Remember: Stories and Pictures of El Dorado County Pioneer Families* (El Dorado, Calif.: El Dorado County Chamber of Commerce, 1977).

198 *the locals preferred to call their home Hangtown:* Herman Daniel Jerrett, *California's El Dorado Yesterday and Today* (Sacramento, Calif.: Press of Jo Anderson, 1915).

199 *California had created a bureau of highways:* Department of Engineering of the State of California/California Highway Commission, Biennial Reports 1912–1920, California State Archives, Sacramento.

201 *By 1919, the Central Valley:* Walter G. Reed, *History of Sacramento County, California* (Los Angeles: Historic Record Co., 1923).

205 *It didn't quite get that big:* Raymond W. Hillman and Leonard Covello, *Stockton Through the Decades* (Stockton, Calif.: Vanguard Press Inc., 1981).

EPILOGUE: THE END OF THE ROAD

214 *Thirty-seven years later, President Eisenhower:* The papers at the Eisenhower Library concerning the creation of the interstate system are fascinating. Ike's memoirs of this period are *The White House Years* (London: William Heinemann, 1963).

215 *by 1955 . . . the death toll was over thirty-eight thousand:* Road deaths in the United States peaked at over 50,000 a year in the 1970s. By 1999 the figure had fallen to 41,611, though by then there were three times as many cars as there had been forty years earlier.

216 *The War Department was now foursquare behind Detroit:* The War Department's 1920 report containing General Drake's observations on the convoy is in the Eisenhower Library.

Detroit was now intimate with the highest echelons of government: Henry Joy knew President Harding personally. A few years earlier, when Harding was an Ohio senator, he'd met Joy to argue for the inclusion of his hometown, Marion, on the Lincoln Highway. Joy refused, but they got on well and a cordial correspondence ensued. "My Dear Mr. Joy," wrote Harding on February 19, 1916, "I quite agree with the wisdom of the policy which you have adopted. I am sure your policy will meet with universal approval."

218 *"practically all of the equipment was in very bad condition":* Bamberger's claim seems disingenuous. Now the war was over, large quantities of heavy vehicles and machinery that the army no longer needed were distributed among the states to assist with their road-building programs. In September, Gael Hoag had seen seven new trucks at work on the cutoff.

219 *"rank repudiation of contract":* In May 1920, Utah's attorney general, Dan Shields, told the Lincoln Highway Association, "Mark you now...that not one single member of the Road Commission of Utah favored that road, because *we knew*, at least *I knew*, that it seemed an unfeasible piece of operation."

It's reasonable to ask, in that case, why he drew up and signed Utah's contract with the association in the first place. Joy sighed and told Bement, "The English language as it is used in Utah is subject to strange interpretations."

Between Grantsville and Wendover: Utah State Road Commission, Biennial Reports 1917–1928, Utah State Archives.

223 *"utter absence of an intelligent system of finances":* W. D. Shills, unpublished manuscript on Goodyear history, University of Akron Archives.

227 *The Victory Highway became U.S. 40; bitter battles continued:* Stanley W. Paher, ed., *Nevada Official Bicentennial Book* (Las Vegas: Nevada Publications, 1976).

228 *the Selfridge Field air base:* The base was built by Henry Joy. When the war began in Europe he bought half a dozen farms, then cleared and leveled the ground for an aviation field. Meanwhile, in early 1915, he set Packard's Experimental Department the task of designing an airplane engine—the Liberty motor—so that when America entered the war two years later, both engine and airstrip were ready and waiting for the military to use.

The base was named for a Lieutenant Selfridge, who'd died when one of Orville Wright's planes crashed in 1907. Had it not crashed, Joy had been slated to ride in it next.

After the war, the government kept the base and refused to pay Joy for the land. He took the government to court and won. As for the charge that Packard had made excessive profits on its contracts for Liberty engines, Joy dismissed it as "too absurd to be given serious consideration. . . . I consider that it is not possible to have any business relations with the government on any reliable basis."

230 *one of the most important men in the story of the American road finally receives his appropriate recognition:* Randall A. Wagner, "Moving Joy," *Lincoln Highway Forum* vol. 9, no. 2, winter 2001–2, pp. 10–15.

231 *Helen Hall Joy died the same year:* Arthur M. Woodford, ed., *Tonnancour: Life in Grosse Pointe and Along the Shores of Lake St. Clair* (Detroit: Omnigraphics Inc., 1994).

Bibliography

ELWELL JACKSON WROTE a daily log of the convoy's progress in his Lincoln Highway guidebook and cabled each day's report to the Ordnance Department in Washington. The Dwight D. Eisenhower Library in Abilene, Kansas, has copies of both the telegrams and the handwritten log. Unless stated otherwise, all of Jackson's observations are from this source. Captain Greany's report is also in Abilene, with a bountiful supply of other material on the convoy, and on Ike's life in general.

Like Jackson, Colonel McClure cabled daily news of their progress to Washington. Sometimes he copied Jackson's messages verbatim; on other occasions he went into greater detail. Copies of his telegrams are in the National Archives, Modern Military Records Branch, College Park, Maryland. Nearly all of McClure's observations derive from this source.

Information about American servicemen around the time of World War I can be hard to come by, as many records were lost in a fire. Despite the losses, the National Personnel Records Center in St. Louis, Missouri, found helpful details, as did the National Archives in Maryland. Further information about Elwell Jackson came from the Pennsylvania State Archives in Harrisburg.

Eisenhower's account of the convoy is in Dwight D. Eisenhower, *At Ease: Stories I Tell to Friends* (London: Robert Hale Ltd., 1968), chapter 11, "Through Darkest America with Truck and Tank." Unless stated otherwise, Ike's contributions are based on this memoir.

Two collections at the University of Michigan in Ann Arbor provided a priceless fund of material. Henry Joy's papers in the Bentley Historical Library contain exhaustive correspondence, autobiographical sketches, newspaper clippings, documents, and photographs. The finding aid for these papers is at: http://www.hti.umich.edu/cgi/f/findaid/findaid-idx?type=simple&c=bhl&view ext&subview=outline&id=umich-bhl-851730. The official papers of the Lincoln Highway Association are at the university's Special Collections Library. They're another rich source on the convoy, as well as on the full course of the association's life and activity, with newsletters, annual reports, minutes of board meetings, invaluable correspondence, and photographs. Many of the passages about Joy and his colleagues, their creation and promotion of the highway, and the arguments over the route are based on material in these two collections.

Another key source was *The Lincoln Highway: The Story of a Crusade That Made Transportation History*—the Official History of the Lincoln Highway Association (New York: Dodd, Mead & Co., 1935). Though not credited to him, this was written by Gael Hoag, the association's field secretary from 1920. Some of Hoag's correspondence, including notes written for him by Carl Fisher and others when he prepared the book, are in the Bancroft Library at the University of California, Berkeley. Another valuable account of the highway is Drake Hokansen's *The Lincoln Highway: Main Street Across America* (Iowa City: University of Iowa Press, 1988). Details of road conditions and hotels and other businesses along the way are in most cases from the 1918 edition of the Lincoln Highway guidebook. Otherwise, the convoy was front-page news from coast to coast. The newspapers I have quoted or paraphrased are listed in the chapter notes.

I first read about the convoy in Daniel Yergin's magisterial history of the oil industry, *The Prize* (New York: Pocket Books, 1993). There were only three paragraphs, but it seemed worth looking into. In the British Library, in the Eisenhower Library, and in countless other libraries from Washington to San Francisco I found the sources listed below.

Bliss, Carey S. *Autos Across America: A Bibliography of Transcontinental Automobile Travel, 1903–1940.* N.p.: Jenkins & Reese, 1982.

A Brief for the Lincoln Highway in Utah and Nevada. N.p.: Lincoln Highway Association, 1923.

Franzwa, Gregory M. *The Lincoln Highway.* Vol. 1, *Iowa.* Tucson: Patrice Press, 1995.

———. *The Lincoln Highway.* Vol. 2, *Nebraska.* Tucson: Patrice Press, 1996.

———. *The Lincoln Highway.* Vol. 3, *Wyoming.* Tucson: Patrice Press, 1999.

Gladding, Effie Price. *Across the Continent.* New York: Brentano's, 1915.

Graf, Lt. Col. William S. "The Great Overland March." *Soldiers* (October 1975): pp. 47–51.

Harstad, Peter J., and Diana J. Fox. "Dusty Doughboys on the Lincoln Highway: The 1919 Army Convoy in Iowa." *Palimpsest*, vol. 56 (May–June 1975): pp. 66–87.

Historic American Highways. N.p.: American Association of State Highway Officials, 1953.

Knowlton, Ezra C. *History of Highway Development in Utah.* N.p.: Utah State Department of Highways, 1964.

Koster, George E. *A Story of Highway Development in Nebraska.* Rev. ed. N.p.: Nebraska Department of Roads, 1997.

Manchester, Albert D. "Coast to Coast with the Doughboys." *Car Collector & Car Classics* (April 1987): pp. 15–19.

McCarthy, Joe. "The Lincoln Highway." *American Heritage*, vol. 25, no. 4 (June 1974): pp. 32–37, 89.

Paxson, Frederic L. "The Highway Movement 1916–1935." *American Historical Review*, vol. 51, no. 2 (1946): pp. 236–53.

Post, Emily. *By Motor to the Golden Gate.* New York: D. Appleton & Co., 1917.

Stevenson, Victoria Faber. *American Highways.* Vol. 1. N.p.: Winship Publishing Co., 1918–19.

Thompson, William H. *Transportation in Iowa: A Historical Summary.* N.p.: Iowa Department of Transportation, 1989.

U.S. Department of Transportation, Federal Highway Administration. *America's Highways, 1776–1976.* Washington, D.C.: U.S. Government Printing Office, 1976.

White, Tom. "The Khaki-Colored Caravan." *NEBRASKAland* (November 1999).

Wickman, John E. "Ike and 'The Great Truck Train'—1919." *Kansas History*, vol. 13, no. 3 (autumn 1990).

The present-day Lincoln Highway Association publishes a quarterly, *Lincoln Highway Forum,* with regular pieces on the history of America's first transcontinental road. Of particular value were:

Earl, Phillip I. "1919 Lincoln Highway Military Convoy: The Nevada Phase." *Forum,* vol. 6, no. 1 (fall 1998).

Harstad, Peter J. "Henry C. Ostermann and the Lincoln Highway." *Forum,* vol. 2, no. 1 (fall 1994).

Oyster, Esther M. "Henry B. Joy: Visionary and Pragmatist." *Forum,* vol. 3, no. 3 (spring 1996).

Illustration Credits

Photograph 1: Dwight D. Eisenhower Library, Abilene, Kansas.

Photographs 2–4, 6–9: Lincoln Highway Collection, Transportation History Collection, Collections Library, University of Michigan, Ann Arbor.

Photographs 5, 10–12: Henry Joy Papers, Bentley Historical Library, University of Michigan, Ann Arbor.

Photographs 13, 23–25, 31: Taken by Dwight D. Eisenhower. Eisenhower Library.

Photographs 14–19, 21–22, 26, 28–30: Taken by First Lieutenant Kenneth C. Downing, one of McClure's adjutants. Eisenhower Library.

Photograph 20: Iowa Department of Transportation.

Photograph 27: Taken by Private Edward J. Mantel, Company F, 433rd Motor Supply Train. Eisenhower Library.

Photograph 32: Source unknown. Eisenhower Library.

Acknowledgments

On Saturday, April 7, 2001, I bought a pea-green 1985 Chevrolet Caprice for $2,000 from Jimmy's Autos, 418 New York Avenue NW, Washington, D.C. It had had one careful owner, and she'd put 107,000 miles on the clock. Jimmy said he could sell me something more expensive, but if all I wanted to do was drive across the country, then that Chevy would get me there.

It did. I spent about $300 on it at Midas in Chambersburg, Pennsylvania, and the service was excellent. Otherwise, when I crossed the Bay Bridge sixty-one days and 5,909 miles later, all it had asked for was one quart of oil. So if you're in D.C. and you need a secondhand car, Jimmy's the man to see.

At journey's end in San Francisco I sold the Chevy to Chad Thompson, the parking valet at the Galleria Park, for $800. Thanks for taking it off me, Chad; I hope it was as good a deal for you as it was for me.

I owe a great debt of gratitude to Deborah Brody at Henry Holt for letting me make this journey, and for making sense of what I came back with. My thanks to my agents Elaine Markson and Rachel Calder for looking after me—and, as always, to Rebecca, Joe, and Megan for putting up with my going away again.

During my research, I didn't meet one single unhelpful librarian. Usually at short notice, in government archives and state and county historical societies, in university and public libraries from one coast to the other, I met no end of courtesy, kindness, wit, and insight, and was given much smart advice and assistance. It made the work a real pleasure.

My thanks first to Herb Pankratz and Kathleen Struss at the Eisenhower Center in Abilene; in Ann Arbor, to Kathy Marquis at the Bentley Historical Library and Kathleen Dow at the Special Collections Library.

Through four weeks in February and March of 2001, these people helped provide the historical bedrock of the book.

In the National Archives in downtown Washington they found Erna Risch's history of the Quartermaster Corps, then put me on a bus to College Park. Mitchell Yockelson at NARA's Modern Military Records Branch was particularly helpful, as were Rich Saylor at the Pennsylvania State Archives in Harrisburg, John Miller at the archives of the University of Akron, and Larry Booher at the National Personnel Records Center in St. Louis.

Hank Zaletel at the library of the Iowa Department of Transportation in Ames was especially informative. Sara Howieson at the Douglas County Historical Society at Fort Omaha went out of her way to try to find material about the convoy's visit there. In Grand Island, Keith Meyer at the Nebraska Department of Transportation was another courteous informant. Thanks too to Christian Zavisca at the *North Platte Telegraph,* and to Melpha Barnica in Big Springs. Moni Hourt in Crawford, Nebraska, is a good friend, a welcoming host, and a fine teacher. Ten years after *Storm Country,* it was good to be in Sioux County again.

The staff at the Wyoming State Archives in Cheyenne was wonderfully helpful; the same goes for the American Heritage Center at the University of Wyoming in Laramie. Joyce Kelley at the Carbon County Museum in Rawlins and Gary Perkins at the Sweetwater County Historical Museum in Green River were rich mines of local knowledge.

In a state where the reconstruction of what happened was particularly tricky, Arlene Schmuland and Val Wilson at the Utah State Archives were fantastically obliging and produced much valuable material. The staff at the Utah State Historical Society were a great help, as was Walter Jones at the University of Utah's Special Collections Library.

The Nevada State Archives are full of good things, and good people to help you find them. Michael Brodhead at the University of Nevada in Reno was kind and informative. Karen Smith and her colleagues in the California history section of the California State Library in Sacramento found me useful sources with impressive rapidity; the staff at the California State Archives was similarly productive. As for the staff at Berkeley's Bancroft Library who found Gael Hoag's papers, bless you.

Last but very far from least, my thanks to the public librarians of America. In big cities and small towns alike, they did everything they could to help. Particular thanks to Tamra Hess in East Palestine, Ohio; Sandy Haynes in Denison, Iowa; Mary Carpenter in Council Bluffs, Iowa; to the woman whose name I never got in Kimball, Nebraska; to Laura McMennamin in Laramie, Wyoming; to Roseanne Revelli in Evanston,

Wyoming; and to Deborah Westler in Stockton, California, who let me go to work despite the fact that her library was closed for staff training that day.

Perhaps the best illustration of the thoughtfulness I encountered comes from Clinton, Iowa. In the library's root cellar, I found everything I needed except the census figures; they were away being microfilmed. At about seven in the evening, I left to drive twenty miles west to De Witt; the next morning I went into the library there and started explaining what I was looking for. The moment my English accent emerged, the woman at the desk said, "Are you Pete Davies?" She knew to expect me because, after I'd left, someone in Clinton had taken the trouble to find the missing census figures, and then phoned them ahead to De Witt.

THE PRESENT-DAY Lincoln Highway Association was formed in the early 1990s, a coming together of conservationists, classic-car enthusiasts, and amateur local historians; it has over one thousand members. Their most notable achievement has been the approval by Congress of $500,000 for the National Parks Service to study how the highway might best be preserved and promoted, both for its own sake and as a tourism generator. This has been set in motion by good people on a shoestring budget; if you want to help, membership information can be had from Lynn Asp, LHA Headquarters, P.O. Box 308, Franklin Grove, IL 61031; (815) 456-3030; lnchwyhq@essex1.com.

The Pennsylvania chapter has the highway marked as a heritage corridor pretty much all through the state. Its *Lincoln Highway Driving Guide* is available from P.O. Box 386, Greensburg, PA 15601; (724) 837-9750.

Many members of the association in Ohio were especially kind and hospitable. My thanks to Jim Ross in Canton, who showed me stretches of the original brick road, and to Bob Lichty, Rosemary Rubin, and Gary Pelger at the Classic Car Museum. Particular thanks to Dave Johnson at the Spread Eagle Tavern in Hanoverton; if you're in eastern Ohio (or anywhere near it) the Spread Eagle is a fine place to stay and has outstanding food.

I'm grateful for the help, knowledge, and advice of Esther Oyster, Mike McNaull, Dick Taylor, and Mike Buettner in Ashland, Mansfield, and Lima. Taylor's lovingly restored 1905 National Automobile can be seen in the foyer of Mansfield City Hall; Buettner has produced a detailed guide to the highway through Ohio.

Pete Youngman took time to visit the Studebaker Museum with me in South Bend, Indiana, and kindly produced a thick sheaf of newspaper articles about the convoy. In Illinois Ruth Frantz, Lynn Asp, and Carl and Sue Jacobson were welcoming hosts, and showed me much of the road through their state. I'd like also to tip my hat to George Otterson at the Baymont Inn in De Kalb for his help and good company.

Lyell Henry in Iowa City and Bob and Joyce Ausberger in Jefferson are hugely well informed about the highway and were generous with their time and knowledge. In Denison, I recommend Bill and Mary Cullen's Ho Hum Motel. Room 6 is a Hansel and Gretel chalet in the corner of the parking lot, and it wins my award for Best Little Motel Room in America. As for the Best Mexican Meal on the Lincoln Highway, that's at La Fiesta in Fallon, Nevada.

In Omaha, Carol Ahlgren is working on the National Park Service study of the highway; she was wonderfully informative, as well as entertaining. Chris Plummer in Wyoming was a more than helpful guide; my thanks also to Vernon Scott at the Virginian in Medicine Bow, Linda Byers at Fort Bridger, and Stan Taggart at Pete's Rock 'n' Rye in Evanston. I'm grateful to Phil Earl in Reno, for his time and insight, and to Leon Schegg in Truckee, California, for his thoughts on the alternate routes around Tahoe.

THE STANDOUT DAY of the trip came in Tooele County in west-central Utah. The Goodyear Cutoff still exists, but you can't drive on it; the military keeps it graveled as part of the Dugway Proving Ground and the Utah Test and Training Range. I'm grateful to Deanna Terry and her colleagues at Dugway for letting me onto the base to see what can be seen. The log bridge built over Government Creek in 1919 still stands by Michael Army Air Field, long unused and perfectly preserved.

While you can't see the cutoff, what you can do is drive the original 1913 route of the Lincoln Highway to the south of it. From Tooele you go south on 36, then west on 199 through Johnson's Pass. Tom See's Willow Springs Lodge in the pass was a work camp for the convicts in 1919; Tom knows a lot about the convoy, and I thank him for sharing his time and knowledge. There's a move afoot by local members of the association to have the pass finally renamed after Carl Fisher; good luck to them.

Orr's Ranch is still in business in Skull Valley, along a county road called (what else?) the Lincoln Highway. It's a stand of poplars in an epic wilderness. Don't turn that way, but keep straight on to the church by the gate into Dugway; this is where the pavement ends. If you're going on from here, take extra gas, water, and food. If you get lost or break down, you may be alone for a while.

Turn south past the church onto the dirt road by a sign for Simpson Springs; another sign tells you you're on the Pony Express Trail. After ten miles, turn west at a T-junction also posted to Simpson Springs. At the springs, the Pony Express station has been restored—a stone hut all alone in a parched and magnificent desolation. Ignore the ominous turn to Death Canyon and carry on with appropriate caution toward Fish Springs. Stretches of the road here are rough and stony, a washboard through rock and dune.

The sagebrush thins out into a baked aridity of dust and sand, then revives on the ascent into the Dugways. As you crest Dugway Pass the Great Salt Lake Desert appears to your north, a broad, dirty-white shimmer under the remorseless sun, and the snowcaps of the Deep Creek Mountains rise up ahead of you.

Past the Dugways, Fish Springs National Wildlife Refuge is the site of John Thomas's ranch. Thomas was by some accounts a rogue and a reprobate, by others a lovable or at least a lively one. He did well out of the highway, selling food, gas, and lodging to the growing trade past his door, and charging people handsomely when he towed them out of mud and sand holes.

In 1914, Thomas recorded a little more than four hundred cars passing by the ranch; by 1916, the year before he died, that number had risen to nearly eighteen hundred. Jay Banta, manager of the Fish Springs Refuge, reckons that by the 1920s, before the Victory Highway was finished, there were more cars coming through here than the twenty-five hundred or so that visit the place each year today. Banta said, "I go out and look at sections of the Lincoln Highway here, and I am so impressed with people then, with how intrepid they were. I'll bet people coming from Orr's Ranch to here had ten flat tires, they had their radiators boil over—and they just dealt with it."

FOUR MILES PAST Fish Springs, take the right fork for Callao (CAL-ee-oh). Run north along the east side of the Fish Springs range, then west toward the looming stacks of black-and-white rock in the Deep Creeks. Callao was settled in 1857; the highway generated two service stations, a store, and a hotel, and the population peaked in the mid-1930s at about one hundred. Today, a map of the town on a wooden sign shows fourteen homes and the Double J Ranch; it's an oasis of green grass and grazing livestock.

Turn north at a T-junction on the west edge of town, following a sign for Gold Hill and Ibapah; five miles along, turn west toward Overland Canyon and Ibapah. The trail rolls into the folds of the Deep Creek Mountains, with the salt desert a vast and forbidding emptiness behind you. It twists up onto Clifton Flats, then drops southwest to join a short stretch of hardtop into Ibapah (AYE-buh-pah). The name's an anglicized version of Ai-bim-pah, meaning "deep, clay-colored water." The settlement was founded in 1859 by Mormon missionaries to the Goshute. It did well out of the Deep Creek mines in the early twentieth century, then faded away. The Sheridan Hotel served the highway here, advertising itself as "a desert resort of merit . . . latchstring out day and night." It's a store now; sometimes it has gas, sometimes it doesn't.

Just south of a monument marking the town's history, the pavement turns left. Carry straight on here, back onto dirt, following a sign for the Nevada state line. Way out in Spring Valley, Tippett's Ranch is a tumbledown collection of wood and stone cabins quietly falling apart in the desert wind. Look to any point of the compass, and there's no other sign of human life past or present. For isolation, severity, and grandeur, in my experience only Namibia comes close to the harsh beauty of this place.

Three miles past Tippett, ignore the right turn marked with a Pony Express sign. Eight miles farther on the trail starts winding up and west into Tippett's Pass, a string of ascending curves to a fork just past the crest. Go right, following the sign for Schellbourne Pass; after seven miles, at an abandoned stone house by a junction, go right again for Schellbourne. The descent out of the pass is dramatic, with steep grades and sharp turns; take a deep breath and consider doing this in a truck in 1919.

The dirt ends at the foot of the pass, joining U.S. 93 for Ely. From the Dugway gate, it's 172 miles; with the brief exception of Ibapah, it's rough dirt and gravel all the way. I spent over eight hours on it, dumbstruck with awe. It's the most beautiful day's drive I've ever had—so perhaps we should thank Utah for building the road to Wendover. After all, if Henry Joy and his colleagues had had their way, this would be an interstate now.

I'M GRATEFUL TO Jay Banta for giving me time to talk at Fish Springs; I'm especially grateful to Jesse Petersen in Tooele, who helped get me onto Dugway and gave me directions along the 1913 road. These two between them probably know everything there is to know about the Lincoln Highway in Utah. Banta says, "I always tell people that the Pony Express is a very romantic entity, but that its impact on history is not particularly consequential. It lasted eighteen months, and it proved you couldn't transport mail economically that way. There are some collateral issues, to do with keeping California in the Union during the Civil War, but it's grossly overemphasized. Whereas the Lincoln Highway—that's a seminal event." Banta and Petersen have both contributed essays to a book about the highway that's currently being edited by Drake Hokansen. I look forward to reading it.

In conclusion, my thanks to all the good people I met on the road across the United States. It is, quite simply, the greatest drive in the world.

Index

William Henry Morgan in, 58–59
  Wooster, 61–62
Ohio River Boulevard, 55
"Old Pacific," 14–15
Olds, Ransom, 11
Omaha Daily News, 106
Omaha (NE), 105–10
Omaha World-Herald, 107, 110
100th meridian, 119–20
Orr, Mathew, 175
Orr's Ranch (UT), 172, 174, 175
Osborne, John, 140
Ostermann, Babe Bell, 33, 217
Ostermann, Henry C.
  death of, 217
  first crossing of, 15
  First Transcontinental Motor Train and,
    9, 38
  at Goodyear Cutoff, 168
  in Indiana, 73
  in Iowa, 85–86, 94, 95
  memorial bench for, 224
  in Nebraska, 114
  in Ohio, 56, 63, 65–66
  in Pennsylvania, 45, 50
  work for Lincoln Highway Association,
    32–33
  in Wyoming, 130
Overland Stage, 27, 136

Pacific Fleet, 203, 207
Packard
  in First Transcontinental Motor Train, 6
  Henry Joy's first, 20–21
  Twin Six, 9
Packard, James Ward, 21
Packard Motor Company
  aviation engines by, 1
  backing of Lincoln Highway, 25–26
  Charles McClure at, 212
  Liberty engine and, 246, 247
  merge with Studebaker, 230
  publicity for Lincoln Highway, 30
  sale to Henry Joy, move to Detroit,
    21–24
  transcontinental crossing of, 14–15
  trucks of, 5
  vehicles for army, 34–37, 235–36
Palace of the Legion of Honor, 210–11
Pancho Villa, 34, 36
Pardington, A. R., 29, 234
Parrott, Big Nose Charlie, 139–40
Patent Motorwagon, 233

Paul, Harry J. (Pvt.), 101
Paul, Walter, 176
pavement
  in California, 201, 206
  "ideal section" of, 224
  in Illinois, 79
  interstate system project for, 214–15
  in Iowa, 84, 88, 96–97, 102–3
  in Nebraska, 118
  in Wyoming, 147–48
"peacock alleys," 83
Pennsylvania
  Chambersburg and Bedford, 47–48
  convoy vehicle problems, 50–51
  Greenmount, 44–45
  Greensburg, 48–49, 50
  hospitality in, 67
  Pittsburgh, 51–53
  road conditions, construction, 45–47
  Sewickley, 53–54
Pennsylvania State Highway Department,
  45–46
Pershing, General, 35, 37
Philistine, 17
Pinto House (NV), 183
Pioneer Monument (UT), 160
Pioneer Trail Association, 193
Pittsburgh (PA), 51–53
Placerville (CA), 198–99
Plum Creek Gazette, 117
Plum Creek Station (NE), 117–19
Pony Express, 27, 155
Prest-O-Lite, 12–13, 239
primary road system, 216, 220, 222–23
Prohibition, 228–29
public relations
  of First Transcontinental Motor Train,
    41–42
  in Iowa, 98–99
  in Nebraska, 112
  in Pennsylvania, 44–45
  in Wyoming, 130
publicity stunts
  for Lincoln Highway, 30–32
  of Packard Motor Company, 14–15

Quartermaster Corps, 4
Quartermaster Review, 212–13

racetrack, 11
racism
  in Nebraska, 106–8, 118–19
  riots, 240

About the Author

PETE DAVIES is the author of a number of critically acclaimed works of fiction and nonfiction, including *Inside the Hurricane* and *The Devil's Flu*. He lives in West Yorkshire, England.